↑MINISTRY
MISSION→

What to look for in a pastor

A guide for pastoral search committees

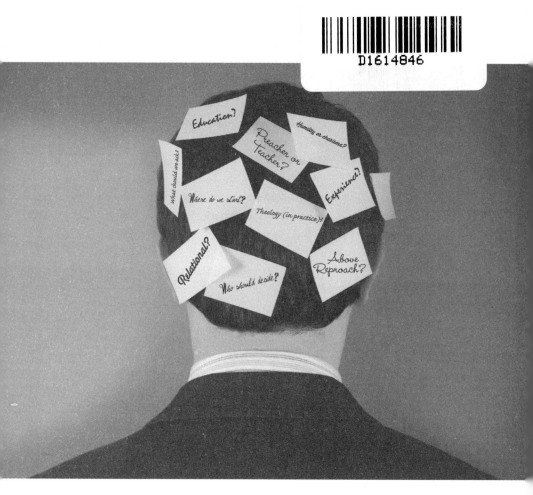

D1614846

Education?

Preacher or Teacher?

Humility or charisma?

What should we ask?

Where do we start?

Experience?

Theology (in practice)?

Relational?

Above Reproach?

Who should decide?

Brian Biedebach

DayOne

© Day One Publications 2011
First printed 2011

ISBN 978–1–84625–268–6

British Library Cataloguing in Publication Data available

Scripture quotations taken from the **New American Standard Bible®**,
Copyright © 1960, 1962, 1963, 1968, 1971, 1972, 1973,
1975, 1977, 1995 by The Lockman Foundation
Used by permission. (www.Lockman.org)

Published by Day One Publications
Ryelands Road, Leominster, HR6 8NZ
☎ 01568 613 740 FAX 01568 611 473
email—sales@dayone.co.uk
web site—www.dayone.co.uk
North American—e-mail—sales@dayonebookstore.com
North American—web site—www.dayonebookstore.com

Cover design by Wayne McMaster
Printed in the United States of America

The time when a church needs its best and most biblical discernment is when choosing a new pastor. But the question is, how does a church without pastoral leadership find pastoral leadership? Brian Biedebach has answered this in What to Look for in a Pastor. *Church-leadership boards, search committees, and congregants will find this resource invaluable in providing needed guidance on this topic. I know of no other volume as saturated with biblical wisdom for finding a pastor. It will help a church not only to find the right kind of pastor, but also to know how to care for the one who is called to care for them.*

Rick Holland, Executive Pastor, Grace Community Church, Sun Valley, California, USA

I've just come out of a pulpit-selection process in which I have been quizzed and questioned by people who knew what their church believed and were anxious to know whether what I believe measured up to their doctrinal position. They pulled no punches as they probed my answers, listened to sermons, and read my responses in order to make sure there was unity in the truth. Would that this was always the way it was, but I can assure you that this is the exception rather than the rule. In other words, this church's process was so unlike the "beauty pageant" that often passes for pulpit selection in many "evangelical" churches today. Brian's work will serve the churches by providing a model of how the enormous responsibility of seeking an undershepherd of the flock of God should be carried out. With a faithfulness to Scripture and a freshness of style, What to Look for in a Pastor *hits the proverbial nail on the head. May the Chief Shepherd use it for His glory and His church's good!*

Liam Goligher, Senior Minister of Tenth Presbyterian Church, Philadelphia, USA, and former Minister of Duke Street Church, Richmond, UK

Brian has written a resource that will be helpful for churches for years to come.

John MacArthur, Pastor-Teacher, Grace Community Church, Sun Valley, California, USA

Commendations

Perhaps no process in all of church life is more fraught with pitfalls and hazards than the task of choosing a new pastor. Pastoral search committees often consist of marginally equipped lay people who are utterly inexperienced when it comes to examining a pastor and evaluating his giftedness. In many cases, members of search committees themselves could not pass the most elementary doctrinal exam, and they are often totally clueless about how to choose a pastor to lead and feed the flock. What to Look for in a Pastor *is filled with sound advice and solid help for churches seeking pastors. Brian Biedebach's book fills a void that has needed to be addressed for a very long time. I'm very grateful to Day One for publishing this book.*

Phil Johnson, Executive Director, Grace To You, Southern California, USA, and internationally known conference speaker and lecturer

Contents

Dedication

To my wife, Sweet Anita. Your love, companionship, honesty, and willingness

to follow me anywhere are my treasured gifts from God.

Since 1957 I have personally been involved either in pastoring a church or training others to function as pastors in a church. During that time, there has never been a period of my life when I have not served on the elder board of a church. I write all of that to say that, during that time, I have been involved in the selection process of a church that needed a pastor in one of three ways. On a few occasions, I was involved because I was the person who was being considered as a possible candidate to pastor a local church. Other times, as an elder in a church, I was involved as a member of a search committee that was looking for a person or persons to pastor the local church to which we belonged. On numerous occasions, I have also had the privilege of giving some counsel to search committees who were seeking guidance about what to look for in selecting a pastor and how to go about securing him.

In this book, Brian Biedebach has done the church a tremendous service by providing biblically based guidelines for helping pastors or want-to-be-pastors to know what their ministry as a pastor should look like. And he has also served us by giving to churches (and the search committees of those churches) a clear presentation of the most important qualifications and directives they should focus on as they select a pastor. I suggest that if pastors and people in churches read and apply the biblical teaching of this book, our churches will reap the benefit of being shepherded by men who will be extremely useful in "equipping … the saints for the work of service" and helping the church to bring the glory to God that He deserves (Eph. 4:12; 3:21).

Wayne Mack, internationally known author and lecturer, currently teaching at Grace School of Ministry in Pretoria, South Africa

Introduction

Recently I met a man named Joe, who works as a purchaser in the finance office of a large church. Anything the church needs—a piano, chairs, microphones, lights, you name it—this man does the research and finds the best product at the best price. For thirteen years this has been his full-time occupation. Imagine how much Joe has saved his church, not only financially, but also in headaches. Because of his diligent skills in stewardship, the church staff have enjoyed great peace of mind in their purchases—they have got just what they needed, at the right time, and for the right price.

After I met Joe, I began thinking, "If only churches were as diligent in how they find a pastor as many of them are in how they purchase items for the church, think how many headaches could be saved!" After all, finding the right pastor must be more important than finding the right piano. But instead of looking to an expert like Joe, most churches rely on the recommendations of an inexperienced and sometimes blinded pulpit committee.

The typical pulpit committee is made up of six or seven church members who hardly know one another and have never before experienced the process of choosing a pastor. Either their previous pastor was with them so long that there never was a need to consider finding a new pastor, or their previous pastor was around so briefly that the church elected a new committee to make sure that the next pastor was a better match for the congregation. Generally speaking, no pulpit committee is well experienced at selecting a pastor. In fact, the few committees that are well experienced have proven by the results of their selections that they should have had more help to find God's best choice.

Pulpit committees often gamble with the selection of their candidates because they usually don't have a clear understanding of biblical guidelines for choosing a pastor. Many pastoral search committees unwittingly have incorrect expectations, erroneous criteria, and a skewed evaluation process. The result is that their churches end up with the wrong man.

To complicate matters, there is much confusion in the church today about what a pastor should be. The characteristics that top the committee's list are often the ones that were lacking in their previous pastor. The pendulum swings from the extremes of one pastor's deficiencies to the next. If people say that their previous pastor was a really good "preacher" but not much of a "people person," members often look for a man with a "pastor's heart." If, on the other hand, he was "all people" but preached ineffectively, the committee looks for a "good communicator." If he was too old or boring, they look for a young, "vibrant" pastor, but if he was inexperienced, they look for someone "mature." On it goes. The problem with this approach is that the committee finds itself driven by what didn't work before, instead of by what the Bible says a pastor should be.

A further issue that makes the process difficult is the lesser view of preaching that is prevalent in churches today. Music, drama, dancing, multimedia presentations, movie clips, and extended announcement sessions are crowding out time that used to be reserved for preaching in many church services. The sermons get shorter, making pastoral searches less and less concerned with how effective the man's preaching is. The committee becomes more concerned with his personality and ability to "host" the Sunday morning service. If we combine this with growing ecumenism and the current trend that devalues the importance of doctrine, it becomes far more difficult to know which direction a church may be headed in with the leader it has chosen. One church member who recognized the confusion and need for direction in pulpit committees has written,

We don't want ministers anymore, we want CEOs. We don't want prophets, we want politicians. We don't want godliness, we want experience. We don't want spirituality, we want efficiency. We don't want humility, we want charisma. We don't want godly authority, we want relational skill. As a result, we have thousands and thousands of churches in this country whose ministers are very qualified to do what the Church has asked of them, but the one thing that hasn't been asked of them is to love Jesus. So they don't. And neither do their people. As a result, it is not just God who is dead ... the Church is dead.[1]

This book is all about helping committees and churches find the right men for their pulpits. It is also a book for pastors to help them keep the right balance between preaching and other shepherding responsibilities that are given to them by God. My prayer is that this book will help your church find the right pastor.

This book is designed to assist pastoral search committees by discussing the issues that surround six fundamental questions: Can this candidate preach effectively? What else should he do? Is he qualified? Is he theologically sound? How does his practical theology compare with his written theology? And, lastly, how do we find this man? Biblically based answers to these questions will help any search committee define what they should be looking for and how they should prayerfully consider candidates.

It should be noted that throughout I use male pronouns without reservation when referring to a pastor. I do this for two reasons. First, I believe that God has called men to be leaders in both the home and the church.[2] This has nothing to do with foolish notions of male superiority or female inferiority. God has simply designed men and women with different responsibilities in mind, and, for His own reasons, He will hold men accountable for their leadership in spiritual matters.[3] A second reason why it is prudent to use male pronouns in this work is because research has shown that the vast majority of churches looking for pastors are looking for a man. In Adair Lummis's extensive research for Duke Divinity School's publication *What Do Lay People Want in Pastors?*, it was affirmed that most churches are looking for a male pastor. In fact, Adair notes that this is the case "even in those denominations which have ordained women to full ministerial status for fifty years or more."[4] Because male pronouns are appropriate in a work like this, please note that it is not my intention to offend anyone with the use of them.

Notes

1 **Mike Yaconelli,** "The Church Is Dead," in *The Door*, Jan./Feb. 1992, 36. Philosophically, Yaconelli and I would disagree about many ministry issues, but this quote is outstanding.

2 The fact that 1 Timothy 3 and Titus 1 use male pronouns and the qualification "one-woman man" is enough to demonstrate that the inspired writers of Scripture understood that church leaders would be men. Ephesians 5:24 is also clear on male leadership in the home: "Just as the church is subject to Christ, so let the wives be to their own husbands in everything"

(NKJV). If men are expected to be the spiritual leaders at home, how could their wives be their spiritual leaders in the church?

3 For further reading on this subject, I recommend **John MacArthur's** *Different by Design: Discovering God's Will for Today's Man and Woman* (Wheaton, IL: Victor Books, 1994). Another great help is **Wayne Grudem,** (ed.), *Biblical Foundations for Manhood and Womanhood* (Wheaton, IL: Crossway, 2002).

4 **Adair T. Lummis,** "What Do Lay People Want in Pastors?" in *Pulpit & Pew*, Winter 2003, 16.

Is He an Expositor?

The first mark of a healthy church is expositional preaching. It is not only the first mark; it is far and away the most important of them all, because if you get this one right, all of the others should follow. This is the crucial mark ... My main role, and the main role of any pastor, is expositional preaching.

Mark Dever, *Nine Marks of a Healthy Church*

The current trend in many churches is to reduce the amount of time that their pastors spend preaching and increase other worship activities. Worship in song and music is often given more time in a service than worship through the preaching of God's Word. Some churches attempt to minister the Word through alternative means (e.g., drama, conversations, and testimonies). This chapter will demonstrate that not only is preaching the best way to significantly change the lives of believers, but also that there is a biblical mandate for the priority of preaching. Biblical preaching, by means of biblical exposition, is the primary responsibility for a shepherd-teacher and it is the Number One characteristic that a pulpit committee should be looking for in a pastor.

Among all the responsibilities of a pastor, his ability to understand, explain, and apply biblical truth is his chief duty. That task alone, more than anything else, will influence what he does and how he does it. It is because I believe that this is one of the most neglected issues today that I have placed this chapter first before dealing with the many other issues that a pulpit committee should consider. Many pulpit committees prematurely decide to call a pastor merely because he claims to be an expositor (a term I define below). They evaluate his preaching primarily by listening to just a few of his sermons (probably recordings). Other committees are convinced that they don't want an expositor, mainly because they don't understand how important an expositor is for their church. Still other committees have no idea what biblical exposition (exposing the Scriptures) is, and have never considered this "theological" term to be an important part of their selection process. Yet, in spite of so much confusion over what a biblical expositor actually is, it is becoming increasingly common for preachers to refer to themselves as "expositors." In the United States, "it has become stylish for preachers today to call themselves 'expository preachers' [and] quite a lot of pressure exists in conservative church circles for preachers to be 'expository.'"[1]

Although it is encouraging to see a growing number of pastors call themselves "expositors," it is important to ask, "Are they really expositors?" If it is "stylish" for preachers to be expositors, the temptation for many preachers to call themselves "expositors," even though they rarely preach expositional messages, must be great. To complicate matters, definitions of expository preaching tend to be long, using language that is difficult for the average church member to understand. Therefore, the need for a clear, concise, yet complete definition of expository preaching is urgent.

Is Expository Preaching Really Essential?

Not long ago, I met a pastor at a conference for church leaders. When this fellow pastor realized that I was a graduate of The Master's Seminary, he asked a question about the exclusivity of expository preaching. He wanted to know whether or not I believed that expository preaching was the *only* biblical method of preaching. After all, the President of The Master's Seminary has written, "The only logical response to inerrant Scripture ... is to preach it *expositionally*" (emphasis his).[2] Those who agree with this statement are essentially saying that any preacher who believes that the Scripture is without error but is not an expository preacher is not a biblical preacher. After all, how could he be biblical if he ignores the "mandate of biblical inerrancy: expository preaching"?[3]

If you are dedicated to exposition you may say "Amen"—but first you should consider the fact that there have been many great preachers over the centuries who are not usually considered to be expositors. Was Charles Spurgeon an expositor? What about Jonathan Edwards? His most famous sermon is arguably based on a passage that has little to do with the topic of his message. As one theologian has noted regarding Edwards' sermon "Sinners in the Hands of an Angry God," "The biblical text for this sermon is Deuteronomy 32:35: 'Their foot shall slide in due time.' Edwards' exposition of the text is very brief. He does not explain the context of this verse. In fact, he does not even indicate that he has selected only one phrase from the verse, which is part of a song of Moses (cf. Deut 31:30)."4

There is a dilemma for those who claim that expository preaching is the only acceptable type of preaching. It revolves around our definition of expository preaching. On the one hand, if we have a broad definition of expository preaching, it is difficult to distinguish expositional preaching from any other kind of preaching. On the other hand, if we have a narrow definition, and still maintain that expository preaching is exclusively biblical, we are likely to end up excluding some preachers who are clearly biblical.

What Is Expository Preaching?

It is futile to attempt to answer the question about the exclusivity of expository preaching without first clearly defining expository preaching. If anyone ever asks you, "Is expository preaching the only biblical kind of preaching?" the appropriate response is, "You must first define expository preaching for me." Usually, your questioner will be unable to give you a clear, concise, yet complete, and proper definition of biblical exposition. From definitions given by expositors themselves, however, it is helpful to identify each one by its scope. Three categories of definitions are *broad definitions*, *narrow definitions*, and *moderate definitions*.

BROAD DEFINITIONS

The broadest possible definition for expository preaching used among preachers today is that "Expository preaching is biblical preaching." Steven J. Lawson virtually says this when he uses the words side by side, making them sound synonymous. Says Lawson, "A return to preaching—*true* preaching, *biblical* preaching, *expository* preaching—is the greatest need in this critical hour."5 Lawson does go on to narrow his definition somewhat, by commenting on J. I. Packer's words:

What exactly is expository preaching? We are hard pressed to find a better definition than the one given by J. I. Packer in *God has Spoken*: "The true idea of preaching is that the preacher should become a mouthpiece for his text, opening it up and applying it as a word from God to his hearers, talking only in order that the text itself may speak and be heard." Packer noted that the preacher must "[make] each point from his text in such a manner that" [quoting from the Westminster dictionary] "the hearers may discern how God teacheth it from thence." This is the true nature of preaching. It is the man of God opening the *Word* of God and expounding its truths so the *voice* of God may be heard, the *glory* of God seen, and the *will* of God obeyed.[6]

Perhaps now you can begin to understand why this is such a key issue for the pulpit committee. Suppose your entire congregation came to church on Sundays excited to hear the Word of God expounded in a way that the "*voice* of God [might] be heard, the *glory* of God seen, and the *will* of God obeyed." What better activity could your church be doing together? Imagine the impact that God's Word would have on you if preaching like that was truly being heard in your church—Sunday after Sunday, year after year!

Lawson's comments, though clear and concise, are still broad in scope. You would be hard pressed to find any biblical preacher who did not agree with Packer's statement about preaching. And what church member wouldn't want a preacher like that? But the committee may still be left searching for the characteristics that set expositional sermons apart from nonexpositional sermons.

MacArthur is also an expositor who seems to have a broad definition. Earlier, I quoted MacArthur as saying that "The only logical response to inerrant Scripture … is to preach it *expositionally*."[7] Immediately after that statement, MacArthur went on to say, "By expositionally, I mean preaching in such a way that the meaning of the Bible passage is presented *entirely* and *exactly* as it was intended by God. Expository preaching is the proclamation of the truth of God as mediated through the preacher."[8] Again, this gives the reader a better idea of what expository preaching is, but it lacks the sharpness that differentiates expository preachers from nonexpositors. It is not difficult to say that expository preaching is the "only logical response to inerrant Scripture," as long as all those who hold an inerrant view of Scripture also use the definition given by MacArthur. But we will see that there is more to MacArthur's definition than the statements mentioned above. For now, though, it is sufficient to note that some definitions of biblical exposition are broad.

NARROW DEFINITIONS

In the same book in which MacArthur gave his broad definition, Richard Mayhue wrote an excellent chapter, much of which was devoted to the definition of expository preaching. His definition was narrower and he was able to clarify some key ingredients. Mayhue differentiates expository preaching from both topical and textual preaching. According to Mayhue, "Topical messages usually combine a series of Bible verses that loosely connect with a theme. Textual preaching uses a short text or passage that generally serves as a gateway into whatever subject the preacher chooses to address."[9] But expository preaching "focuses predominantly on the text(s) under consideration along with its (their) context(s). Exposition normally concentrates on a single text of Scripture, but it is sometimes possible for a thematic/theological message or a historical/biographical discourse to be expository in nature."[10] Mayhue goes on to list ten marks of what expository preaching is not. This list can be helpful for us, enabling us to make clear evaluations as we listen to a sermon to determine whether or not it is expositional. Mayhue writes,

One way to clarify expository preaching is to identify what it is not:

1. It is not a commentary running from word to word and verse to verse without unity, outline, and pervasive drive.

2. It is not rambling comments and offhand remarks about a passage without a background of thorough exegesis and logical order.

3. It is not a mass of disconnected suggestions and inferences based on the surface meaning of a passage but not sustained by a depth-and-breadth study of the text.

4. It is not pure exegesis, no matter how scholarly, if it lacks a theme, thesis, outline, and development.

5. It is not a mere structural outline of a passage with a few supporting comments but without other rhetorical and sermonic elements.

6. It is not a topical homily using scattered parts of the passage but omitting discussion of other equally important parts.

7. It is not a chopped up collection of grammatical findings and quotations from commentaries without a fusing of these elements into a smooth, flowing, interesting, and compelling message.

8. It is not a Sunday-school-lesson type of discussion that has an outline of the contents, informality, and fervency but lacks sermonic structure and rhetorical ingredients.

9. It is not a Bible reading that links a number of scattered passages treating a common theme but fails to handle any of them in a thorough, grammatical, and contextual manner.

10. It is not the ordinary devotional or prayer-meeting talk that combines running commentary, rambling remarks, disconnected suggestions, and personal reactions into a semi-inspirational discussion but lacks the benefit of the basic exegetical–contextual study and persuasive elements.[11]

Mayhue later summarizes several pages of definitions by listing five minimal elements of expository preaching:

1. The message finds its sole source in Scripture.

2. The message is extracted from Scripture through careful exegesis.

3. The message correctly interprets Scripture in its normal sense and context.

4. The message clearly explains the original God-intended meaning of Scripture.

5. The message applies the Scriptural meaning for today.[12]

It is significant to note that, although Mayhue is a strong advocate of expository preaching, he does not say that topical or textual preaching is unbiblical. What he does say is that "Neither the topical nor the textual method represents a serious effort to interpret, understand, explain, or apply God's truth in the context of the Scripture(s) used."[13]

When Iain Murray wrote about Martyn Lloyd-Jones's expository preaching, his definition of expository preaching was so narrow that for an entire decade virtually no one else in England besides Lloyd-Jones would have qualified as an expositor. Murray wrote,

In the 1950s ML-J [D. Martyn Lloyd-Jones] was virtually alone in England in engaging what he meant by "expository preaching." For preaching to qualify for that designation it was not enough, in his view, that its content be biblical; addresses which concentrated upon word-studies, or which gave running commentary and analyses of whole chapters might be termed "biblical" but that is not the same as exposition. To expound is not simply to give the correct grammatical sense of a verse or passage, it is rather to set out principles which the words are intended to convey. True expository preaching is, therefore, *doctrinal* preaching, it is preaching which addresses specific truths from God to man. The expository preacher is not one who "shares his studies" with others; he is an ambassador and a messenger, authoritatively delivering the Word of God to men. Such preaching presents a text, then, with that text in sight throughout; there is deduction, argument, and appeal, the whole making up a message which bears the authority of Scripture itself.[14]

Bryan Chapell is another expositor with a narrow definition of expository preaching. Notice in the following quote that Chapell first gives a broad definition and then (in the same paragraph) goes on to present a narrow definition:

A sermon is not expository simply because it addresses a subject in the Bible. Neither does quoting numerous Scripture references in a sermon make a preacher an expositor ... A sermon that explores any biblical concept is in the broadest sense "expository," but the *technical definition of an expository sermon* requires that it expound Scripture by deriving from a specific text main points and subpoints that disclose the thought of the author, cover the scope of the passage, and are applied to the lives of the listeners [emphasis his].[15]

Further, Chapell comments on topical sermons, saying,

A topical sermon may creatively add redemptive truth to the message since the preacher is not bound to disclose the precise meaning of a specific text in such a message. The much repeated characterization of Spurgeon that "no matter where he began in Scripture, he always took a shortcut to the cross," exemplifies a method that bypasses the direct statements in the text. This is not to say that a topical sermon necessarily leads to unbiblical conclusions or to inappropriate redemptive connections. Such an approach simply progresses without clear biblical authority.[16]

It should be noted that Mayhue, Lloyd-Jones, and Chapell are all three strong advocates for expository preaching. Richard Mayhue believed that, as "the twentieth century sets and a new millennium dawns, we must reclaim the science and art of expository preaching for the coming generation."[17] Lloyd-Jones clearly proposed that "a sermon should always be expository."[18] And Chapell says that "for the beginning preacher and for a regular congregational diet no preaching type is more important [than expository preaching]."[19]

In spite of their passion for expository preaching, many who hold narrow definitions do not go so far as to say that nonexpositors are unbiblical. Bryan Chapell even says, "Other types of preaching that proclaim biblical truth are certainly valid and valuable …"[20] Chapell was also quick to say that topical sermons were not necessarily "unbiblical … or … inappropriate"[21] after he used Spurgeon as an example of a topical preacher. So far, it would seem that, the narrower your definition of expository preaching, the more you accept other forms of preaching.

MODERATE DEFINITIONS: THE MIDDLE GROUND
In the book *The Company of Preachers*, Richard Lischer said, "How one defines any activity will dictate one's attitude toward the task and its execution."[22] This applies to the exclusivity of expository preaching. Those with a broad definition can say that expository preaching is the only biblical method. Those with a narrow definition can say that it is the best form of several legitimate forms of preaching. There is, however, a third option. If one holds a moderate definition, one can say that all biblical preaching is expositional but pure exposition is the most biblical form of preaching.

Essentially, this is what Bryan Chapell did when he wrote about "the broadest sense ... [and] the *technical definition of an expository sermon*"[23] in the same sentence. He noted that there are two ways that people refer to expository preaching: broad and technical. Broadly speaking, all biblical preachers are expositors, even though they might not expound a given text of Scripture. Technically, only those who truly expound a passage of Scripture should be called "expositors." It is important for your search committee to look for an expositor in the most technical sense of the word. The more he expounds Scripture, the more your congregation will grow in the grace and knowledge of Jesus Christ.

MacArthur also raised the question of a "middle ground" position when he commented about Charles Spurgeon. He stated that "Spurgeon was not a pure expositor,"[24] despite what James F. Stitzinger wrote in the same book: "Charles Haddon Spurgeon is highly regarded as a preacher and expositor."[25] How can Stitzinger and MacArthur, in the same book, hold two opposing opinions about the same man? Was Spurgeon an expositor or not? Stitzinger said he was.[26] MacArthur agreed, but said that Spurgeon wasn't a "pure expositor." Chapell used him as a prime example of a topical preacher.[27] The answer can only be that Stitzinger, MacArthur, and Chapell have different definitions of what an expositor is. When it comes to Spurgeon, MacArthur leans toward a moderate definition because he uses the word "pure." He thus implies that Spurgeon was indeed an expositor. Therefore Spurgeon logically responded to an inerrant Scripture, but the implication is that Spurgeon could have been a better preacher (MacArthur even uses the term "unsurpassed") if he had been devoted to a verse-by-verse expository form.[28]

Astonishingly, Spurgeon seems to be the barometer that helps a listener determine the broadness of a man's definition of "expositor." If your candidate is familiar with the preaching of Charles Spurgeon, you should ask him if he thinks that Spurgeon was an expositor. If he believes that Spurgeon was an expositor, he probably has a very broad definition of expository preaching. If he denies that Spurgeon was an expositor, his definition of expository preaching is likely to be quite narrow. If your candidate uses a moderate or qualifying word or phrase (such as "not technically" or "not purely") to describe Spurgeon's partial role as an expositor, his definition is one that must lie in the middle.

I prefer a moderate definition for this very reason. Though Spurgeon was a phenomenal preacher and especially gifted in creativity,[29] it is difficult to call Spurgeon a pure expositor, even though Spurgeon's preaching was indeed biblical. Therefore, here is my definition: "Expository preaching is setting forth the meaning and message of the biblical text. In its purest form, it also includes an outline derived from the text, an explanation of what the original author meant, and an application from the text for the audience." This definition has the best components of both broad and narrow definitions. At the same time, it emphasizes the importance of expository preaching.

Why Is Expository Preaching so Important?

Danny and I grew up together in the same small town. We were in the same classes in elementary school. We moved up in Sunday school together until we graduated high school in 1987. Danny got married, became a father, and joined the police force in Southern California. Though everyone knows that the police force is a dangerous profession, I was still shocked to learn in September 2004 that Danny was killed in the line of duty.

He left behind two young daughters, a loving wife, a brother, and both parents. It was devastating for his family. However, in January 2005, at a church prayer and praise meeting, Danny's mother was one of the first to stand up to give a testimony. What would she say after losing her son and months of suffering? Her words were few but priceless: "God is good," she said, and then she added, "all of the time."

I recently told this story to a friend of mine, who responded, "Wow, what she said is really powerful!" He was very encouraged by this story of praise to the all-powerful, sovereign God who is truly good "all of the time." But he said something else that challenged my thinking about the importance of expository preaching. He said, "I know you're a preacher and all, but sometimes a story like that is probably worth more than 100 sermons."

This leads to a very important question about preaching. I don't want to discount the testimony of Danny's mother in the slightest. It is a truly inspiring, encouraging testimony from a faithful servant of Christ. It also portrays a biblical mindset. But, at the end of the day, what is more valuable for God's people to hear: inspiring stories or expositional preaching of God's Word? Is it really possible that a touching story could be more valuable for a Christian than 100 sermons? If so, expository preaching must not be that important, and I should spend more time each week finding inspirational stories and less time studying God's Word.[30] Good illustrations do have their place—but are they more valuable than expounding God's Word?

The bottom line is that your pastor will spend his time doing what he believes is most effective for the spiritual growth of his congregation. Some pastors will have inspirational stories that dominate their preaching. They do that, I suppose, because they think that inspirational stories change lives. Other pastors will spend most of their time in the pulpit explaining the text and giving great detail about the historical background, the precise meaning of the words, and how the grammar affects the passage's interpretation. Those expositors who do that (myself included) do so because they believe that the more their congregations understand the text, the more they will be transformed into the image of Jesus Christ. I am not talking about intentionally boring preaching with no illustrations or applications. But I am talking about the kind of preaching that is concerned that the congregation understands the text, rather than being temporarily moved by a tear-jerking illustration.

The reality is that no inspirational story is worth 100 expositional sermons because an expository sermon unleashes the very power of God. The long-term benefits for spiritual growth and maturity are found only in expository preaching. God changes lives, and the primary means by which He does this is His Word, not inspirational stories. Bryan Chapell confirms this:

God fully manifests the dynamic power of his Word in the New Testament where he identifies his Son as the divine *Logos*, or Word (John 1:1). By identifying his Son as his Word, God reveals that his message and his person are inseparable. The Word embodies him. This is not to say that the letters and the paper of a Bible are divine, but that the truths Scripture holds are God's vehicle of his own spiritual activity. God's Word is powerful because he chooses to be present in it and to operate through it.

Through Jesus "all things were made" (John 1:3), and he continues "sustaining all things by his powerful word" (Heb. 1:3). The Word uses his word to carry out all his purposes.[31]

Because the power of God is carried through the understanding of God's Word, expository preaching is far greater than any inspirational story because expository preaching sets forth the meaning and message of God's Word. Again, inspirational stories have their place (especially ones that illustrate biblical truths), but they cannot take the place of or surpass faithful expositional preaching. This is true, even though the impact of a single story may be felt with more emotion at a certain time.

John Calvin wrote, "We owe to the Scripture the same reverence which we owe to God; because it has proceeded from Him alone, and has nothing belonging to man mixed with it."[32] This is why the more a preacher expounds the Word of God to his congregation, the more his congregation will grow closer to God. The higher the view of God's Word that a man has, and the more he preaches it accurately and authoritatively, expounding the meaning of each text to his congregation, the more faithful a preacher he is.

Sadly, though, there are preachers today who do not believe that merely expounding a text of Scripture is a consistent or reliable way to feed their flocks. Barbara Brown Taylor wrote, "When a door opens in a sermon, it is because God has consented to be present. Sometimes it happens and sometimes it doesn't."[33] Apparently, in Taylor's opinion, expository preaching is not a consistent way to bring nourishment to a church. But true expository preaching *always* brings nourishment to a body of believers because the goal of pure exposition is to help the congregation understand Scripture. Everything that is needed for life and godliness is gained through the knowledge of God revealed in His Word (2 Peter 1:3). The same Word that caused the disciples' hearts to "burn within" in Luke 24:32 when Jesus "explained to them the things concerning Himself in all the Scriptures" (v. 27) is alive today. It merely needs to be explained and understood by a believing heart in order for spiritual renewal to begin (Ps. 119:34).

For some reason, though, many pastors today have lost faith in biblical exposition. They don't believe that biblical exposition is what the church needs most. What the church really needs, according to them, is not biblical understanding that will lead to obedience, but something spontaneous that will excite it and cause it to tremble. Taylor is one of these preachers. When she describes her technique for sermon preparation, she reveals that exposition of the Word is not, in her opinion, "fresh." Read carefully the following account:

Every preacher has a different routine for preparing a sermon. My own begins with a long sitting spell with an open Bible on my lap, as I read and read and read the text. What I am hunting for is the God in it, God for me and for my congregation at this particular point of time. I am waiting to be addressed by the text by my own name, to be called out by it so that I look back at my human situation and see it from a new perspective, one that is more like God's. I am hoping for a moment of revelation I can share with those who will listen to me, and I am jittery because I never know what it may show me. I am not in control of the process. It is a process of discovery, in which I run the charged rod of God's Word over the body of my own experience and wait to see where the sparks will fly. Sometimes the live current is harder to find than others but I keep at it, knowing that if there is no electricity for me, there will be none for the congregation either. This means that I never know ahead of time what I will preach. If I did, then my sermons would be little more than lessons, expositions of things I already know that I think my listeners ought to know too. While there are preachers who do this sort of thing well, I am not one of them. I do not want to scatter pearls of wisdom from the pulpit; I want to discover something fresh—even if I cannot quite identify it yet, even if it is still covered with twigs and mud. I want to haul it into the pulpit and show others what God has shown me, while I am still shaking with excitement and delight.[34]

For Taylor, the idea of preaching consecutively, verse by verse, through a book of the Bible is dull. The church doesn't need "wisdom," she says, but rather "something fresh." She does not see how biblical exposition can have power enough to excite the congregation. To be sure, there is nothing desirable about dull preaching. I agree with her that the pastor should be excited about what he is going to preach from the pulpit. In fact, if the pastor is not convinced that his text is the richest, most nourishing passage to be preached that Sunday morning, he is likely to preach a dull and boring sermon. But it is wrong to equate biblical exposition with ineffective preaching. Ineffective preaching is a result of poor sermon preparation. All of God's Word is "living and active and sharper than any two-edged sword, and piercing as far as the division of soul and spirit, of both joints and marrow, and able to judge the thoughts and intentions of the heart" (Heb. 4:12). Therefore, if a pastor wants to preach a sermon that cuts to the heart, he only needs to unearth the great truths buried in every passage and expound them properly. Some passages require more digging than others, but every passage in the Bible is relevant for believers today. Verse-by-verse exposition is ideal, not because it helps the pastor choose a text for his next sermon (though that may be a benefit), but because it helps the congregation and the pastor to be familiar with the entire context of every sermon preached. The more the context is understood, the better the passage is understood; and better understanding of a text will result in greater spiritual nourishment.

Having served as a missionary in Africa for nearly ten years, I have seen signs of physical malnutrition firsthand. I have seen countless children with bloated stomachs because they are not getting the right nutrients. Many of them have an orange tinge to their hair because of malnutrition. I have helped to establish several homes for abandoned babies. Dozens of abandoned infants who were too weak to crawl or do anything on their own have been nurtured by our church members, and I've performed funerals for many of them in cemeteries that have hundreds of fresh graves in the baby section (small, three-foot graves). My heart aches for the many dying children in Africa.

I am, however, no less concerned about the multitudes of church members who sit under teaching like that described above. Perhaps you are reading this book right now and thinking, "Aren't you being a little harsh with your evaluation of this preacher [Taylor]? I mean, it sounds like she is earnestly searching for relevant passages and thoughts to share with others and get them excited about God. What is wrong with that?" To make sure you understand how essential it is for your congregation to be fed by an expositor of the Word, please allow me to point out some dangerous components of Barbara Brown Taylor's sermon preparation. Doubtless her intentions seem sincere, but her methodology may leave a congregation spiritually malnourished.

The first red flag raised by Taylor's description is that, when she is reading a passage in preparation to preach, she is "hunting" for the "God in it."[35] Yet 2 Timothy 3:16–17 says that "All Scripture is inspired by God and profitable for teaching, for reproof, for correction, for training in righteousness; so that the man of God may be adequate, equipped for every good work." This means that there are no ineffective or dull parts of Scripture, and the preacher needs only to unfold and expound any portion to God's people and they will benefit. In Acts 20:27 Paul told the Ephesian elders, "I did not shrink from declaring to you the whole purpose of God" (Acts 20:27). It concerns me when a preacher says that it is necessary to "find God" in Scripture, when all of it is God-breathed. Taylor says that she is "hoping for a moment of revelation," when she is reading a complete revelation of God's Word. She no longer needs to hope; she only needs to read and she will have endless moments of revelation. Yes, it is true that some passages need more study than others. A genealogy, for example, may not be as clear to most of us initially as a pastoral epistle. But both are found in God's Word and both can be preached in a meaningful, applicable way that will benefit His church.

A second concern that is typical in the preparation of many preachers is the idea that their own personal experience should be the guiding force in sermon preparation. Taylor said, "I am waiting to be addressed by the text by my own name, to be called out by it so that I look back at my human situation and see it from a new perspective, one that is more like God's." The problem with this is that God's Word speaks to more situations than one person can possibly experience. I have no doubt that personal application is essential for a preacher, and I do not discount that at all. The preacher must look to his own heart and apply the truths he is studying as he studies. Otherwise, his own heart will surely grow cold and pharisaic. But this does not mean that I should preach only those passages that address my own human situation. Countless times, while preaching verse by verse through a particular section of Scripture, I have had someone come up to me and say, "That passage spoke directly to my soul; it applied to my current situation so precisely that if I didn't know you were preaching through a book of the Bible, I would have thought that you chose that text specifically for me."

Sometimes, people to whom I am giving counsel ask me if I chose a Sunday morning passage because I knew of their particular situations. Ironically, not only do I never choose passages because of individual situations, but most of the time I never think of those particular counseling situations when I am preparing a message. The reason why I often hear people say how much the passage has meant to them after they have heard it preached is because they now understand the passage more deeply than they ever did before. Their preacher has endeavored to explain and expound the text of Scripture with such clarity and passion that they now understand what it meant to the original recipients and how it can be applied to their own situations. My congregation is thankful that I do not "run the charged rod of God's Word over the body of my own experience and wait to see where the sparks will fly." I could never experience what all my congregation members have experienced. If I only expounded texts that related emotionally to my own experience, myriads of experiences and situations would go unaddressed in our church family.

I must also make it perfectly clear that experience should have no part in the interpretation process. The typical "Bible study" these days involves a "leader" who begins by reading a verse from Scripture. He then turns to the person on his right and says, "What does this verse mean to you?" That person then shares his or her thoughts. The same question is asked to each person in the circle and quite often several different "meanings" are shared until the question comes back to the "leader." At which point, he often says, "Well, thank you for coming tonight. This certainly was an enlightening study." This scenario makes me want to pull out my hair.

In fact, when I am in a Bible-study scenario like that and someone asks me, "What does this verse mean to you?" I am tempted to say, "It means that *you* obviously didn't do any preparation for this Bible study." The truth is that it doesn't matter what the text means to me, or to Bob, Sally, or Joe. What matters is "What does this verse *mean*?" What did it mean to the original recipients? What is its historical background? How are the key words in this passage used elsewhere in Scripture, and what do they mean in this context? Interpretation is all about finding the meaning of the text, and there is only one meaning to every passage.[36] There may be hundreds of applications, but only one meaning. The power of God's Word is unleashed in the lives of believers when they begin to understand what the text before them means. Meaning is extremely important; if it weren't, preachers could just stand up and read a Greek or Latin translation of the text to an English-speaking congregation and the "Word" would have been spoken forth. But we know that the "Word" hasn't really been spoken forth in such situations because nobody has really understood it. Likewise, a Bible study or sermon in which no one understands the passage at hand is certainly an inadequate attempt to expound the Word of God.

It frightens me to hear someone claiming to be a preacher saying, "I never know ahead of time what I will preach. If I did, then my sermons would be little more than lessons, expositions of things I already know that I think my listeners ought to know too."[37] This philosophy is the exact opposite of the one that a preacher should have. Again, I am not saying that pastors should be boring and stale; nor am I saying that sermon preparation time should be mechanical and without a sweet time of devotion. I believe that a boring sermon from God's Word is an oxymoron. Every verse in God's Word was put there for a reason and, in its context, each verse is so life-transforming that it should never be preached in an uninteresting or lackluster manner. But it is a recipe for disaster to suggest that a pastor should go into the pulpit not knowing what he is going to say, so that he can remain fresh.

The average pastor has a few favorite sermons virtually memorized and can basically walk into any pulpit and "shoot straight from the hip" without any notes or preparation. His message may even be biblical, powerful, and just what that congregation needs to hear. But eventually he is going to run out of ammunition. Pretty soon, he will be saying the same things and just trying to repackage them in a new presentation. What may be acceptable in one pulpit he visits could starve his congregation at home if he tries to "wing it" week after week. The only way for a pastor to nourish his congregation with fresh food from God's Word is to study the Scriptures diligently each week. It can be a tedious and laborious task to read the historical background for a passage and diagram the text (so that the main points preached are the main points from the text). It is difficult to craft a message that will present a passage from Scripture accurately, passionately, and in a way that can be easily applied to each person's situation. But this is the job of a shepherd-teacher. Charles Spurgeon once said, "I scarcely ever prepare for my pulpit with pleasure. Study for the pulpit is to me the most irksome work in the world."[38] And yet this preacher from the late 1800s was known and is still known today as "The Prince of Preachers." Preparation is hard work and requires discipline and diligence, but it can also be a sweet time of communion with God. The following story from Spurgeon himself illustrates this:

There is a story told of me and some person who desired to see me on a Saturday night, when I had shut myself up to make ready for the Sabbath. He was very great and very important, and so the maid came to say that someone desired to see me. I directed her to say that it was my rule to see no one at that time. Then he was more important still, and said, "Tell Mr. Spurgeon that a servant of the Lord Jesus Christ desires to see him immediately." The frightened servant brought the message, but the sender gained little by it, for my answer was, "Tell him I am busy with his Master, and cannot see servants now."[39]

It should be noted that few preachers could respond to a visitor as Spurgeon did and not get fired. The loving response for most pastors would be to sacrifice an hour of study in order to minister to someone who showed up unexpectedly with a need. Evidently, Spurgeon's popularity forced him to guard his study time with such tenacity that it demonstrated his commitment to serving his congregation through serious study.

The ability to find a sermon outline from the text, research the historical background and context, interact with commentaries, and prepare a message on a weekly basis that exposes the true meaning and application of each text is an essential quality that a pastor needs to have. The more devoted he is to the ministry of the Word, the better he will be able to shepherd your flock. The most valuable service a man can do for you is to preach the whole counsel of God. And there is no better way to preach the whole counsel of God than through expository preaching. John MacArthur wrote that consecutive expositional preaching is even better:

Preaching verse by verse through books of the Bible is the most reliable way to teach the whole counsel of God. If I am obligated to teach the whole new covenant message and all of the mystery unfolded, the only systematic way that I know to teach it all is to take it the way it comes, one book at a time from beginning to end. If I were to approach the goal of teaching the whole New Testament in random fashion, it would be a hopeless maze to lead people through. On the other hand, if I am committed to teaching the Word of God systematically so that all of the revelation of God is brought before His people, the only reasonable way of doing that is to go through it one book at a time.[40]

Expository preaching is the most biblical method of preaching because it is the best way to expound the powerful Word of God. Broadly speaking, any preaching that does not expound God's Word is not biblical preaching. Expository preaching not only sets forth the meaning and message of the original text, but, in its purest form, includes an outline from the text, an explanation of what the original author meant, and an application from the text for the listener.

Notes

1   **Jack Hughes,** *Expository Preaching with Word Pictures* (Fearn: Mentor, 2001), 14.
2   **John MacArthur,** "The Mandate of Biblical Inerrancy: Expository Preaching," in **John F. MacArthur, Richard Mayhue,** and **Robert L. Thomas,** (eds.), *Rediscovering Expository Preaching: Balancing the Science and Art of Biblical Exposition* (Dallas: Word, 1992), 23.
3   Ibid. 22.
4   **Glenn R. Kreider,** "Sinners in the Hands of a Gracious God," January 1, 2004, at: bible.org.
5   **Steven J. Lawson,** *Famine in the Land: A Passionate Call for Expository Preaching* (Chicago: Moody, 2003), 17.
6   Ibid.
7   **MacArthur,** "Mandate," 23.
8   Ibid. 23–24.
9   **Richard Mayhue,** "Rediscovering Expository Preaching," in *Rediscovering Expository Preaching*, 9.
10 Ibid. 9.
11 Ibid. 10. These ten suggestions were originally derived from **Faris D. Whitesell,** *Power in Expository Preaching* (Old Tappan, NJ: Revell, 1963), vii–viii.

12 Mayhue, "Rediscovering Expository Preaching," 12–13.

13 Ibid. 9.

14 Cited in **Mayhue,** "Rediscovering Expository Preaching," 12.

15 Bryan Chapell, *Christ-Centered Preaching: Redeeming the Expository Sermon* (Grand Rapids, MI: Baker, 1994), 128–129.

16 Ibid. 273.

17 Mayhue, "Rediscovering Expository Preaching," 20.

18 D. Martyn Lloyd-Jones, *Preaching and Preachers* (Grand Rapids: Zondervan, 1972), 72.

19 Chapell, *Christ-Centered Preaching*, 22.

20 Ibid.

21 Ibid. 273.

22 Richard Lischer, "The Promise of Renewal," in **Richard Lischer,** (ed.), *The Company of Preachers: Wisdom on Preaching, Augustine to the Present* (Grand Rapids, MI: Eerdmans, 2002), xiii.

23 Chapell, *Christ-Centered Preaching*, 128–129.

24 MacArthur, "Frequently Asked Questions about Expository Preaching," in *Rediscovering Expository Preaching*, 340.

25 James F. Stitzinger, "The History of Expository Preaching," in *Rediscovering Expository Preaching*, 36.

26 Ibid.

27 Chapell, *Christ-Centered Preaching*, 273.

28 MacArthur, "Frequently Asked Questions," 340.

29 Ibid. It should be noted that MacArthur shows immense respect for Spurgeon and explains that one of the reasons why he (MacArthur) does not do more topical messages as Spurgeon did is because "I could never produce such inspiring, clever, creative topical sermons week in and week out as he did."

30 I currently spend at least half my pastoral ministry time studying. It takes me about 10–15 hours to prepare one expositional message. This is painstaking work for me at times, since I am the type of person who prefers to be out visiting and fellowshipping with people rather than alone studying in my office. But I believe that a dynamic, clear exposition of God's Word on Sunday morning and evening is the way I can best serve my congregation.

31 Chapell, *Christ-Centered Preaching*, 19.

32 John Calvin, *Commentaries on the Epistles to Timothy, Titus, and Philemon*, in *Calvin's Commentaries*, vol. 21, trans. by **William Pringle** (Grand Rapids, MI: Baker, 2005), 249.

33 Barbara Brown Taylor, "Preaching," in Richard Lischer, (ed.), *The Company of Preachers:*

Wisdom on Preaching, Augustine to the Present (Grand Rapids, MI: Eerdmans, 2002), 49.

34 Ibid. 50.

35 Ibid.

36 For an extensive treatment of this subject see **Robert L. Thomas,** *Evangelical Hermeneutics: The New versus the Old* (Grand Rapids, MI: Kregel, 2002).

37 Taylor, "Preaching," 50.

38 Cited in **Tom Carter,** *Spurgeon At His Best* (Grand Rapids, MI: Baker, 1988), 162.

39 Ibid.

40 MacArthur, "Frequently Asked Questions," 340.

The Balance of Responsibilities

Our Lord's favorite metaphor for spiritual leadership, a figure He often used to describe Himself, was that of a shepherd—one who tends God's flock. Every church leader is a shepherd. The word *pastor* itself even means "shepherd." It is appropriate imagery. A shepherd leads, feeds, nurtures, comforts, corrects, and protects. Those are responsibilities of every churchman.

John F. MacArthur, Jr., *Shepherdology*

Oftentimes, when people describe their pastors, they begin by talking about what he is not. "He's not a really good *preacher*," they say, "but he is an excellent *pastor*." The opposite response is, "He's not much of a *pastor,* but, boy, can he *preach*!" When people make this latter statement, it is clear that they themselves don't feel shepherded by their pastor, but they appreciate his preaching. In fact, I had one lady tell me that her pastor really relates to bikers and people from rough backgrounds in her church, but pretty much ignores the rest of the congregation. She seemed happy with that because she had such a high respect for his preaching ministry. At the other end of the spectrum, a person once boasted to me about a pastor who had "built an entire congregation primarily through home visitation." That pastor was a quiet man who was not a good preacher at all, but he was endearing and caring and he visited each member's home frequently on a regular rotation.

I hope that you have gained from the last chapter how important it is to have a high view of expository preaching. If your pastor is going to be excessive in one part of his ministry, let it be the diligent study of God's Word, as he prepares to bring forth the Word in his preaching. There is no greater service a pastor can do for his congregation than to delve into the deepest depths of God's Word and then expound the truths he discovers to his congregation in a manner that is passionate, accurate, and clearly understood by every ear. Charles Jefferson (1860–1937) wrote, "We sometimes hear it said of a minister: 'He is a good pastor, but he cannot preach.' The sentence is self-contradictory. No man can be a good pastor who cannot preach, anymore than a man can be a good shepherd and still fail to feed his flock."[1] Indeed, preaching is a vital part of shepherding.

This does not mean that the pastor does not have any other responsibilities. I have to admit that, when I began studying for this chapter, I was surprised to discover that a pastor's other responsibilities are all closely related to his preaching ministry. This is why I have spent so much time writing about the importance of preaching. However, by emphasizing the priority of preaching, I in no way want to discount the importance of other pastoral responsibilities. When selecting a pastor, your pastoral search committee needs to consider a balance of responsibilities. In this chapter I shall discuss not only what the goal of your pastor should be, but also what his biblical responsibilities (besides preaching) should be, in order to help him reach his goal.

What Is Your Shepherd's Goal?

Ephesians 4:11–12 says, "And He gave some as apostles, and some as prophets, and some as evangelists, and some as pastors and teachers, for the equipping of the saints for the work of service, to the building up of the body of Christ." The main subject of Ephesians 4:1–16 is the church walking in unity. In this passage of Scripture, Paul calls believers to "preserve the unity of the Spirit" and to "walk in a manner worthy of the calling" (4:1–3). Paul then lists areas of unity, such as "one Lord, one faith, one baptism, one God ..." (4:4). Finally, Paul explains how to build and maintain unity in the church through various gifts provided by God (4:7–16). One of the gifts that God has given your church for edification is your pastor-teacher.

In Ephesians 4:11, Paul mentions four positions in the church. Two no longer exist but the other two are present in the church today. The two that are not currently practiced in the church today are the offices of apostles and prophets. One of the reasons why we know that these offices are no longer being practiced is because Paul has already explained what their roles were (Eph. 2:20). Apostles and prophets had three primary responsibilities according to the Word of God: to serve as a foundation, to serve as a conduit, and to give confirmation.

First, the apostles and prophets served as the foundation for the church. The picture in Ephesians 2:20–22 is of a building. Those who are redeemed by Christ's work on the cross are the bricks (vv. 21–22). They are being fitted together on top of a foundation. Christ is the cornerstone and the apostles and prophets are the foundation. Notice the words "having been built": the tense implies that the foundation has already been laid.

A second responsibility of the apostles and prophets was to serve as a conduit for God's Word (Eph. 3:5). Again, the verb describing this action of the apostles and prophets indicates past action. So the apostles and prophets received revelation from God and then declared it to His people.

Third, the apostles and prophets were responsible for giving confirmation of that Word through signs, wonders, and miracles (Heb. 2:3–4; 2 Cor. 12:12). As we have seen, the apostles and prophets are mentioned in the book of Ephesians earlier than 4:11, and they are also mentioned elsewhere in the New Testament. It is clear that all the responsibilities given to them have been fulfilled: the foundations for the church have been laid (Eph. 2:20) and God's Word has been fully revealed (2 Tim. 3:16). Therefore, there is no need for further conduits of God's revealed Word—"His divine power has granted to us everything pertaining to life and godliness" (2 Peter 1:3).

An additional consideration is that nowhere in Scripture is there an instruction for apostles or prophets to make other apostles or prophets. Also, nowhere in Scripture are church members instructed to be apostles or prophets. So it is clear from Scripture that those offices (though gifts from God and vitally important for the foundation of the church) have been fulfilled and there is no need for them anymore.

However, the other two positions that God has given to the church are still in existence today: evangelists and pastor-teachers. Evangelists are those who proclaim the good news, especially in areas that have not yet heard the gospel. In Acts 21:8, Philip is called an evangelist. In 2 Timothy 4:5, Timothy is told to "do the work of an evangelist." As we study the New Testament evangelists, we find that they are more like today's missionaries and church planters, rather than being what we normally think of when we hear the word "evangelist." Crusades and revivals may have their place, but the biblical picture of an evangelist probably looks less like Billy Graham and more like a missionary who is involved in church planting and strengthening. Other evangelists might stay in their home churches and help to bring people in. "The work of an evangelist is to preach and explain the good news of salvation in Jesus Christ to those who have not yet believed. He is a proclaimer of salvation by grace through faith in the Son of God."[2] Timothy was a good example of this, because for him, part of doing the "work of an evangelist" meant being identified with a local church in a prolonged ministry. He also dealt with problems in the church (like false doctrine, disorder in worship, and materialism). But one of his major roles was to proclaim salvation through Christ to those who were lost.

The fourth position that God has given to the church as a gift is that of pastor-teacher. Some commentators separate these as two separate offices, but both the context and the structure of the verse seem to imply that it is one office. As I mentioned at the beginning of this chapter, it is common to hear people talk about pastoring and teaching as two separate responsibilities. Although it may be true that not every teacher is a pastor, the biblical standard for all pastors is that they are also teachers.

The term "pastor" comes from the same word that is sometimes translated "shepherd." Furthermore, there is no distinction in Scripture between the offices of elder, bishop, and pastor. The qualifications for these offices are the same (1 Tim. 3; Titus 1), and included in these qualifications is the ability to teach. Also the terms are sometimes used interchangeably: 1 Peter 5:1–2 brings all the terms together when Peter instructs all elders to be good bishops as they pastor. While all elders are required to be able to teach, in Scripture there seem to have been some elders who took on the bulk of the preaching ministry (1 Tim. 5:17). Homer Kent has noted, "The pastor-teacher describes the person whose responsibilities are usually localized, in contrast to the evangelist."[3]

Grammatically, Ephesians 4:11 seems to group pastors and teachers together because in the Greek text there is no definite article in front of the word "teachers." Most Bible translators have highlighted this grammatical distinction by stating that God has given "*some as* apostles, and *some as* prophets, and *some as* evangelists, and *some as* pastors and teachers" (notice that the word "teachers" doesn't have "some as" in front of it, presumably because it is so closely associated with the term "pastors").4 Many commentators have written about the significance that there is only one article for pastors and teachers.5

The significant question in Ephesians 4:11 regarding those who are gifted by God in both shepherding and teaching is, "What exactly do pastors do to equip the saints?" There are some who say that preaching is everything and that there is nothing that a pastor can do for his congregation that is more important than prayer and the preaching of the Word. Others state quite plainly that "shepherding includes instruction but probably is most concerned with administration and various ministries to the flock."6 If the latter statement is more accurate, the question at hand needs to be adjusted. For the sake of argument, suppose that the office of "pastor-teacher" describes those who are gifted in both shepherding and teaching while serving full-time in the church today. What, then, is the priority? What does the pastor-teacher do to equip his flock? If pastoring is mainly "administration and various ministries," what kind of balance should a pastor have regarding his pulpit ministry? Is it 50–50?

One can conclude from Ephesians 4:11 that there does need to be a balance in the life of a pastor-teacher between various shepherding responsibilities and the shepherding responsibility of preaching. Of course, this balance will vary, depending on the size of your church and the number of pastors on staff, but there does need to be one. It would be rare for a pulpit committee to look for a pastor-teacher who only preaches. One could question if that would even be biblical. After all, prayer is a vital part of the pastoral ministry. A willingness and competence to counsel is an essential characteristic of a church leader. A pastor who never visits the sick or never is involved with mercy ministry is neglecting his own responsibility as a believer to live out his faith (James 1:27).

Occasionally, pastors will quote Acts 6:1–7 to justify not doing any ministry besides preaching and prayer. It is true that the early church leaders devoted themselves to "prayer and to the ministry of the word" (Acts 6:4). Some pastors refer to that verse to justify their decision to not get involved in any administrative decisions. The greater context of the verse, however, reveals a different picture altogether. This *was* an administrative decision by the church leaders. The pressing issue in that church was that some of the widows were being overlooked in the daily serving of food because of their race. The twelve apostles made it clear to the congregation that it would not be prudent for them to spend most of their time serving tables instead of in prayer and the ministry of the Word, but they did not abandon the issue: they made some administrative decisions. They found men who were able to devote their time to the food ministry. They appointed the men to look after that ministry. Not only that, to assume that they never again checked up on the situation (or gave oversight) is presumptuous on our part. Indeed, they were administrators. Furthermore, it is also presumptuous to assume that the ministry of the Word was limited to preaching.

The pertinent question is, "What are the biblical responsibilities of a pastor?" What is his job exactly? What is he supposed to do in order to adequately equip his congregation for works of service? Great insight on this subject has been given to us by Charles Jefferson. In the late 1800s and early 1900s he was pastor of Broadway Tabernacle in New York City. In his excellent book *The Minister as Shepherd*, he listed seven "works" or essential responsibilities of a pastor. Warren Wiersbe values Jefferson's book on shepherding so much that he says it is one of those books "... I try to read again each year ... It reminds me of my privileges and responsibilities as one of God's shepherds, and it makes me want to do a better job of preaching the Word and pastoring my flock. And it always convicts me."[7] Jefferson's seven responsibilities provide us with an excellent structure in which we can better learn what pastoring is all about. Each "work" is summarized in the remaining outline of this chapter.

Jefferson examined the ancient Near-Eastern responsibilities and characteristics of shepherds and compared them to the biblical implications for pastors. Shepherding is an appropriate theme since "The Old Testament frequently describes Israel as God's flock (Ps. 77:20; 78:52; 80:1; Isa. 40:11; 63:11; Jer. 13:17; 23:2–3; 31:10; Ezek. 32:4ff; Mic. 2:12; 5:4; 7:14; Zech. 10:3), and the New Testament pictures the church as a flock with the Lord Jesus Christ as its Shepherd (John 10:1ff.; Heb. 13:20; 1 Peter 2:25; 5:2–4)."[8] Also, both Paul and Peter are found in the New Testament instructing church leaders to "shepherd the flock" (Acts 20:28; 1 Peter 5:2). While the following areas of responsibility are largely based on Jefferson's insights, the order and some of his terminology have been changed for clarity. I have, however, included a number of quotations from his book, because his undying words paint such a vivid portrait of a complete pastoral ministry.

So, what are the biblical responsibilities of a shepherd?

A Good Shepherd Feeds His Flock

Preaching should be the primary ministry of your pastor. It is one of the best ways in which a pastor can care for his flock. For some, however, this concept is not easy to accept. Members of your congregation may sometimes feel that preaching is more of an artistic or oratorical act and that true shepherding takes place outside the pulpit. Nothing can be further from the truth. Consider these words from Charles Jefferson:

Many would not call preaching pastoral work at all, but what is it if it is not pastoral? No part of a pastor's work is more strictly, genuinely pastoral than the work of preaching. When the minister goes into the pulpit, he is the shepherd in the act of feeding, and if every minister had borne this in mind, many a sermon would have been other than it has been. The curse of the pulpit is the superstition that a sermon is a work of art and not a piece of bread or meat. It is supposed to be a declamation or an oration or a learned dissertation, something elegant and fine to be admired and applauded and talked about by eulogizing saints, or carped at by stiff-necked, unreasonable sinners. Sermons, rightly understood, are primarily forms of food. They are articles of diet. They are meals served by the minister for the sustenance of spiritual life.[9]

There is no doubt that the biblical model of church leadership is the preaching and teaching of God's Word. The Great Commission of Jesus Christ was to make disciples of all nations, and the two tasks He mentioned which explain how one makes disciples are "baptizing them ... [and] teaching them" (Matt. 28:19–20). Discipleship is all about teaching baptized believers all that Christ has commanded. The primary method that Jesus' disciples used to teach what Christ had commanded was the preaching of God's Word. Preaching was the first response of Peter in

Acts 2 as the foundations for the church were being laid. It was the first of four devotions to which the church was committed in Acts 2:42. In Acts 7 Stephen preached and expounded several Old Testament passages in order to proclaim Christ. Preaching was the first action that Paul took when he entered a new town. He preached first to the Jews in the synagogue and then to the Gentiles. Throughout church history, preaching to people has been recognized as the main concern of the church minister. It is a historical fact that whenever the church has wavered in its priority of preaching, it has suffered. It is not coincidental that the darkest period in the history of the Christian church (the medieval period, 476–1500) was also "perhaps the sparsest for expository preaching."[10]

Because expository preaching is so essential for the church, many church leaders today are crying out for its proper place of primacy in the pastoral ministry. As Dallas Theological Seminary's professor emeritus J. Dwight Pentecost once exclaimed,

The great need across evangelicalism is exposition of the Scriptures. I sense there is a departure from that, even among some of our own grads, who are entertaining the people, giving the people what they want, whereas we are called to teach the Word. It is the Word that is the power of God to salvation, it is the Word that is the power for Christian living, and I would want them to make the Word of God the center of their ministry. It may not be popular, it may not build mega-churches, but it will fulfill that to which they are called upon to do in ministry.[11]

Oftentimes, in the ancient Near East, it was not easy for a shepherd to find food and water for his flock. As Jefferson noted, "The water in Asia is often gotten out of wells, and drawing it is part of the shepherd's work. The grass varies with the seasons, and the shepherd is ever changing the location of his flock."[12] Both of these examples imply work that is very time-consuming and strenuous. Indeed, your pastor's job is also one of discipline and labor. As he plumbs the depths of God's Word throughout the week in sermon preparation, it will be like finding fresh water for a thirsty congregation. As he searches the Scriptures for a better understanding of God's truth, his presentation of that to you will be like the provision of healthy fields of nourishment. His shepherding ministry to you is often accomplished in his study.

In Ezekiel 34 the prophet was instructed to prophesy against the spiritual leaders of Israel who were responsible for "shepherding" God's people. At the top of a long list of complaints, God said that they did not feed His sheep but instead were interested only in themselves: "You eat the fat and clothe yourselves with the wool, you slaughter the fat sheep without feeding the flock" (Ezek. 34:3). Still today, we need shepherds who are willing to labor diligently so that Christ's sheep can be fed.

A Good Shepherd Watches Over His Sheep

A former professor once told me that the pastorate had the possibility of becoming the most rewarding or the laziest job a person could have. At the time, I had not yet been a pastor and I didn't understand the contrast he was making. It seemed odd that he would contrast laziness with reward. The connection between the two, however, is quite clear to me now. When a pastor becomes lazy, often it is not in the diligence of his study, but in his watchfulness over his sheep. It is not that it is easy for pastors to become idle and inactive; the danger for pastors occurs when their priorities get out of order and they neglect something that should be at the top of their list. One of the pastor's priorities that can easily get lost in his day-to-day duties is "watching." Familiarity breeds contempt; as long as everything seems safe, it is easy to stop keeping a lookout for danger. But the shepherd who neglects his watch is sure to end up with a hurting flock. Consider these insights from Jefferson:

The Eastern shepherd was, first of all, a watchman. He had a watch-tower. It was his business to keep a wide-open eye, constantly searching the horizon for the possibilities of foes … An alert wakefulness was for him a necessity. He could not indulge in fits of drowsiness, for the foe was always near. Only by his alertness could the enemy be circumvented. There were many kinds of enemies, all of them terrible, each in a different way. At certain seasons of the year there were floods. Streams became quickly swollen and overflowed their banks. Swift action was necessary in order to escape destruction. There were enemies of a more subtle kind—animals, rapacious and treacherous: lions, bears, hyenas, jackals, wolves. There were enemies in the air; huge birds of prey were always soaring aloft ready to swoop down upon a lamb or a kid. And then, most dangerous of all, were the human birds and beasts of prey—robbers, bandits, men who made a business of robbing sheep-folds and murdering shepherds.[13]

In Acts 20, Paul met with the Ephesian elders while he was passing through Miletus. He used this brief meeting as an opportunity to encourage them and strengthen them for their ministry as overseers. Among his exhortations to them was this prophetic warning: "For I know this, that after my departure savage wolves will come in among you, not sparing the flock. Also from among yourselves men will rise up, speaking perverse things, to draw away the disciples after themselves. Therefore *watch*, and remember that for three years I did not cease to warn everyone night and day with tears" (Acts 20:29–31, NKJV). Paul specifically instructed those church leaders to "watch." By this, he meant that they were to be alert. Jesus had given this same command in Matthew 24:42 regarding the timing of His Second Coming and the Day of the Lord. It is also the same command Jesus gave to His disciples in Mark 14:34 while He was praying at Gethsemane. They were to be alert as Jesus prayed, but instead they fell asleep.

The concept of watchfulness is not difficult to understand. It is the opposite of being totally unaware of what is going on around. In the context of a sheepfold, or a church family, the pastor is to have a constant sense of alertness to the dangers that are around his people and where their hearts might be straying. Again, our mentor, Charles Jefferson, says it well:

Many a minister fails as a pastor because he is not vigilant. He allows his church to be torn to pieces because he is half asleep. He took it for granted that there were no wolves, no birds of prey, no robbers, and while he was drowsing the enemy arrived. False ideas, destructive interpretations, demoralizing teachings came into his group and he never knew it. He was interested perhaps in literary research; he was absorbed in the discussion contained in the last theological quarterly, and did not know what his young people were reading, or what strange ideas had been lodged in the heads of a group of his leading members. There are errors which are as fierce as wolves and pitiless as hyenas; they tear faith and hope and love to pieces and leave churches, once prosperous, mangled and half dead.[14]

The obvious implication is this: if your pastor is going to be watchful, he needs to be near his sheep. He needs to be among them. His friendships are among the body and his fellowship is within the body he shepherds. It is impossible for a pastor who is distant and removed to be watchful.

A Good Shepherd Protects His Sheep

The natural response for a pastor who is watching will be to protect. Since so many dangers await the church, it will be impossible for a pastor who is close to his congregation to turn a blind eye. Ultimately, it is God who protects His sheep. He is the Great Shepherd and, because He is so mighty, His sheep can say, "Even though I walk through the valley of the shadow of death, I fear no evil, for You are with me; Your rod and Your staff, they comfort me" (Ps. 23:4). Yet, as under-shepherds, pastors must also provide corrals of safety for their congregations and ward off intruders with evil intent. As Jefferson has written,

The safeguarding of the sheep is a prime function of pastoral work. How to protect the young men of the community from overwhelming temptation, how to shelter the girls of a village or city from unnecessary dangers, how to shield the wage-earner from the gambling den and the liquor saloon, how to keep amusements and recreations from degenerating into forms of demoralization, how to curtail evils which cannot be annihilated, and how to guard boys and girls against influences which stain the mind and eat out the bloom of the heart; all this work of prevention is pastoral work, and what work is more important and more difficult?[15]

A pastor who is proactive in the protection of his flock will have to spend less time picking up the pieces of lives ravaged by the wiles of the worldly. In biblical times, a shepherd would often spend hours, even days, preparing protective shelters or sheepfolds where the sheep could rest. He would also build barriers near dangerous overhangs to prevent his sheep from going the wrong way. Those who didn't construct secure sheepfolds paid the price for their hasty work by mending wounds after an attack.

Those who neglected to build protective barriers near steep cliffs or dangerous parts of a river bank were sure to lose lives that could have been spared. As Jefferson noted, "We have spent too much time in coaxing half-dead sheep back to life again, and not enough time in building barriers against the wolves."[16]

A pastor can construct protective barriers many different ways in the church. In his teaching ministry he can warn against certain dangers, but he must do more. In his counseling ministry he can show a church member how dangerous his or her lifestyle or attitude is, but he must do more. He needs to be the kind of man who will help construct barriers for sheep that are likely to stray.

When Charles Jefferson was pastoring, in the late nineteenth and early twentieth centuries, it was often easier to protect the sheep because many communities were less fragmented. If a pastor wanted to protect his sheep from drunkenness, he could go and stand in front of the tavern on a Friday night. If a traveling speaker was influencing some of his young people, the pastor could address the specific issue that was big in the community. Today, there are so many issues facing the church, and in many cases churches are much larger. It is simply impossible for a pastor to go and stand in front of every tavern. It is a poor use of a pastor's time to expose every charlatan that is out there. Your pastor needs to be studying God's Word and teaching its truth to you so that you will be able to recognize falsehood and make discerning decisions. Your pastor's heart must still be one that desires to protect. This should be evidenced in his preaching and, on a more personal level, in his counseling.

On several occasions I have had young men in the church ask me to help them flee from sinful desires relating to their pasts—their days before they submitted their lives to Christ. Whether their struggles are drugs, alcohol, or some other vice, it is only part of the solution to direct them to relevant passages; I can help set up barriers to prevent them from going back down those paths. Perhaps that means I should set up a financial accountability partner for them. It usually means that I at least give them some assignments for further biblical study and then meet with them again to help them gain a deeper understanding of God's Word and of who God is. It also could mean that I need to schedule a meal or a meeting with them again so that I can ask them how they are managing with their struggles. In some cases, I have had to go with them to help confront family members or friends who had led them astray.

A Good Shepherd Guides His Sheep

When it comes to church leadership, some people think their pastors must be "visionaries" or "go-getters" who are going to start building projects, new outreaches, and other such works. This is a wrong idea about church leadership. While it is certainly not wrong for your pastor to be a "visionary," that is not what real guidance is all about. Spiritual guidance requires spiritual depth. As Jefferson has noted,

A minister must always go in advance of his people. He must lead them in thought. It is tragic when a minister is not the intellectual leader of his people. If his conceptions are those of the average man, if his ideas are the safe and commonplace ideas of the general community, if in his attitude to great reforms he is not in advance of the crowd, if in pulling down strongholds of evil, many are more aggressive than he, he is not a shepherd.[17]

The only way for a shepherd to be the leader of his people is for him to spend more time studying God's wisdom than his people do. Spiritual leadership is dependent not only upon a desire to lead, but also upon a depth of knowledge, character, and wisdom. Your pastor needs to know Christ more intimately than you do if he is going to guide you. Discipleship cannot be driven by someone less mature. Again, Jefferson has said it well: "Mules and hogs can be driven, but not sheep; their nature is to follow."[18] He later adds, "Not every minister knows how to lead ... Such men are always cutting, lashing, forcing, and therefore always getting into trouble. They are continually quarrelling with their people and for no other reason than that they do not know how to lead."[19] If your pastor is going to make disciples, he first needs to be a good disciple.

Jesus commanded his disciples to make other disciples (Matt. 28:19–20). Discipling others is something that every Christian should be involved in, but especially pastors. Pastors should be willing to stay in their churches for a lifetime but always training others to assist, take over, or start somewhere else. One of the struggles that many pastors have is to find the time to make disciples.

Over a five-year period, while I was pastoring in South Africa, I had the opportunity to disciple twelve men. Each one had committed between one and four years to assist in our local outreach ministries. Some of these men were also in seminary but others simply had a heart for support ministry and wanted to be better equipped. It was my desire to build them up so that they, in turn, could build up others, but one thing held me back: time. I was already spending twenty to thirty hours per week preparing sermons and Bible Studies. On top of that I was counseling, doing church administration and visitation, and I had a family with young children. How could I possibly carve out enough time to disciple these young men in a qualitative way?

I found the answer by double-dipping: by combining discipleship time with sermon preparation time. It was usually a struggle for me to get started on my sermons early in the week. I was pretty faithful in taking Mondays off to spend completely with my wife and children, so, by the time I got into the office on Tuesday, I already had a backlog of phone messages, emails, and other issues which needed attention. Wednesdays were usually study and reading days for me. Thursdays were administrative. On Fridays I tried to finish up for Sunday, and on Saturdays I tried to catch up when I was behind—and I usually was. So the only way I found that I could spend real quality discipleship time with these young men was to have them help me with something I already had to do—prepare sermons.

The result was better than I ever could have imagined. Each Tuesday morning, at 10:00 A.M., the guys would arrive at my office. That would give me about two hours to get my office in order before they arrived. We would begin our time by discussing ministry responsibilities for the week and then we would pray together for the week ahead and for the passage we were about to look at. Since I preach by consecutive exposition, I always know what my next passage will be. If my previous Sunday sermon ended at John 15:11, I was going to carry on the next week with John 15:12 and the verses that followed it. Each Tuesday morning, then, my interns and I would turn to the passage that I would be preaching that next Sunday. I would usually write the passage on the whiteboard and we would indent any subordinate point so that we could see the main points of the passage. Each of us would then take a blank sheet of paper and try to come up with an outline and thesis statement (or proposition) for the passage. Our outlines would come directly from the text and we would discuss the truths associated with each passage. This would give me a working outline for my Sunday sermon. Sometimes, further exegetical work would show me that I needed to make some adjustments, but it was helpful for me to have a starting outline from the text.

That is not all we accomplished each week. First, because God's Word was the topic of conversation, we all grew spiritually, and discipleship was taking place. Second, the questions the young men were asking me helped me to ponder relevant issues in the text—some of which I may never have recognized. Third, I was invigorated and excited about my upcoming sermon, and it was only Tuesday! Fourth, in addition to all of that, these young men were learning to get outlines from the text. This was a skill that will help them with sermon and Bible-study preparation the rest of their lives. Spending that time each week with interns is like killing four birds with the same stone.

Pastors are not all wired the same way. I am a people person, and working with a group of men like that helped me to understand the text better. Some pastors may work better alone. The important thing is that your pastor is someone who will find the time to disciple other men without compromising the time he needs for his other responsibilities. How he implements that is up to him, but he must not neglect his duty to disciple. Discipleship is a command for all believers, not just pastors. But if the pastor is not setting an example, others will not follow.

A Good Shepherd Nurtures Sheep that Are Suffering

If you close your eyes and try to picture a shepherd, you may well think of a man wearing robes, holding a staff in one hand, and, with his other hand, holding on to the leg of a small, weak lamb that is resting on the shepherd's shoulders. Perhaps we think of this picture because artists have ingrained that pose into our minds. But the picture tells us something about what a shepherd is: he is someone who cares for those in his flock who are weak or hurting. As Jefferson notes,

A shepherd in Israel was a physician to the sheep. Sheep, like human beings, have diseases, and like all other living creatures on our planet, they are liable to accident and misfortune. They cut themselves, their feet get sore, they break their legs, they fall—the victims of distempers and infirmities of many kinds. The Asian shepherd was a healer of the diseases of his flock. There was usually at least one of his sheep which was lame and ailing, and upon this invalid the shepherd bestowed more abundant care.[20]

Just as a Near-Eastern shepherd was expected to show abundant care to the lambs that were ailing, so a pastor today needs to show extra care to those in his flock who are ailing.

This means that, when a family has a crisis, the pastor is there. If there is a death in the family, the pastor is there. If there has been a major accident or incident of crime, the pastor needs to be one of the first people there if it is at all possible. One of the ways in which a pastor can show his flock that he really cares is not only by visiting those who are injured, but also by having a "first response" policy when it comes to visitation. Early on in my pastoral ministry, I did not see the importance of this type of policy. I always planned to visit those who were in the hospital, and most of the time I was able to visit them before they were released. But I found that there was an extra-special sense of appreciation when I made it my policy to try to be the first one to arrive during a time of crisis. As other members of our church would come later, the injured person would often say in a comforted way, "My pastor has already been here and prayed with me." A good shepherd will find ways to let his congregation know he cares about them. Visiting the sick and ailing is one of the clearest ways he can show how much he cares.

The amount of follow-up your pastor does depends on the size of your church. All elders have the same responsibility to shepherd the flock (Heb. 13:17). When a member of a small congregation has a major trial, a visit from the pastor might be expected. In a larger-sized church, a phone call from the teaching pastor may be sufficient—especially if it is accompanied by a visit from another elder. Many congregations today have more than

1,000 members. Depending on the week, a teaching pastor in such a church may not have the time to even call. In these cases, another elder or staff counselor should make himself available to the member in need. As long as the leadership as a whole takes care of you when you are in need, you can be grateful for the shepherding in your church.

All problems experienced in this life are either spiritual or physical. Emotional problems are related to your spiritual state. Mental problems may be related to physical irregularities or spiritual issues. If your current struggle is physical, your pastors and elders should be praying for you and with you. They should make sure that you receive good medical treatment. If your struggle is spiritual, those church leaders who know God's Word should be counseling you from His Word. There is no greater wisdom, or comfort, for spiritual problems than that which God has provided for us in the Bible.

One aspect that greatly surprised me when I began my pastoral ministry was that counseling was a lot like preaching. After seminary, I was not especially looking forward to counseling, partly because it seemed like such a massive responsibility and partly because I preferred to devote more time to preparation and preaching. In a small church, however, the pastor often has no other option and needs to counsel. I can remember how delighted I was when I first started counseling: it was like preaching! In some senses it was completely different—no pulpit, not nearly as many people, and no way to thoroughly prepare. But in many other ways, counseling coincided with preaching. One of my first counseling cases involved a family who had several issues to deal with, the major one being forgiveness. As I sat there and listened intently to their struggle, I recalled a sermon that I had preached on the issue of forgiveness. When it was my turn to respond, I jumped up, had them turn to the passage I had previously preached, and I walked them through the passage. I even outlined the main points for them on the whiteboard: "3 steps to forgiveness from Luke 17:3–4." Step 1 was to "confront;" step 2 was to "forgive—if the person repents;" step 3 was to "repeat steps 1 and 2 as often as necessary."

Not only did this family respond well to this counsel from God's Word, as they were equipped with a new way to deal with offences, but also their son was saved! As I concluded the session I spoke about our greatest need for forgiveness—forgiveness for our sins through faith in Jesus Christ. Their high-school-aged son told me that he didn't think he was a real Christian. Then and there he committed his life to Christ and he has been growing spiritually ever since. He is one of my greatest joys in ministry. Do you see the similarities to preaching? I explained the text, verse by verse, we discussed the applications, and someone even came to faith in Christ. It was all through the ministry of the Word in counseling.

Over the years, not every counseling session has ended with a conversion. Some have been much tougher than others. In many cases, a person has left my office unwilling to repent of his or her sins and to trust in Christ. In those cases I have sometimes shown people who entered my office thinking that they were Christians that they weren't really Christians at all, and they have left my office sadder than when they arrived. But, in love, I have shared the truth of God's Word with them, and they are surely better off for knowing where they stand before God. This is part of your pastor's responsibility, and he needs to be willing and able to counsel others.

A Good Shepherd Rescues Sheep that Are Lost

One of the most familiar "shepherding" parables in Scripture is that of the lost sheep. Jesus used it on two occasions. In Luke 15, Jesus told the parable in order to teach about God's concern for unbelievers. God rejoices over unbelievers He rescues in the same way that a shepherd rejoices when he finds a lost sheep. He calls together his friends and neighbors and says to them, "Rejoice with me, for I have found my sheep which was lost!" (Luke 15:6). Jesus said that likewise "there will be more joy in heaven over one sinner who repents than over ninety-nine righteous persons who need no repentance" (Luke 15:7). Charles Jefferson noted that some ministers do not demonstrate a great desire to reach the lost, but are only concerned with those already in the fold:

They soliloquize thus: "Why do they not come in? If they are outside it is their own fault. The church is open. The Word of God is preached. The sacraments are administered. This is enough." That is a style of argument that brings relief to a certain type of ministerial mind. Such ministers have few converts … they do not feel any special call to the straying sheep of the house of Israel. They like the sheep who do not stray. They are fond of good sheep who behave well and give the shepherd no trouble by getting lost. It is a great bother to go after a sheep that has broken away—a sacrifice which it is hardly necessary to make.[21]

The reality is that your minister should be willing to make those sacrifices. He needs to understand that part of his job is to be "on call" all of the time. My wife understood that before she married me. When we were dating, she said to me, "I really have to think about this; it would be different if you were a plumber. Then I would know what I was getting into, but as a pastor you will be called upon at any time, for any kind of problem." She married me anyway. Even after counting the cost of marrying a minister, she decided I was worth it. As providence would have it, we lived for a time next door to a plumber and his family. On occasion, I would take great delight in pointing out to my wife that she could have married the guy next door—who, I might add, was often called out in the middle of the night to help people with problems as well! Many professions require availability around the clock. What is sad, however, is when pastors decide that they are too professional for that kind of rescuing service.

Though it is clear in Luke's passage that Jesus refers to the ninety-nine as unbelievers, in Matthew's Gospel He uses the same parable to illustrate the kind of love, patience, care, and concern God has for every believer in his kingdom. In Matthew 18:12–14 the greater context relates to how believers treat one another. A good shepherd will go after one of his straying sheep, no matter how weak or injured he might be. He is unconcerned about himself. He is willing to put himself in danger, if necessary, to go after one of his lambs. Of course, his rescuing ministry begins by knowing that one of them is missing. This kind of alertness, sensitivity, and care is an essential part of pastoring. Again, as Jefferson says so well, "The minister who allows one sheep to drop out of his flock without a wound in his heart and without lifting a hand to bring that sheep back is not a good shepherd."[22]

A Good Shepherd Loves His Sheep

George Whitefield, the famous British preacher of the 1700s, was not very romantic. In fact, his first marriage proposal to the woman who would later become his wife was so uninspiring that she rejected him. He had written to her, "For, I bless God, if I know anything of my own heart, I am free from that foolish passion which the world calls love. I write only because I believe it is the will of God that I should alter my state ..." Alter his state? That sounds as romantic as an income tax return. No wonder he had to ask her again! His failed proposal was proof that a promise of commitment is a far cry from true love.

At the other end of the spectrum, high emotion and infatuation do not add up to true love either. Feelings come and go, and if that is all your love is based on, what will prevent you from coming and going as well? This is extremely relevant for pastoral search committees because the entire committee can "fall in love" with a particular candidate prematurely. You have a committee that offers a job, security, a new sense of identity, and new surroundings. You also have a candidate who probably needs all that and likes the attention he is getting from the committee. "Finally," he thinks, "I have found a group of people who appreciate my preaching." Furthermore, he finds the idea of starting over quite appealing. This is especially likely to be true if it is a larger church, paying a larger salary, and with better accommodation, than in his previous pastorate. If you are not careful, your choice might be made for entirely wrong reasons—with temporary infatuation and misconceptions from both sides. When the honeymoon is over, the effectiveness of the preacher might be over as well. If your church is small, you should consider a fresh seminary graduate who can grow with your congregation. Even though your congregation may have to exercise some patience early on, if he has a long-term commitment to your people, you may be better off in later years.

If your pastoral candidate is already pastoring his own congregation, it may be agonizing for him to consider leaving his flock in order to minister to yours. His reasons for considering your church should be compelling, regardless of his love for his current congregation. In past centuries, to approach a pastor of another church and ask him to consider becoming the pastor of your church was considered to be inappropriate. In the eighteenth century, for example, churches in New England worked together to encourage lifelong relationships with pastors and congregations. As one historian notes,

Permitting a minister to change pastorates because there was an opening in a wealthier community or in one of the several pulpits that automatically made its occupant a colony-wide clerical and social leader would have meant opening the ministry up to precisely the worldly ambitions for wealth, fame, and power that were thought to be antithetical to both the spiritual and the public character of the office. [23]

One example from the early nineteenth century records that financial penalties were imposed for those who recruited pastors and took them away from their congregations:

The recruitment practices of the churches respected the ideal [of] permanency. A church that needed a minister did not violate the sanctity of another church's settled pastorate. In fact, the [restriction] against raiding was such that in 1782 when Yale College called the Reverend Samuel Wales from the First Church in Milford, Connecticut, to become the professor of divinity, his church refused to dismiss him (even though he was not a very popular preacher) until Yale agreed to pay the church a £200 indemnity. A number of churches might well compete for a young man of talent, piety, and promise, but once he settled he left the pool of available candidates. And even if a church had wanted a settled minister, no council would have been likely to release him from his original charge.[24]

Because churches at that time agreed not to pillage one another's pulpits, fewer pastors left their churches over discontentment issues. Also, fewer churches encouraged their pastors to leave. If they did let their pastors go, or if their pulpits were empty, whatever the reason, "the church generally had no choice but to look to fresh ministerial graduates who had no pastoral experience whatsoever."[25] The churches' only options were to keep their pastors and work through their difficulties, or start over with other men who were so young and inexperienced that it might take them years to reach the churches' present level of pastoral care.

Unconditional love for his own congregation became a responsibility and a duty of each pastor. Churches and ministers of that day were deeply committed to each other. As a result of that commitment, there was more pressure to practice church family love. When conflict did arise, leaving the church was the last option to be considered by all. It was far more common then than it is today for pastors to spend their entire ministerial careers shepherding one congregation.[26] Today, I am convinced that many churches and pastors part company too swiftly. They don't work through difficult times, resolved to love at all times. There is a great temptation for a pastor to look for greener pastures prematurely instead of practicing his duty of ongoing love for his congregation. As one pastor has written well, "Love is a responsibility that, when rightly practiced, reignites feelings of joyous affection and strong passion. Right feelings are produced in the laboratory of responsibility and duty, to one another, and before God."[27] His words, written for young couples, have a great application for pastors and their congregations. If your pastor is committed to his congregation for the long haul and he properly practices love for his church family, feelings of joyous affection will continue to be reignited throughout his ministry. There may be times when those feelings are weaker, but a longstanding commitment to practice love will help to restore them.

One of the most loving acts a pastor can do for his congregation is to pray with and for it. Prayer must permeate all that your pastor does on a daily basis. God has chosen to use prayer as one of the primary means by which He works. God does not need your pastor's prayer to do His work, but He has chosen prayer to be an instrument of grace. Just as a musician may use a piano to bring forth beautiful music, so God uses prayer to transform the lives of His people.

When pastors (or any one of us) neglect prayer, it is sin, pure and simple. Not only does God's Word instruct us to pray (Eph. 6:18; 1 Thes. 5:17), but also the many examples in Scripture of faithful praying leaders summon all church leaders to be disciplined in prayer. In 1 Samuel 12, Samuel spoke forth the Word of the Lord concerning the wickedness of Israel when they asked for a king. The people of that day heard God's message from Samuel, but additionally the message was confirmed to them by a thunderous display of God's might. The people responded in godly fear and said to Samuel, "Pray for your servants to the LORD your God, so that we may not die, for we have added to all our sins this evil by asking for ourselves a king" (1 Sam. 12:19). Samuel not only comforted God's people with words, but he also made two promises to them: to teach them and also to pray for them. He recognized that if he neglected to pray for them, it would be sin. In 1 Samuel 12:23 he said, "Far be it from me that I should sin against the LORD in ceasing to pray for you; but I will instruct you in the good and right way."

Too many pastors today, who are committed to teaching their congregations the "good and right way," sin against the Lord because they do not pray enough for God's people. One of the reasons why pastors neglect prayer is that they are not sufficiently disciplined in their daily lives. It was D. Martyn Lloyd-Jones who said, "Everything we do in the Christian life is easier than prayer."[28] He was right. The Christian life needs to be a disciplined life. This is especially true for church leaders. Compare the life of a believer with that of an unbeliever and you will find that discipline is one of the distinguishing marks of the believer. As Lloyd-Jones noted, "The man of the world knows nothing of … self-discipline. He just yields to every impulse, gives himself over to lust and passion … He knows nothing about discipline. The man who disciplines himself stands out, and has the mark of greatness upon him."[29] If it is true that even a man who lives for himself stands out with greatness because of discipline, how much more should Christians be disciplined? Christians, who have all been spiritually renewed, live not for themselves but for Christ. Lack of self-discipline is a mark of spiritual weakness. Therefore, it is of the utmost importance that spiritual leaders live disciplined lives. Since prayer may be the most difficult spiritual discipline to implement, it must be a priority in every pastor's life.

I have never been able to be self-disciplined in prayer without being self-disciplined in other areas of my life as well. The times when I am eating right, exercising, studying God's Word, and caring for others are the times when my prayer life is at its best. But if one area of my life is out of whack (if I am being lazy, gluttonous, etc.), it would truly be rare to have my prayer life going well.

I have emphasized the importance of self-discipline and prayer because they are essential components of a pastor's life. They are usually a barometer of how effectively he is doing his job. We all know that prayer is important as a natural demonstration of love. Alexander Strauch put it well when he wrote, "Loving leadership is incomplete without intercessory prayer. The Scriptures say, 'Let love be genuine,' and then go on to say, 'be constant in prayer' (Romans 12:9, 12). Praying for people is an act of love. Genuine love desires to pray for people. Hypocritical love promises to pray but doesn't."[30]

Those who pray for a new pastor need also to pray that he loves his people enough to pray for them. A balanced prayer life requires great discipline. A disciplined pastor needs your prayer support and encouragement as well.

A Word of Caution

The man you look for to shepherd your church should be someone who can equip your people for works of service primarily through an excellent preaching ministry. In addition to his high view of God's Word and preaching, he needs to be attentive to his people, as he is their watchman. He must not only watch: he must protect and guide his people as well. His caring heart will be evident by the way he nurtures those who are weak, and by the way he rescues those who are lost or wandering. In everything he does, his genuine love for the people of the church must be evident. When a search committee gains a better understanding of what a truly effective pastor should be like, there may come a sense of hopelessness. Can we really find anyone like this?

But remember, especially if you are a church hiring a young pastor: it often takes time to learn how to shepherd a flock with genuine care. The special attention that may be needed by the congregation is not always easy for a new pastor to recognize. When it is recognized, maintaining a proper balance between the pulpit ministry and other shepherding ministries will be a challenge for him. I urge churches to be patient with young pastors. Our friend Charles Jefferson shepherded the same congregation for nearly forty years. He wisely reminded his readers,

It is by no means easy for a young man to become a Shepherd. And he ought not to be discouraged if he cannot become one in a day or a year. An orator he can become without difficulty. A reformer he can become at once. In criticism of politics and society he can do a flourishing business the first Sunday. But a Shepherd he can become only slowly, and by patiently travelling the way of the cross.[31]

Finding a man who understands what shepherding is all about is the first step toward finding a man who will become a mature shepherd. The chances are that, if he is already a mature shepherd, he may not be available to come to your church because he is committed to his own congregation. But if an applicant understands these responsibilities and desires to grow in each of the areas, he is a suitable candidate for your congregation.

Notes

1 **Charles Jefferson,** *The Minister as Shepherd* (Fincastle, VA: Scripture Truth, 1989), 63.
2 **John MacArthur,** *Ephesians* (MacArthur New Testament Commentary; Chicago: Moody, 1986), 143.
3 **Homer Kent, Jr.,** *Ephesians: The Glory of the Church* (Chicago: Moody, 1971).
4 Emphasis in all Scripture quotations has been added.
5 For an excellent discussion of this issue, see **Harold W. Hoehner,** *Ephesians: An Exegetical Commentary* (Grand Rapids, MI: Baker Academic, 2002), 544. Some hold that the grammatical construction of one article followed by two plural nouns which are separated by καὶ. indicates a certain distinction. Wallace, for example, holds that in such cases the first is the subset of the second—meaning in this case that "all pastors are to be teachers, though not all teachers are to be pastors" (**Daniel B. Wallace,** *Greek Grammar beyond the Basics* [Grand Rapids, MI: Zondervan, 1996], 284). This is precisely what I have already pointed out. Hoehner, however, has a beneficial word of caution. He repeatedly reminds his readers that Paul is writing in Ephesians 4:11 about "gifts and not offices." The caution, then, is that one should not necessarily assume that there is a biblical office of pastor-teacher just because God has gifted certain individuals to both shepherd and teach. The noteworthy point here for the pulpit committee, however, is that if you are going to hire a pastor, he had better be able to preach, because all pastors are to be preachers.
6 **Hoehner,** *Ephesians*, 545. He goes on to say, "Teaching includes instruction in doctrine and its application to daily life but the teacher may not have all the administrative and shepherding responsibilities of the pastor."
7 **Warren Wiersbe,** "Introduction," in **Charles Jefferson,** *The Minister as Shepherd* (Fort Washington, PA: CLC Publications, 2006), 5.

8 **John MacArthur,** *Acts 13–28* (MacArthur New Testament Commentary; Chicago: Moody, 1996), 224.

9 **Charles Jefferson,** *The Minister as Shepherd* (Fincastle, VA: Scripture Truth, 1989), 61–62.

10 **James F. Stitzinger,** "The History of Expository Preaching," in **John F. MacArthur, Richard Mayhue** and **Robert L. Thomas,** (eds.), *Rediscovering Expository Preaching: Balancing the Science and Art of Biblical Exposition* (Dallas: Word, 1992), 45.

11 Quoted in **Steven J. Lawson,** *Famine in the Land: A Passionate Call for Expository Preaching* (Chicago: Moody, 2003), 50–51.

12 **Jefferson,** *The Minister as Shepherd*, 59.

13 Ibid. 41–42.

14 Ibid. 43–44.

15 Ibid. 46.

16 Ibid.

17 Ibid. 49.

18 Ibid. 47–48.

19 Ibid. 48.

20 Ibid. 50.

21 Ibid. 56.

22 Ibid. 58.

23 **Donald M. Scott,** *Pastors and Providence: Changing Ministerial Styles in Nineteenth-Century America* (Evanston, IL: Seabury-Western Theological Seminary, 1975), 4; cited in **Paul V. Harrison,** "Pastoral Turnover and the Call to Preach," in *Journal of the Evangelical Theological Society,* 44/1 (March 2001), 93.

24 **Donald M. Scott,** *From Office to Profession: The Transformation of the New England Ministry, 1750–1850* (Philadelphia: University of Pennsylvania Press, 1978), 6.

25 **Harrison,** "Pastoral Turnover," 93.

26 Ibid. 90.

27 **Jim West,** *The Art of Choosing Your Love* (Palo Cedro, CA: Christian Worldview Ministries, 1994), 20.

28 **D. Martyn Lloyd-Jones,** *Studies in the Sermon on the Mount*, vol. 2 (Grand Rapids, MI: Eerdmans, 1960), 46.

29 Ibid.

30 **Alexander Strauch,** *A Christian Leader's Guide to Leading with Love* (Littleton, Co: Lewis & Roth, 2006), 117.

31 **Jefferson,** *The Minister as Shepherd*, 32.

The Character of the Man

Spiritual leaders are not elected, appointed, or created by synods or church assemblies. God alone makes them. One does not become a spiritual leader by merely filling an office, taking coursework in the subject, or resolving in one's own will to do the task. A person must qualify to be a spiritual leader.

J. Oswald Sanders, *Spiritual Leadership*

Thus far, I have written primarily about certain gifts and responsibilities. I purposely started with those chapters because many churches typically don't think about the man's gifts and responsibilities as much as they think through the qualifications of the man. From the outset of this chapter, then, I must make it clear that the character qualities of your pastor are of primary importance as you select the right man for your congregation. Indeed, if he is not qualified biblically, he is useless to you as a shepherd-teacher. While you may be familiar with these biblical qualifications from 1 Timothy 3 and Titus 1, I urge you not to skip over this section of the book. For the better you understand these qualifications, the easier it will be for you to interview and select potential candidates.

Some may question whether this is really an important issue for *church members*. It is obvious that it is important for *church leaders*, but why is it so important for church members? The answer is simple: if the leaders are the only ones who know the qualifications, the members will never know for themselves if the leaders are really qualified. An elder board that goes off-track needs to be held accountable by godly members of the congregation. Furthermore, if the members do not know what the biblical qualifications are, how will they know if their church is hiring a qualified man? Many churches are so out of touch with these qualifications that many members are confused regarding some conclusions that should be obvious to them.

A few years ago, the well-known pastor of the largest church in a city where I was pastoring divorced his wife for no biblical reason. Three months later he announced his engagement to another woman in the congregation. Less than a year later, they were married. To this day, he continues to pastor with the approval of his church leaders and members. During all this time, Christians, even those from my own congregation, were asking the question, "Doesn't this disqualify him for ministry?" I was surprised that people were even asking the question. In this chapter, we will see that the Bible's response to that situation is clear.

There are other questions that are relevant to a leader's qualifications. Since I started training for the pastorate, people have told me, "You'd better be careful: pastors' kids can be quite rebellious." My children are under the age of four. It is not uncommon to see them (and hear them) rebel against my wife and me. Does that disqualify me for ministry? What if one of them becomes a rebellious teenager? What about pastors' children who are grown and at least in their twenties or thirties but do not confess Christ? Can that disqualify a man from being an elder? There are many issues associated with qualified leadership, and I have tried to cover the most relevant in this chapter.[1]

God has a high standard for the leaders of His church. Many churches today are either ignorant about them or deny that they exist. Nothing damages Christ's work as much as when a church ignores His instructions regarding leadership. For if the leaders of the church are straying spiritually, doctrinally, or morally, you can be sure that the church will not be far behind.

It was for this reason that Paul left Titus on the island of Crete. Paul's pattern of ministry began with him preaching to convert Jews in a synagogue. If some of them came to Christ, or if they started to stone him, he would move on and preach to the Gentiles, leading many of them to Christ. Next Paul would spend time with the young believers, nurturing them and encouraging them in the faith. Finally, before moving on, he would typically provide them with loving, mature, spiritual leaders. An example of these last steps can be found in Acts 14:

After they had preached the gospel to that city and made many disciples, they returned to Lystra and to Iconium, and to Antioch, strengthening the souls of the disciples, encouraging them to continue in the faith, and saying, "Through many tribulations we must enter the kingdom of God." When they had appointed elders for them in every church, having prayed with fasting, they commended them to the Lord in whom they had believed.

(Acts 14:21–23)

The receptivity and the maturity of the congregation would often determine how long Paul would need to stay. If the church was under attack, or taking a long time to respond to God's Word, Paul would often leave one of his traveling companions to strengthen it while he moved on. That is clearly what was going on in Crete with Titus. In Titus 1:5–9, Titus was given two priorities that help us understand why God's standard for church leadership is so high. Titus was instructed to straighten out problems within the church, and to appoint qualified elders to lead the church.

Prior to leaving Titus in Crete, Paul had remained on the island to sort out some of the problems. But there were problems that still remained. So Paul left Titus and instructed him to set in order the things that were left unfinished (Titus 1:5). The Greek verb translated "set in order" is the same word from which we get "orthodontist." An "orthodontist" sets teeth in order and an "orthopedic surgeon" sets broken bones, but Titus was instructed to "set in order," or "straighten out," certain problems within the church. From the content of the letter to Titus, we see that these problems included both doctrinal issues (1:10–11) and behavioral problems (1:16). *It is critically important for a pulpit committee to understand this concept, because if your church is currently in the midst of heavy doctrinal issues or dealing with severe behavioral problems, now may not be the right time to look for a pastor.* Instead, your church may very likely need someone like Titus—an interim pastor. When a congregation tries to appoint a new pastor too quickly, it can be one of the primary reasons why the new man fails to lead the church properly.[2]

A second priority for Titus was to appoint qualified elders (1:5b–9). Appointing qualified elders would certainly help to straighten out problems, so these two priorities are obviously related. Some churches may find it easier to establish elderships than others. Notice that Paul says he commanded Titus to establish elders "in every city" (1:5). This suggests that much of the island had been evangelized by Paul and that a number of local churches had been established. It is also significant that "every city" was to have qualified leaders because it implies that it is important for every congregation to have godly men who are not only able to exhort, but who also will be godly examples for the members of the congregation. In verses 6–9 of Titus 1, Paul mentions four areas of qualification for every Christian who desires to serve as an overseer.

Spiritual Reputation

An elder must be "above reproach" (v. 6a).

This first qualification centers around an overarching term that is defined by all of the character qualities listed after it. Alexander Strauch explains what it means to be "above reproach":

> To be above reproach means to be free from any offensive or disgraceful blight of character or conduct … When an elder is irreproachable, critics cannot discredit his Christian profession of faith or prove him unfit to lead others (Neh. 6:13). He has a clean moral and spiritual reputation. Since all God's people are called to live holy and blameless lives (Phil. 2:15; 1 Thes. 5:23), since the world casts a critical eye at the Christian community (1 Peter 3:15–16), and since Christian leaders lead primarily by their example (1 Peter 5:3), an irreproachable life is indispensable to the Christian leader.[3]

In his *Expository Dictionary of New Testament Words*, W. E. Vine says that the term "above reproach" implies "not merely acquittal, but the absence of even a charge or accusation against a person."[4] In other words, being above reproach does not merely mean that you could go to trial and be found "not guilty"; it includes the idea that nobody would point an accusing finger at you. Occasionally I am asked by men who want to be elders, "What about my promiscuous past?" Let's say a young man had committed fornication as a young Christian teenager. Does he qualify to be an elder some day? The issue has a lot to do with "Is he above reproach now?" What if the young lady he had previously had sexual relations with wanted to attend his church under his leadership? Would she be able to point a finger at him for the way he had treated her? What about her husband now, if she is married? What about the potential elder's wife?

Would she be able to enjoy sweet, unhindered fellowship with her husband's former girlfriend? I believe that in some rare cases, a potential elder in this situation could qualify—in time. But in most cases, he would already be disqualified because he is not currently above reproach. To be above reproach does not mean that you are perfect, but that your spiritual character has been consistent long enough that no one would be able to point an accusing finger at you.

This qualification of an elder is so important that Paul repeats it twice in Titus 1 (v. 6 and again in v. 7). As mentioned in an earlier chapter, it should also be noted that Paul uses the terms "elder," "pastor," "overseer," and "bishop" interchangeably. Passages like Titus 1 make it clear that an "elder" (v. 5) is the same thing as a "bishop" (NKJV) or an "overseer" (NIV, NASB, v. 7). This is significant for every church, because it reminds us that an elder is expected to have the same spiritual qualities as a pastor.

There are some churches where you will find a picture of the "senior pastor" high up on the wall. Below him are his associates, and then the church staff and elders. The individual photos form a pyramid that might give someone the impression that the pastor is the C.E.O. But, biblically, elders are the overseers of the church. Pastor-teachers are simply elders who are especially gifted in communication and exhortation. Their gifts don't mean that they are more important than any of the other elders (or anyone else, for that matter). But the biblical model is of a plurality of elders who lead together. They will not be perfect men, for such men do not exist. They will, however, be leaders who cannot be accused of sinful character flaws because they have each sustained a reputation for being blameless. As we continue to examine the remaining four characteristics, it will be easier to understand the role played by this overarching characteristic of being "above reproach."

Marital Fidelity
An elder must be "the husband of one wife" (v. 6b).

Another way of saying "the husband of one wife" is that he is a "one-woman man." Still another way of putting it is "he is dedicated to sexual purity." The literal Greek translation is "one-woman man," or "one-wife man" (three words in Greek: *mias gynaikos, andra*). There are only four possibilities for what this phrase could mean. First, it could mean that elders must be married. Second, it could mean that elders must not be polygamists. The third possibility is that elders may marry only once. Fourth, and finally, it could simply mean that an elder must be above reproach in his marriage.

Occasionally I have met people who stand by the first option—that an elder must be married. Part of the argument runs, "How else could the elder fulfill the biblical requirement of being a one-woman man?" One church planter I know who held this position even took it a step further. He not only believed that all elders must be married, but he also used the same argument and applied it to "having children who believe." He took this to mean that he had to have at least two children (plural) and that they both had to be old enough to assure the congregation that they were legitimately saved by demonstrating consistent, fruitful living. To him this passage meant that he needed to be married and have grown children (all of whom were genuinely saved) before he could qualify to be an elder. Since his children were still young, he himself, according to his position, did not yet qualify to be an elder—and neither did anyone else in his congregation. Furthermore, he was thinking that it could be ten to twenty years before he found anyone who was qualified to be an elder.

The problem with this view is that the apostle Paul wouldn't have qualified to be an elder in this man's church either. Remember that it was Paul who instructed Titus to appoint elders. In 1 Corinthians 7:8–9 Paul wrote, "But I say to the unmarried and to the widows that it is good for them if they remain even as I. But if they do not have self-control, let them marry; for it is better to marry than to burn with passion." Back in 1 Corinthians 7:7 Paul had written, "Yet I wish that all men were even as I myself am. However, each man has his own gift from God, one in this manner, and another in that." Now you would think that if Paul were listing the advantages and disadvantages of being single (which he does in 1 Corinthians 7), he would have mentioned that being single is a disadvantage for some because it disqualifies them from being elders or deacons—if that were indeed the case. The fact is that most Christian men who pursue eldership are married and have children. Scripture simply requires that these men have their homes in order and that their marriages are good examples of what a marriage should be. But these qualifications obviously do not apply to elders who are single or childless.

The second possibility for what it means to be a "one-woman man" is that elders must not be polygamists. To be a polygamist means that you have more than one wife at a time. Some commentators believe that Paul used the phrase "one-woman man" because he was trying to discourage polygamy. On the surface, this seems like a pretty good possibility. The problem is that it is not consistent with a related statement found in 1 Timothy 5: "A widow is to be put on the list *only* if she is not less than sixty years old, having been the wife of one man [or, more literally, a "one-man woman"]" (1 Tim. 5:9). This passage, you may recall, listed several qualifications for a widow to receive assistance from the church. It is highly unlikely that Paul would have mentioned that, in order for a widow to receive assistance, she couldn't have been married to more than one man at a time. A woman who has more than one husband at the same time is guilty of polyandry. One might picture a woman who at one time was married to eight husbands. Is it reasonable to think that Paul's purpose in 1 Timothy 5 was to say, "Women who were once polyandrous don't qualify for help from the church"? That is not a reasonable conclusion because polyandry was abhorrent to the Jews of that day. It was despised by the Romans and it certainly wasn't a big problem in the early church. Therefore, since it is very unlikely that Paul would have addressed polyandry by mentioning a "one-man woman," it is also unlikely that Paul was addressing polygamy by referring to a "one-woman man."

The third possibility for our phrase is that elders may marry only once. Again, there are some prominent commentators who say that Paul was teaching that elders could marry only once in a lifetime. Before you latch on to this position, you should first realize that this would also mean that an elder who remarries after his wife's death would no longer be eligible to be an elder. A man who married young, got divorced, and then later became a Christian could never become an elder or a deacon if he married again—so we are setting down pre-conversion requirements. It would also disqualify a Christian man who got married, divorced on biblical grounds, and then was remarried according to biblical grounds.

The problem with this position is that it adds more to the requirement than is in the text. The phrase "husband of one wife" simply does not indicate whether or not Paul meant "one wife in an entire lifetime" or "one wife at a time." And it is not right to impose on people limitations that are not clear in Scripture. That is legalism. In other words, if we say that a man who is divorced on biblical grounds and who is free to remarry later will no longer be a "one-woman man" (because "husband of one wife means for a lifetime"), we are also obligated to dismiss an elder who is a widower but chooses to remarry. Yet most would agree that a widower is free to remarry and is still eligible for eldership. Either a "one-woman man" means one wife in an entire lifetime or it means one wife at a time. Still another consideration is that Paul did clearly explain some ground rules for divorce and remarriage in 1 Corinthians 7. The whole counsel of Scripture must be considered here. It is important that we don't add something that goes against what Scripture says elsewhere.[5]

Let's look now at the fourth possibility of what it means to be a "one-woman man": that an elder must be above reproach in his marriage. The phrase "husband of one wife" is meant to be a positive statement that says "this man's marriage is an example of a faithful, dedicated marriage." The man is faithful and true to one woman. What would disqualify a man from being recognized as faithful and true to one woman? If he were involved in polygamy, concubinage, homosexuality, and/or any other questionable sexual relationship. What is important is that we are serious about God's standard for elders. We don't need to add anything to God's requirements, but, at the same time, each member of Christ's body needs to be aware of what God expects of church leaders and desires for us all.

We have an obligation before God to know and understand what His Word says regarding church leadership. We need to look at each candidate individually and then make wise, scripturally sound decisions. These are rarely easy situations; indeed, they are usually heart-wrenching. One of the goals of the pulpit committee should be to evaluate the character of the candidate in a way that honors Christ. It may not be easy to raise some subjects, but a wise application and a well-thought-out interview process will help. (See Appendix B: Good Questions to Ask a Prospective Senior Pastor.)

Faithful Parenting

An elder must have "children who believe, not accused of dissipation or rebellion" (v. 6c).

I once heard the following quote: "Parents spend two years teaching their children to walk and talk, and then spend eighteen years trying to teach them to sit down and be quiet." When one of those kids who refuses to learn is a pastor's kid, it is big news around town.

An older pastor friend of mine once told me about his son, Junior. When Junior was a teenager, he started to come home late in the evenings and hang out with kids in the wrong crowd. It became evident that Junior wasn't living his life the way that Christ would live. So one day my pastor friend sat his son down and said, "Junior, I have spoken to the church leadership and I have decided to step down from the pastorate for a while." When Junior asked why, his dad said, "I know that you are not living your life the way that the Lord would want you to live, and I feel like I need to do something else for a time." After a few moments of silence, Junior looked up at his father and said, "Daddy, don't stop preaching—I'm going to start living for the Lord again."

It is rare to hear stories like that. But what does the Bible say about this kind of thing? Did my pastor friend do the right thing? Should all pastors do what he did if they find themselves in the same situation?

What about pastors and elders whose children never genuinely commit their lives to the Lord? Should they force them to live like Christians? If their children refuse to shape up, does that mean that they, the fathers, are disqualified? At what age would it disqualify them? What about grown children who are in their twenties or thirties and do not confess Christ: can that disqualify a man from being an elder? These are all questions that motivate us to carefully examine what the Bible says about a pastor's ability to lead his own family (family administration).

When someone raises the subject of the pastor's home, you will find that there are four common misconceptions about what the Bible requires of elders. The first is one that we have already mentioned—that elders are required to have children. A second is that all elders are automatically disqualified if their children are not saved. Third, there are those who assume that elders should automatically be disqualified if they have unfaithful adult children. Finally, a fourth misconception that looks at the opposite side of the coin is that elders cannot be disqualified by the behavior of their children.

When I first started pastoring, I was single. The leadership of the church that hired me had to work through the issue of hiring a single pastor. Typically, those who believe that elders are required to have children also believe that elders must be married first—otherwise, how could he be "a one-woman man"? Also, in reference to Titus 1:6, how could he have "children who believe, not accused of dissipation or rebellion"?

As I have already noted, if this were a true requirement (to have a wife and children) then Paul himself wouldn't have been qualified to be a church leader. Many of the twelve apostles might also have been disqualified. Therefore, qualifications regarding marriage and children should not be taken as commands to get married and have children. Rather, these qualifications are simply standards for church leaders who *are* husbands and fathers. A man is not necessarily disqualified if he doesn't have a wife, but he is disqualified if he has a wife and is not devoted to her. Likewise, he is not disqualified just because he doesn't have children, but he would be disqualified if the children he had were not faithful children. This leads us to our next misconception.

Some believe that elders are disqualified if their children are not saved. This misconception is not helped by the fact that some versions say "children who believe" (Titus 1:6, NASB and NIV). I think a better translation is found in the NKJV: "having faithful children." The Greek word here is *pistos* and it can be translated either actively ("believing") or passively ("faithful," "trustworthy," or "dutiful"). An example of the word being translated actively can be found in 1 Timothy 6:2: "Those who have believers [*pistos*] as their masters must not be disrespectful to them because they are brethren, but must serve them all the more, because those who partake of the benefit are believers [*pistos*] and beloved. Teach and preach these principles." Second Timothy 2:2 is an example of this word being used passively: "The things which you have heard from me in the presence of many witnesses, entrust these to faithful [*pistos*] men who will be able to teach others also."

The context of Titus 1:6 implies faithfulness. Notice that there is a contrast in Titus 1:6. The elder has "faithful children" (NKJV) who are "not accused of dissipation or rebellion." Is the contrast between believing and unbelieving children? No, rather it is between obedient, respectful children and lawless, uncontrolled children. The terms here ("dissipation," which is wild living, and "rebellion," which is insubordination) stress the behavior of the children, not their eternal state.

A second reason why this passage is most likely speaking about faithfulness is because of its parallel passage in which Paul refers to "one who manages his own household well, keeping his children under control with all dignity" (1 Tim. 3:4). Here Paul is clearly talking about behavior. The elder is required to have his children "under control." This should help us when we ask ourselves, "Is Paul speaking about the status of their souls, or the kind of behavior that they are exhibiting?" In 1 Timothy he is saying that the children should be under control and in Titus he is saying the same thing—only positively: they should be "faithful" or "trustworthy."

A third reason why I do not believe that an elder is required to have children who are saved is because of the impossible burden that would then be placed upon an elder. In Strauch's book on eldership, he writes on this issue,

Those who interpret this qualification to mean that an elder must have believing, Christian children place an impossible burden upon a father. Even the best Christian fathers cannot guarantee that their children will believe. Salvation is a supernatural act of God. God, not good parents (although certainly used of God), ultimately brings salvation.[6]

John 1:12–13 offers biblical support for Strauch's statement. That passage says, "But as many as received Him, to them He gave the right to become children of God, even to those who believe in His name, who were born, not of blood nor of the will of the flesh nor of the will of man, but of God."

A good friend of mine who is a member of a Reformed church recently made an interesting comment to me when I told him that my wife was expecting another child. His response was "Great! Another child for the kingdom!" My response to that was, "We are praying so." I am not being pessimistic; I just think it is a little arrogant to say that every one of my offspring will go to heaven simply because I am a believer. If that were the case, maybe my wife should have forty-two children. The truth is that I can't guarantee the salvation of any of my children. But I can guarantee that they will not be involved in wild, disobedient, and unruly living. That is a promise I can make to them because I am committed to shepherding them. The Puritans referred to family households as "little churches." And this agrees with what it says in 1 Timothy 3:4–5, where Paul speaks of "one who manages his own household well, keeping his children under control with all dignity (but if a man does not know how to manage his own household, how will he take care of the church of God?)." The implication there is that a Christian man can know how to rule his own household. He can do this by not provoking his children and by not being an authoritarian dictator. Rather, he is to be a loving but firm shepherd. And if he doesn't know how to manage his own household, how then can he be a steward in the church?

A third issue involving elder qualification and children has to do with adult children. The question arises, what happens when an elder has a son or daughter who is grown up and out of the house, but is known for wild living or an immoral lifestyle? Does this disqualify the elder? The answer to this is not easy.

The tense that Paul used in both Timothy and Titus seems to indicate that he is speaking about children who live under the roof of the elder. First Timothy 3:4 refers to "one who manages his own household well, keeping his children under control with all dignity." Titus 1:6 speaks of "having children who believe, not accused of dissipation or rebellion." "Having" and "keeping" are in the present tense. This seems to indicate that the children are presently in the home and under their father's authority.

Paul doesn't write that the elder "had kept" his children in submission or that he "had" faithful children. The picture seems to be that, presently, his children are in submission and faithful. In fact, the Timothy passage is especially clear ("manages his own household"). Some commentators have suggested that in Timothy, Paul is referring to younger children and in Titus he is referring to older children.[7] This seems unlikely. It is more reasonable to accept that Paul has the same qualification in mind in both passages; he simply states it differently.

Having said this, there is another biblical principle that needs to be considered here—one that involves the human conscience. In his book *The Vanishing Conscience*, John MacArthur writes about the importance of educating your conscience with biblical knowledge so that it can make informed decisions. At the same time, he reminds his readers:

> If your conscience is too easily wounded, don't violate it; to do so is to train yourself to override conviction and that will lead to overriding true conviction about real sin. Moreover, violating the conscience is a sin in itself ([1 Cor. 8:12], cf. Rom. 14:23). Instead, immerse your conscience in God's Word so it can begin to function with reliable data.[8]

Even though I believe that it is possible for one man with unbelieving, even rebellious, adult children to qualify for eldership, it may not be the case for every man. If a man's conscience is preventing him from being an elder because he knows that his grown children are not living for the Lord, we should never try to coerce him into pursuing eldership, especially if he feels that he can have a greater impact on his children by waiting to become an elder. Remember, eldership is an office that is to be desired or aspired to (1 Tim. 3:1). It is more important for a potential elder to be sensitive to his conscience than it is for your church to have him in leadership.

Should an elder be disqualified if he has unfaithful adult children? Not necessarily. This, however, is an issue that each elder is going to have to work through and act upon with a clear conscience. For one man, it may be fine. For another, it would be wrong for him to pursue eldership at that time.

A fourth misconception about elder qualification and children is that elders cannot be disqualified by the behavior of their children. For the first three misconceptions, I have defended the elder:

- A man can be an elder even if he doesn't have children.
- A man can be an elder even if his children are not saved.
- A man can be an elder even if his adult children are unfaithful.

I don't want to give the impression, however, that the children of elders have nothing to do with elder qualification. On the contrary, the words used in Titus 1:6 ("dissipation" and "rebellion") are very strong and emphasize the importance of this qualification. If your child is involved in disorderly living or rebellion, it is a very serious issue.

When I was a teenager, a friend's mother sometimes joked that she would let him do just about anything as long as he had a sweater on. "Mom, we're going to go vandalize some public property and then try to get the police to chase us around town," he would jest. She would then reply, "OK, honey, just don't forget your sweater!" If she had been serious, it would have been an appalling indictment on their family. Wild and rebellious children are a terrible reflection on a home, particularly on a father's ability to guide and care for others. And a man who aspires to be an elder but has rebellious children under his authority is not an eligible candidate for such a position.

In Titus 1:7, it is clear that there is no room in the church leadership for an elder who is a poor shepherd at home ("For the overseer must be above reproach, as God's steward …"). Immediately after talking about leadership in the home, Paul once again reminds his readers that elders must be "above reproach." An elder is God's "steward" (literally, "house manager"). In ancient times, only the most faithful servant in a palace would become the *oikonomos* (house manager). This is a great picture of what elders actually do. The church does not belong to them but they manage it, care for it, and shepherd it, for the King. Since an elder is required to manage God's household, it logically follows that he must first manage his own household well.

Sum Characterization

An elder must be "not self-willed, not quick-tempered, not addicted to wine, not pugnacious, not fond of sordid gain, but hospitable, loving what is good, sensible, just, devout, self-controlled, holding fast the faithful word which is in accordance with the teaching, so that he will be able both to exhort in sound doctrine and to refute those who contradict" (vv. 7–9).

This fourth area of qualification for every Christian who desires to serve as an overseer has to do with his overall or general character. In Titus 1:7–8, Paul lists five negative and seven positive attributes that are to mark the church elder. The elder is characterized by what he *is not* to be and what he *is* to be.

HE IS NOT SELF-WILLED

To be self-willed is to be arrogant. It is the opposite of being gentle or forbearing. Alexander Strauch wrote, "A self-willed man wants his own way. He is stubborn, arrogant, and inconsiderate of others' opinions, feelings, or desires. A self-willed man is headstrong, independent, self-assertive, and ungracious, particularly toward those who have a different opinion."[9] This is precisely the man that your church needs to keep out of its leadership team. Charles Swindoll tells the story of a young pastor who was quite gifted:

His preaching was a cut above the rest and as his congregation began to swell, so did his head. One day, as one of the church members was leaving, she shook his hand and said, "You're becoming one of the greatest expositors of this generation, pastor." As he squeezed his head into the car and slid behind the steering wheel, his weary wife beside him and all the kids stuffed into the back seat, he could not resist telling the story. "Mrs. Franklin told me she thought I was one of the greatest expositors of this generation," he said proudly, caught up in the heady swirl of the woman's exaggerated comment. No response. Fishing for affirmation, he glanced at his silent wife with a weak smile and said, "I wonder just how many 'great expositors' there are in this generation?" Unable to set the record straight, she said quietly, "One less than you think, my dear."[10]

Great preachers and great elders alike are not to be self-willed! They are stewards of Christ's church. They are not masters or owners of the church, but servants. Second Peter 2:9–11 says,

The Lord knows how to rescue the godly from temptation, and to keep the unrighteous under punishment for the day of judgment, and especially those who indulge the flesh in its corrupt desires and despise authority. Daring, self-willed, they do not tremble when they revile angelic majesties, whereas angels who are greater in might and power do not bring a reviling judgment against them before the Lord.

The self-willed person is really only interested in promoting himself. He acts like a self-made man. He seeks self-glorification. The self-willed man is not so much concerned about following the Word of the Lord as he is about being seen as a leader and commander. A good example of this reckless leadership style is King Saul. In 1 Samuel, Saul was asked by God's prophet Samuel,

"Why then did you not obey the voice of the LORD, but rushed upon the spoil and did what was evil in the sight of the LORD?" Then Saul said to Samuel, "I did obey the voice of the LORD, and went on the mission on which the LORD sent me, and have brought back Agag the king of Amalek, and have utterly destroyed the Amalekites. But the people took some of the spoil, sheep and oxen, the choicest of the things devoted to destruction, to sacrifice to the LORD your God at Gilgal." Samuel said,

"Has the LORD as much delight in burnt offerings and sacrifices
As in obeying the voice of the LORD?
Behold, to obey is better than sacrifice,
And to heed than the fat of rams.
For rebellion is as the sin of divination,
And insubordination is as iniquity and idolatry.
Because you have rejected the word of the LORD,
He has also rejected you from being king."

(1 Sam. 15:19–23)

In this Old Testament account of God's dealings with Israel's king, we find a self-willed, self-promoting attitude. Saul is more concerned with looking like a victor than he is about paying close attention to God's instruction. There is no place for a self-willed leadership style among the leaders of Christ's church.

HE IS NOT QUICK-TEMPERED
One of God's characteristics is that He is "slow to anger" (Exod. 34:6; Ps. 86:15) and this must also be true of His stewards. Proverbs 29:22 says, "An angry man stirs up strife, and a hot-tempered man abounds in transgression." A hot-headed man will stir up all kinds of strife in the

74 What to Look for in a Pastor

church leadership when he lets his temper fly. A quick-tempered man uses ugly, angry words when he is provoked and this will only cause disunity to grow in the church.

In 1999, a seminary board in the Midwest was forced to go through the unpleasant experience of firing the seminary president because of his problem with anger. After two months of investigation and agonizing interviews, they made a decision to fire him for "misappropriation of anger." One report noted, "The action came following 13 hours of a closed executive session in a special ... meeting of the board, attended by 31 of the seminary's 34 trustees."[11] The former president had been employed by the seminary for less than five years. The obvious lesson is that the better you know your candidate before you hire him, the less stress you are likely to have after he is hired. Periodic outbursts of anger and the use of profanity is typically part of a sinful pattern in someone's life. When you interview those who have provided references and others who know your candidate well, you need to ask them if he is characterized by gentleness—even under stressful situations. Gentleness is one of the biblical qualifications of an elder (1 Tim. 3:3). It is one of those godly characteristics needed in a church environment that sometimes involves confrontation. As Proverbs 15:1 says, "A gentle answer turns away wrath, but a harsh word stirs up anger."

HE IS NOT ADDICTED TO WINE

An elder must be above reproach in his use of alcohol. Drunkenness is clearly sin in the Bible (Isa. 5:11; Eph. 5:18; 1 Peter 4:3; Gal. 5:21). Furthermore, someone who is persistently drunk needs to be confronted by the church leadership. If they really care about the person, they will confront him or her and, if need be, discipline him or her. So, naturally, there can be no hint of alcohol abuse in the home of a church elder. However, it is important that we don't add to the Bible and put certain restrictions upon church elders: the Bible never forbids alcohol. Yet one passage is often overlooked when one is considering alcohol use as a church leader. Proverbs 31:4–5 says,

It is not for kings, O Lemuel,
It is not for kings to drink wine,

Or for rulers to desire strong drink,
For they will drink and forget what is decreed,
And pervert the rights of all the afflicted.

If it is not wise for kings and princes to drink wine because they might end up with a perverted sense of justice, how much more important is it for church leaders to avoid alcohol as much as possible?

Again, I do not want to be legalistic here. If your pastoral candidate says that he enjoys an occasional glass of wine with dinner, that alone should not raise any red flags. He certainly has the freedom to do that. At the same time, Proverbs 20:1 warns, "Wine is a mocker, strong drink a brawler, and whoever is intoxicated by it is not wise." For me and my wife, it has always been easier to simply avoid alcohol altogether. The question for us has never been "How much would be too much?" We simply avoid it completely. It is just one more temptation (or mocker) that we have chosen to keep out of our home.

HE IS NOT VIOLENT—NOT "PUGNACIOUS"

A pugnacious man is a fighter. He is a bad-tempered, irritable, out-of-control individual. The Greek word used here comes from a word meaning "to strike"—which suggests that this person is prone to hit you. A man may be known as being violent when an unbeliever, but as a Christian this cannot be his characteristic. This is especially true of an elder. Elders are often at the very center of tense situations, and if an elder is a pugnacious fighter, he will not solve problems, but rather he will exacerbate them. A pugnacious attitude will never solve a tense issue in a godly manner. As James 1:19–20 says, "Everyone must be quick to hear, slow to speak and slow to anger; for the anger of man does not achieve the righteousness of God."

HE IS NOT GREEDY FOR MONEY

Wherever there is religion, there are usually those who are interested in personal financial gain. Paul pointed out that false teachers are overly interested in money and financial gain (Titus 1:11). According to Luke 16:14 and Mark 12:40, the Pharisees were lovers of money who devoured widows' houses. The chief religious leaders of Jesus' day turned the temple into a merchandise market for their own profit (Mark 11:15–17).

Paul also warned in 1 Timothy 6:10, "For the love of money is a root of all sorts of evil, and some by longing for it have wandered away from the faith and pierced themselves with many griefs." Your pastor, then, cannot be the kind of man who is always interested in money. He cannot be a man who needs to control the church finances. He cannot be a man who refuses financial accountability. If a church leader sets his heart on money, it will inevitably lead to publicly disgracing the Lord's name.

By contrast, an elder needs to be someone who is content with God's provision. Hebrews 13:5 says, "Make sure that your character is free from the love of money, being content with what you have; for He Himself has said, 'I will never desert you, nor will I ever forsake you.'" First Timothy 6:7–9 says, "For we have brought nothing into the world, so we cannot take anything out of it either. If we have food and covering, with these we shall be content. But those who want to get rich fall into temptation and a snare and many foolish and harmful desires which plunge men into ruin and destruction."

HE IS HOSPITABLE

If you were to ask a number of people what the qualifications are for church leaders, most people would come up with "able to teach" and "above reproach." There may even be some people who mention false qualifications (seminary degree, must be married, etc.). It is likely that few people, if any, would say, "He must be hospitable." And yet this important quality is expected of all church leaders.

Titus 1:7–8 says, "For the overseer must be above reproach as God's steward, not self-willed, not quick-tempered, not addicted to wine, not pugnacious, not fond of sordid gain, but hospitable." It is the first positive quality mentioned in contrast to what the pastor should *not* be. Strauch comments,

The biblical shepherd is a shepherd of people—God's precious blood-bought people. And like Christ, the Chief Shepherd, the church shepherd must give himself lovingly and sacrificially for the care of God's people. This cannot be done from a distance, with a smile and a handshake on Sunday morning or through a superficial visit. Giving oneself to the care of God's people means sharing one's life and home with others. An open home is a sign of an open heart and a loving, sacrificial, serving spirit.[12]

A pastor who has the idea that he should maintain a high level of privacy either has the wrong idea about pastoring, or he has the wrong job. It is not easy, however, to be so open with an entire congregation. One pastor friend of mine had a member of his congregation come into his home during a deacons' meeting and publicly accuse him, belittling him for his apparent failures. Months afterwards that pastor shared with me, "I never want to put myself, or my family, in such a vulnerable position again." He is not the first pastor to be hurt like that and he won't be the last. But that kind of vulnerability is part of shepherding.

HE IS A LOVER OF WHAT IS GOOD
This is closely related to hospitality. The key Greek word here is *philagathos*, which is defined as "one who willingly and with self-denial does good, or is kind." William Hendricksen explains the word as "ready to do what is beneficial to others."[13] A lover of what is good is unyielding in the goodness of his activities.

Job's friends admitted that Job was a lover of goodness. Job 4:3–4 says,

Behold you have admonished many,
And you have strengthened weak hands.
Your words have helped the tottering to stand,
And you have strengthened feeble knees.

Of course, our greatest example of one who loves goodness is Jesus Christ. In Acts 10:38 it is written, "God anointed Him with the Holy Spirit and with power, and … He went about doing good." In short, the pastor who loves what is good cares about others, and does everything he can to help them.

He is loving and kind toward all and he doesn't sink to the kind of behavior that says, "I hate that person and I just want to get back at him for what he did to me." The opposite of a lover of good is a lover of self. Paul prophesied that, in the last days, "men will be lovers of self, lovers of money, boastful, arrogant, revilers, disobedient to parents, ungrateful, unholy, unloving, irreconcilable, malicious gossips, without self-control, brutal, haters of good …" (2 Tim. 3:2–3).

HE IS SOBER-MINDED—"SENSIBLE"
In Greek, the word translated as "sensible" (or "sober-minded," NJKV) is a compound of the words "save" and "mind." It describes a person who is both sensible and cool-headed. It is related to self-control, the exercise of good judgment, discretion, and common sense. The opposite of a sober-minded person is someone who allows circumstances, immorality, or foolishness to distract him from decisions he needs to make. And so the sober-minded man will avoid things that are outright immoral, trivial, unspiritual, and unproductive. He is devoted to his priorities.

HE IS JUST
The Greek word translated "just" could also be translated "righteous," but it is about fairness in this context. The elder of a church cannot show partiality or favoritism. And when making decisions, he needs to reflect the character of God in being both just and fair. First John 1:9 says, "If we confess our sins, He is faithful and righteous to forgive us our sins and to cleanse us from all unrighteousness." God is a just God and His undershepherds also need to display this quality.

I think again of Job, who was known to be a man of justice. Job 29:14–17 says,

I put on righteousness, and it clothed me;
My justice was like a robe and a turban.
I was eyes to the blind
And feet to the lame.
I was a father to the needy,
And I investigated the case which I did not know.
I broke the jaws of the wicked
And snatched the prey from his teeth.

Upon a first reading of those verses you might say, "So much for not being pugnacious!" But the truth is that Job was probably speaking figuratively here about how he dealt with the unjust as an elder in his ancient community. Job is really a good example for us of what an elder should be like because his life was a model of the Old Testament elder. In Job 1:1 it says, "There was a man in the land of Uz, whose name was Job; and that man was blameless, upright, fearing God and turning away from evil."

The concept of an elder is described in the New Testament, but those who were familiar with the Old Testament had an idea of what an elder did in his community. The Jews had been raised with the concept of a leader in the community who was wise, cared for his fellow citizens, and could make decisions with great discernment. The elders in your church, by the grace of God and with the wisdom of His Word, should be community leaders within your congregation. They should care for your members and know how to apply God's wisdom during trying times.

HE IS HOLY—"DEVOUT"

The idea here is that the elder is to be firmly committed to God and His Word. He lives a life that is separated unto God and pleasing to God. Culture and circumstances might change, but the leaders in the church need to be faithful and devout. One of the terrible facts about Israel's history is that many of the kings were neither just nor devout and, as a result, the people were led astray. Godly commitment is the idea here: one who can truly lead people in righteousness and devotion to God.

HE IS SELF-CONTROLLED

I have always loved a quote I heard some years ago: "The steel of manly character is forged in the fires of control and denial." Self-control and self-denial are essential qualifications for an elder. If he doesn't feel like going to church—he must be there. If he doesn't feel like preparing for his sermon or lesson—he has no option. If he doesn't feel like getting up for the prayer meeting or visiting someone who needs attention, it doesn't matter—this is his responsibility. Every area of his life needs to be under control. It is helpful to think of self-control like an air-filled tire. If there is an area of your life that is out of control, it is like a hole in that tire. It does you no good to say that your life is under control except in one area—"I am completely out of control when it comes to _____ [eating, drinking, anger—whatever]." That is like saying, "This tire is perfectly good for holding air except for one hole there." It doesn't matter if you have plugged up 100 holes in that tire and they are sealed airtight; if you let the one remain, your tire will not function properly. It is the same way with self-control. Either a man is self-controlled in every area of his life, or he is not able to function properly in his responsibilities.

Solomon said in Proverbs 25:28, "Like a city that is broken into and without walls is a man who has no control over his spirit." Leaders who lack discipline frustrate their fellow workers as well as those they lead. Not only are they poor examples, but they cannot accomplish what needs to be done. Consequently, their flocks are poorly managed and lack adequate spiritual care.

HE IS COMMITTED TO EXHORTATION

The need for pastoral exhortation is something that is not thought about much in churches today. Someone who exhorts is someone who is able to lovingly yet firmly urge others toward obedience and conformity to God's Word. The Greek word translated as "exhort" in Titus 1:9 is *parakaleo*. Understanding this word will help you to better understand what exhortation is all about.

Exhorting someone is much more than just telling him or her what to do. You might say to someone, "The Bible says, 'Love your neighbor,' and you are not loving your neighbor right now, so I exhort you to start loving him!" While that sounds a lot like exhortation, and may fit the description of exhortation, it really falls short of the Bible's definition of exhortation. Exhortation has more to do with coming alongside someone to help him or her than it does with ordering someone to do something. *Parakaleo* means "to come alongside of." The word was used in ancient times to describe the defense counsel or advocate who pleaded the case of the accused.

You may recall in John 14 that Jesus referred to the Holy Spirit as a *parakletos* (from the same word). In English we say, "Paraclete" or "Helper." The Lord promised in John 14:26, "But the *Helper*, the Holy Spirit, whom the Father will send in My name, He will teach you all things, and bring to your remembrance all that I said to you." So a big part of exhortation is coming alongside someone for the purpose of giving strength and help.

Your pastor should be able to come alongside those who are contradicting the Word of God and, by sound doctrine, help them get back in tune with God's Word. This is an issue of spiritual health. The word translated "sound" in "sound doctrine" (Titus 1:9) is the word from which we get our word "hygiene." It is hygienic, or healthy, doctrine that the elders are to use in order to help those in their care to stay close and obedient to God's Word.

It is for this reason that any Christian ministry must flow out of the priority of preaching and teaching God's Word. John Stott said this about preaching:

Expository preaching is a most exacting discipline. Perhaps that is why it is so rare. Only those will undertake it who are prepared to follow the example of the apostles and say, "It is not right that we should give up the preaching of the word of God to serve tables … We will devote ourselves to prayer and to the ministry of the Word" (Acts 6:2, 4). The systematic preaching of the word is impossible without the systematic study of it. It will not be enough to skim through a few verses in daily Bible reading, nor to study a passage only when we have to preach from it. No. We must daily soak ourselves in the Scriptures. We must not just study, as though through a microscope, the linguistic minutiae of a few verses, but take our telescope and scan the wide expanse of God's word, assimilating its grand theme of divine sovereignty in the redemption of mankind. "It is blessed," wrote C. H. Spurgeon, "to eat into the very soul of the Bible until, at last, you come to talk in Scriptural language, and your spirit is flavored with the words of the Lord, so that your blood is Bibline and the very essence of the Bible flows from you."[14]

Elders of the local church need to hold so firmly to the Word of God that if you were to prick them with a needle, their blood would be "Bibline." It is essential that church elders hold fast the faithful Word, for that is the means by which they will effectively exhort (help, encourage, urge) their flocks to stay away from false doctrine.

Closely related to the word "exhortation" is "refutation." Your pastor needs to be able to refute those who oppose sound doctrine—to "refute those who contradict" (Titus 1:9). To refute means to "speak against." It is becoming rarer and rarer to find church leaders who are willing to speak out against false doctrine. In a time when it is not popular to confront others about their doctrine, John MacArthur has written a great synopsis of the preacher's responsibility to refute:

The dual role of the godly preacher and teacher is to proclaim and to defend God's Word. In the eyes of the world and, tragically, in the eyes of many genuine but untaught believers, to denounce false doctrine, especially if that doctrine is given under the guise of evangelicalism, is to be unloving, judgmental, and divisive. But compromising Scripture in order to make it more palatable and acceptable—whether to believers or unbelievers—is not "speaking the truth in love" (Eph. 4:15). It is speaking falsehood and is the farthest thing from godly love. It is a subtle, deceptive, and dangerous way to contradict God's own Word. The faithful pastor must have no part in it. He himself tolerates, and he teaches his people to tolerate, only sound doctrine.[15]

Closing Remarks on Qualification

These four areas of qualification are not negotiable. If you find someone who appears to be the perfect candidate but he does not qualify in one of these categories, he is not God's man for your church. God will provide a man with an honorable spiritual reputation. His marital relationship will be pure. He will be a faithful parent who provides God's loving instruction in his home. The sum character of this man will be above reproach in every area, including exhorting others scripturally—standing up for and defending the truth. This is his character.

One of the surprising failures of pulpit committees is that they often do not consider the biblical qualifications of a man with sufficient depth. Oftentimes, the man's references are not even called. The pulpit committee needs not only to read the man's references and call the man's references to confirm them, but also to take a third step: the references themselves should be asked to give you the phone numbers of others who know the candidate well. It should be obvious that if the candidate is required to submit references, he will most likely submit people who will give him glowing recommendations. As you contact those people, ask for the phone numbers of others who may have had difficulty or conflict with this candidate. This is one of the least things a committee should do to try to ensure that their candidate meets the biblical qualifications for eldership.

Notes

1 For a more in-depth study of these issues, I highly recommend **Alexander Strauch,** *Biblical Eldership: An Urgent Call to Restore Biblical Church Leadership* (Littleton, CO: Lewis & Roth, 1995).

2 For those committees that might benefit from an interim pastor, one resource that may be helpful is **Roger S. Nicholson,** (ed.), *Temporary Shepherds: A Congregational Handbook for Interim Ministry* (Bethesda, MD: Alban Institute, 1998).

3 **Strauch,** *Biblical Eldership,* 189.

4 **W. E. Vine,** *An Expository Dictionary of New Testament Words* (Old Tappan, NJ: Fleming H. Revell, 1966), 131.

5 For further study on this issue, read **John MacArthur's** comments on 1 Corinthians 7:10–17 in *1 Corinthians* (MacArthur New Testament Commentary; Chicago: Moody, 1984). Also, see Jay E. Adams, *Marriage, Divorce, and Remarriage in the Bible* (Grand Rapids, MI: P&R, 1986).

6 **Strauch,** *Biblical Eldership,* 229.

7 **John MacArthur** states, "If a man's children are too young to understand the gospel and to trust in Jesus as Lord and Savior, then the standard given to Timothy applies … As children grow older and the issue is no longer control, the more demanding criteria in Titus 1 come into play" (*Titus* [MacArthur New Testament Commentary; Chicago: Moody, 1996], 30).

8 **John MacArthur,** *The Vanishing Conscience* (Dallas: Word, 1994), 49.

9 **Strauch,** *Biblical Eldership,* 232.

10 **Charles R. Swindoll,** *The Tale of the Tardy Oxcart* (Dallas: Word, 1998), 222.

11 **Joel Belz,** "Farewell to Anger," *World Magazine,* 14/38 (Oct. 2, 1999), 37.

12 **Strauch,** *Biblical Eldership,* 194.

13 **William Hendricksen** and **Simon J. Kistemaker,** *Exposition of Thessalonians, the Pastorals, and Hebrews* (New Testament Commentary; Grand Rapids, MI: Baker, 1995), 346.

14 **John R. W. Stott,** *The Preacher's Portrait* (Grand Rapids, MI: Eerdmans, 1961), 30–31.

15 **MacArthur,** *Titus,* 51–52.

The Theology of the Man

I have heard of a preacher who thought that whatever came into his head was good enough for his people. On one occasion he informed one of his officers at the end of his sermon that he had never thought of it before he entered the pulpit. The good elder replied, "I thought so while listening to you."

Charles Haddon Spurgeon, from *Spurgeon At His Best*

I have three goals for this chapter. First, I would like to alert you to the importance of your pastor's theology. Second, I want to help you become more familiar with sound theology in general. Finally, this chapter is an effort to assist you in the identification of your church's doctrinal position and of how that may or may not be aligned with your candidate's position.

Theology is something that many church members know little about. We live in a time when many Christians often say, "Let's agree to disagree about doctrinal issues, and not let them keep us from working or fellowshipping together." Indeed, throughout church history there have been many unnecessary splits over minute doctrinal issues in the church. This doesn't mean, however, that doctrine is not important. Knowing what you believe, and why you believe it, is extremely important if you want to stand firm in your faith. Paul warned Timothy that times would come when people would "not endure sound doctrine, but according to their own desires, because they have itching ears, they will heap up for themselves teachers; and they will turn their ears away from the truth, and be turned aside to fables" (2 Tim. 4:3–4, NKJV). He told Titus that every church leader is required to "[hold] fast the faithful word as he has been taught, that he may be able, by sound doctrine, both to exhort and convict those who contradict" (Titus 1:9, NKJV). A church member who does not pay close attention to his or her theology is like a man walking along a slippery slope. He is likely to slip and fall down into murky waters. He has nothing upon which to hold to keep him from falling into those waters—and there is nothing he can grab to pull himself out.

Many church doctrinal statements are so brief that many of the church members who are familiar with them do not know why they should believe them. They can recount truths such as, "I believe that the Bible is the infallible Word of God; I believe that there is one God, eternally existent in three persons; I believe in the deity of Jesus Christ, His virgin birth, sinless life, and bodily resurrection ..." but they may have a difficult time telling you *why* they believe those things. How do they know for sure that the Bible is infallible? What passages in Scripture prove that God exists in three persons? How could Jesus have been both fully God and fully man? These are questions many church members would have difficulty answering.

At the back of this book, in Appendix A, I have included a detailed doctrinal statement from Grace Community Church, Sun Valley, California. I can remember the first time I read that doctrinal statement. I was about to finish my Bachelor's degree in Biblical Literature and I was looking for a seminary that would provide further training in expository preaching. The Master's Seminary had this doctrinal statement in its catalog.

There was no comparison between the detail and depth of this statement and that of the much briefer statements I read in the catalogs from other seminaries. I can remember thinking to myself several times as I read this statement, "That is exactly what I believe and that is exactly why I believe it." I had never read it stated so well, and so clearly. In many ways it is like a mini-theology book, with easy-to-understand theological statements and categories. Furthermore, it has numerous Scripture references that back up each point.

If your church's doctrinal statement is not as detailed as the one in Appendix A, I recommend that you use the doctrinal statement from Grace Community Church when interviewing your pastoral candidate. Even if your leadership does not completely agree with a statement of faith like that of Grace Community Church, it may be advantageous for you to use it. In fact, if there is a point of disagreement, it will help you to identify candidates who might merely affirm what they think you want them to agree with. Ask your candidate to read a copy of the statement and then tell you what he agrees with—and what he disagrees with. It is always good to have clarity on matters on which there is agreement as well as disagreement. Compare his responses with the responses of your church leaders. Are they like-minded? You will also be able to compare his answers with the responses of other applicants.

How to Identify Your Church's Doctrinal Position

If you desire a clear understanding of where your church stands doctrinally, it is important to be familiar with the history of Fundamentalism. Now, some people are easily put off by the thought of reading about this. Others may say that the only thing more boring than a chapter on theology is a chapter about the history of theology. However, before you decide to skip this chapter, let me explain why a basic understanding of the history of Christian Fundamentalism will be extremely helpful.

If you surveyed every evangelical church in your city or country, you would find a wide spectrum of theological beliefs. At the far left of the spectrum you would find Post-Conservative Evangelicals[1]—those who believe that the original manuscripts of the Bible had errors. At the other end of the spectrum (on the far right) you would find Maxi-Fundamentalists—those who believe that the 1611 edition of the King James Bible is the only inspired, inerrant version. Between those two extremes, there are a variety of churches with varying viewpoints about Scripture. The differences between those viewpoints determine with whom a church is willing to associate. Extreme Post-Conservative Evangelicals may believe that it is wrong to evangelize Muslims because they think that Islam is a valid path to heaven. Extreme Maxi-Fundamentalists may insist that new believers read only the King James Version from 1611. Both of those groups (and most groups in between) can trace their church history back to the first half of the twentieth century and the split between Liberals and Fundamentalists. Knowing how your church arrived at its present position can help you find the right pastor. Understanding this history will either help you to better identify a like-minded pastor, or it may cause you to recognize that your church has drifted theologically. This may be a good time for your church leadership to look for a pastor who is more conservative, theologically, than many people in your church. While this may make for a difficult transition, and some members will not be happy, hiring the right man to draw your congregation closer to a sound theological position will be a great blessing. The key question that you need to ask regarding your church is, "How accurately does our doctrine line up with God's Word?" Scripture is the standard for pure doctrine. Some churches need to be drawn closer to the right—if the right is closer to Scripture. Other churches need to be drawn closer to the left—if the left is closer to Scripture. Whichever way your church needs to be drawn, knowing the history of your church's theological position will help you greatly. Determine where your church stands in the spectrum of churches.

The Great Split between the Liberals and the Fundamentalists, 1920s–1930s

At the beginning of the twentieth century, materialism and scientific naturalism were on the rise in America. In an attempt to make Christian doctrine compatible with the changing culture, individuals were exchanging the true gospel for a "social gospel." The result was a rising tide of Liberalism within the church.

The true gospel confesses that Christ was God in the flesh, sent down to live a perfect life for the benefit of mankind. God's Word says that "all have sinned and fall short of the glory of God" (Rom. 3:23) and that "the wages of sin is death" (Rom. 6:23). This puts man in a very precarious position. He is a sinner, and therefore God requires that he die, both physically and spiritually. Eternal hell is indeed what we all deserve because we are all sinners. God is perfectly holy and requires perfect obedience to His Law (Matt. 5:48; James 2:10). As sinners, there is no hope for salvation if our faith is in our own good works (Eph. 2:8–9; Titus 3:5; Isa. 64:6).

The good news is that Christ lived a perfect life (He never sinned) and, therefore, never had to die. But He chose to die so that those who trust in Him as Lord may be redeemed, delivered, and saved from the wrath of God. As Romans 5:8 says, "God demonstrates His own love toward us, in that while we were yet sinners, Christ died for us." God "made Him who knew no sin to be sin on our behalf, so that we might become the righteousness of God in Him" (2 Cor. 5:21; see also John 3:16 and 1 Peter 2:24). Christ not only died for the sins of those who will repent, He also rose from the grave and has ascended into heaven (1 Cor. 15:4).

The most important question a person can ask is, "Have I genuinely repented of my sins, submitted my life to Jesus Christ as Lord, and trusted in His work on the cross to pay the penalty demanded for my sins?" God's Word demands that our commitment to Christ must be more than a cognitive decision—one that is in our heads, not really in our hearts. A genuine commitment to Christ requires faith in Christ and true repentance (Isa. 55:7; Luke 9:23; Rom. 10:9–10; Acts 17:30). Someone who says, "I believe in Jesus," but never really submits his or her life to Him as Lord is not really a Christian. Trusting in Christ means a change of heart—turning from your sins and following Christ as Lord. Jesus Christ died on the cross to deliver sinners who would trust in Him as Lord from the wrath of God. This is the true gospel.

The social gospel, on the other hand, was a movement in the late 1800s and early 1900s. It applied Christian principles to social issues. Advocates of the social gospel were concerned about the poor, those enslaved to alcohol, racial tensions, and other social issues. Of course, there is nothing wrong with reaching out to the poor and outcast. Indeed, Jesus was a great example of this during His life on earth and Christians should be ministering to the physical needs of those around them. But Christ came to do far more than meet social needs—He came to save sinners.

Historically, some churches lost that perspective and focused only on the social welfare of the people in their communities. They neglected God's Word and downplayed sin altogether. Sin was believed to be a problem, at least in part, because of society. Reforming society became the goal of the Liberal church. As a result, the credibility of the Bible was questioned in many areas. Many were more concerned about caring for the downtrodden than about whether or not the Bible was true. Even Darwin's theory of evolution was preferred to the creation account of Genesis 1–2 by many Liberals. This, again, was due to the pressure they felt from atheistic scientists who embraced a philosophy of scientific naturalism.

Liberalism is alive and well today. An example of contemporary Liberalism can be found in the words of Bart Ehrman, Professor of New Testament studies at the University of North Carolina. Ehrman is a graduate of Wheaton College and Princeton Theological Seminary. But in 2006, Ehrman told his students at the University of North Carolina,

"Sometimes Christian apologists say there are only three options to who Jesus was: a liar, a lunatic, or the Lord. But there could be a fourth option—legend."[2] Ehrman takes Liberal theology to an extreme, suggesting that Jesus Christ never really walked upon this earth.

During the 1930s, those who had a high view of God's Word tried to separate themselves from those who were dedicated to a gospel that was merely "social." Churches were going Liberal in just about every major denomination in existence at that time. Baptists, Presbyterians, and Congregationalists were all discovering that some churches in their own denominations were further away doctrinally than conservative churches from other denominations and traditions. Millard Erickson has noted that, in order to be strengthened in their faith, many of these conservative Christians from all denominations would

attend Bible conferences, [and] summer gatherings that combined preaching and teaching with recreation. At one of these [the Niagara Conference] a list of basic beliefs was drawn up, which those attending considered to embody the core of what it meant to be a Christian in terms of doctrinal teachings. This process of articulating the essential Christian doctrines was repeated in other circles, and in time they were called the "fundamentals" of the Christian faith.[3]

During this time, the distinction between those who held on to certain biblical "fundamentals" and those who did not became clearer, and those who did not hold on to them were referred to as "Liberals." "The term 'Fundamentalist' was probably coined by Curtis Lee Laws, editor of the Baptist *Watchman-Examiner* ... to identify a person who insisted on the indispensability of these very basic doctrines. This word quickly caught on and a grassroots movement was transformed into virtually a political party within denominations and a segment of society in general."[4] If your church does not consider itself to be "Liberal" today, your church history is a part of the massive branch known in the early part of the twentieth century as "Fundamentalism."

The Split between the New Evangelicals and the Fundamentalists, 1920s–1940s

Shortly after World War 1, two separate groups branched out from what used to be known as Fundamentalism. One group preserved the name "Fundamentalist" and the other group became known as "Evangelicals." The Fundamentalist group was known for its "political causes as well as [its] efforts to fight modernism in the churches."[5] Though the Fundamentalists were losing major training institutions (such as Princeton in 1929) to the Liberals, new seminaries were established by emerging Evangelicals. Dallas Theological Seminary was established in 1924, and Westminster Theological Seminary was established about five years later. The split between the new Evangelicals and Fundamentalists did not happen overnight (for example, many considered Dallas Seminary to be a Fundamentalist school for many years). In time, however, many Christian leaders expressed dissatisfaction with the Fundamentalist movement. As Erickson has observed,

A handful of leaders began to speak critically of the shortcomings of fundamentalism and to call for a renewal of sorts. One of these was Harold John Ockenga, pastor of the historic Park Street Church in Boston. He published an article, "Can Fundamentalism Win America?" in *Christian Life and Times*, in which he answered the question essentially by saying, "not as presently constituted."[6]

Carl F. H. Henry, who in the 1950s became the first editor of *Christianity Today*, was also concerned about Fundamentalism's shortcomings. The separatism that characterized the extreme Fundamentalists was a major issue for Ockenga, Henry, and many other church leaders. Those who saw Fundamentalism drifting toward separatism began their own movement and became known as "New Evangelicals."[7] These Evangelicals were committed to biblical scholarship, had a high view of God's Word, and had a heart for social action, but they were not in favor of a separatist attitude regarding fellow Christians.

It should be noted that not all Fundamentalists were extreme separatists. J. Gresham Machen differed from most Fundamentalists on

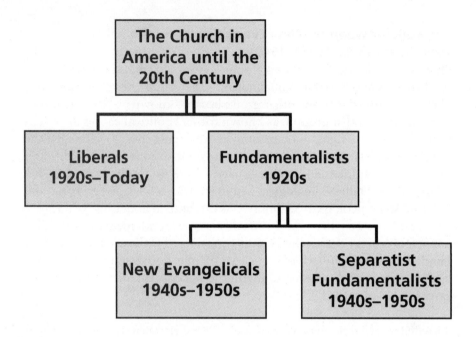

certain issues (such as eschatology), but was indeed a Fundamentalist "in principle."[8] Though he disliked the term, he was concerned with the historic truths of the Christian faith. In response to non-Fundamentalists, Machen has been quoted as saying, "Do you suppose that I do not regret my being called by a term that I greatly dislike, a 'Fundamentalist'? Most certainly I do. But in the presence of a great common foe, I have little time to be attacking my brethren who stand with me in defense of the Word of God. I must continue to support an unpopular cause."[9]

In 1942 the National Association of Evangelicals was founded. "It was intended to be an alternative to the liberal National Council of Churches, but without the negativism of the American Council of Churches."[10] The American Council of Churches was the Fundamentalist association founded by Carl McIntire and others.

Another Evangelical seminary which should be mentioned is Fuller Theological Seminary, founded in 1947 in Pasadena, California. This seminary, the special project of radio evangelist Charles H. Fuller, ... was intended to carry on his evangelistic and evangelical emphasis, combined with the very best of biblical and theological scholarship. It was designed to be a West Coast version of what Princeton Theological Seminary had been in the late 19th century. Ockenga was the first president ... [Carl] Henry was one of four original faculty members.[11]

Fuller Theological Seminary was a flagship college that brought strength and influence to the armada of Evangelicalism. The Fundamentalists remained closely associated—but on the right. The Liberals were far away on the left. Many mainline churches in America decided to ride the middle of the Evangelical wave.

Divisions within the Separatist Fundamentalists from the 1950s until Today

Since 1950 we can identify at least three categories of Separatist Fundamentalists that still remain today—the Maxi-Fundamentalists, the Assertive Fundamentalists (sometimes referred to as the Militant Fundamentalists), and the Moderate Fundamentalists.[12] Precise details of these categories are too abundant for the purpose of this chapter.[13] The distinguishing marks of these three separate groups can, however, be identified, which is helpful for churches today. By mentioning specific individuals and institutions within these three groups, I risk offending some. My intention is not to cause more division, or to pigeonhole a particular person or institution. Indeed, some institutions have shifted from one category to another since terms like these were first used. I am also aware that, at many institutions, faculty and students represent a spectrum of beliefs. Therefore, it is assumed beforehand that some of the lines between these categories will be naturally blurred (some institutions, for example, might easily qualify for more than one category). Nonetheless, in order to help your church identify where it is on the spectrum, I will still attempt to connect specific seminaries or colleges with each category.

Another challenge to categorization is that it is an enormous task. It would be impossible to accurately identify every church for each category: there are just too many churches with varying associations. When George

W. Dollar wrote his book on the history of Fundamentalism in 1973, he stated that there were "thirteen thousand churches in the nation that would call themselves Fundamentalist, which, at an average of 350 members, would yield an aggregate of four million members."[14] In order to make this section as helpful as possible without offending anyone, I attempt to define each category. I also note some distinguishing characteristics of each category. In addition, I attempt to mention a theological training institution in that category. Often, pastors and/or churches can tell you how they are similar to or different from the overall stance of a given institution. This is my goal. If your pastoral candidate can tell you where he stands in relation to a doctrinal spectrum of institutions, it should give you a better idea how he will fit into your church.

Maxi-Fundamentalists

Those who make up this group today seem to believe that they are the only "real" or "true" Fundamentalists. They have separated themselves further to the right than any other Christian fellowship, but have avoided becoming heretical. It is for this reason that some have characterized them as "us four, no more, shut the door." Not all are that exclusive. A doctrinal distinctive of a Maxi-Fundamentalist is that he or she believes that the "Authorized Version" (The King James Version) of the Bible is the only legitimate version for churches to use today. Not all "King James only" church leaders are Maxi-Fundamentalists, but it would be a rare exception to find a Maxi-Fundamentalist who is not "King James only."

An example of a Christian college that could be described as Maxi-Fundamentalist is Pensacola Christian College. In the Articles of Faith for both the college and Pensacola Theological Seminary, the first article is:

We believe that the Bible is the verbally inspired and infallible, authoritative Word of God and that God gave the words of Scripture by inspiration without error in the original autographs. God promises that He will preserve His Word; Jesus said, "*but my words shall not pass away*"—Matt. 24:35. We believe God has kept that promise by preserving His infallible Word in the traditional Hebrew and Greek manuscripts and that the Authorized Version (*KJV*) is an accurate English translation of the preserved Word of God.[15]

Further down in their doctrinal statement they also say,

Without meaning to be unfriendly or unkind, we feel it only fair to say that Pensacola Christian is not a part of the "tongues movement" and does not allow students to participate in or promote any charismatic activities.

Pensacola Christian College is committed to the plenary, verbal inspiration of the Bible, and it is our practice to use only the Authorized Version (KJV) in the pulpit and in classroom instruction. We believe the Textus Receptus is a superior text, and it is used for Greek instruction.

Pensacola Christian College boasts an enrollment that includes students from all fifty states, as well as from more than sixty foreign countries. More than four thousand students attend this college. Each student that attends agrees to a very conservative code of conduct that includes a ban on attending movie theaters.

Assertive Fundamentalists

Assertive Fundamentalists are sometimes referred to as "Militant Fundamentalists" (even among themselves) because of their commitment to "contend earnestly for the faith" (Jude 1:3). However, it is important to note that the term "Militant Fundamentalist" among Christians should in no way be confused with the type of violent militancy common among other faith groups today. A Militant Fundamentalist Christian has nothing to do with jihad or suicide bombers. To say that certain Christians are "Militant Fundamentalists" or "Assertive Fundamentalists" is simply to say that they have a strong commitment to exposing the spiritual dangers around them. They expose them in word, not with military action. "A militant Fundamentalist of the historic type is one who interprets the Bible literally and also exposes all affirmations and attitudes not found in the Word of God. He must both expound and expose. Biblical exposition is vital and essential, but alone is not enough."[16] The implication is that there will be public, vocal exposure of anyone whose doctrine does not line up with Fundamentalist doctrine. Quite often, they will expose and condemn not only those whose doctrine is lacking, but also anyone who maintains fellowship with a "middle-of-the-road" Christian.

A distinctive of this group is a high commitment to expose those who teach error. One Christian Fundamentalist organization that could be considered "militant" is a ministry associated with Bob Jones University. In a statement that is linked to Bob Jones University's website, a Fundamentalist is described as "someone who, among other things, is a born again believer who exposes and separates from all ecclesiastical denial of [the foundational truths of the historic Christian faith], compromise with error, and apostasy from the Truth; and earnestly contends for the Faith once delivered."[17] Bob Jones University, which also has more than four thousand students in its graduate and undergraduate programs, has often been associated with "Assertive (or Militant) Fundamentalists." Even the president of another Fundamentalist seminary has said that Bob Jones University is "a clearly militant fundamentalist institution."[18] The context of his statement was one that saw Assertive/Militant Fundamentalism in a positive light: Assertive/Militant Fundamentalists are those who are "outspoken" about the fundamentals of the Christian faith.

Moderate Fundamentalists

This is a difficult group to describe. In many ways, they are similar to the Assertive/Militant Fundamentalists. They have the same history, and in the past many of them enjoyed fellowship with those who are now Assertive/Militant Fundamentalists. In many ways, Moderate Fundamentalists are very similar to Conservative Evangelicals. Their major defining mark would not necessarily be doctrine, but history. Because of this, many Moderate Fundamentalists find themselves in between the boxes of Conservative Evangelicals and Militant Fundamentalists. The Assertive/Militant Fundamentalists won't have fellowship with them because their theology is too Evangelical. The Conservative Evangelicals are wary of them because, historically, they followed the Fundamentalists. So the lines between Conservative Evangelicals and Moderate Fundamentalists may be blurred more than those between any other two groups. For this reason, it is important to keep in mind that I am trying only to establish a spectrum of theological positions. "Spectrum" is a good term because it gives a picture of institutions that vary by degrees, sometimes bleeding into one another or overlapping.

An institution that matches the description of Moderate Fundamentalist is Temple Baptist Seminary, a graduate division of Tennessee Temple University. Since 1946 and 1948, the University and Seminary, respectively, have been going strong. The 2006–2007 Temple Baptist Seminary Catalog states, "From the outset, the Seminary has been committed to upholding the biblical faith historically believed by fundamental Baptists."[19] What their catalog states about their view of God's Word is something with which most Conservative Evangelicals and Assertive/Militant Fundamentalists would also agree. This is their well-written and detailed statement about the Holy Scriptures:

We believe in the verbal inspiration and authority of the Scriptures. We believe that the Bible reveals God, the fall of man, the way of salvation, and God's plan and purpose in the ages

a. Inspiration and Revelation

We affirm that the Holy Scriptures (the Old and the New Testaments) in all its parts (all sixty-six books) down to every word of the autographic text of the original documents were given by divine inspiration (Acts 1:16; Hebrews 10:15–17; 2 Timothy 3:16), in the sense that holy men of God "were moved by the Holy Spirit" to write the very words of God (2 Peter 1:20–21). This inspiration was plenary—inspired equally in all parts (1 Corinthians 2:7–14; 2 Peter 1:21), verbal—inspired in every word, and God-breathed—the very words of God (2 Timothy 3:16). The written Word of God, therefore, in its entirety is revelation of God, complete in its internal harmony and unity (1 Corinthians 14:37; John 10:35).

We deny natural inspiration, partial inspiration, thought and not words inspiration, the theory that the Bible just contains the Word of God, and also the view that the Bible only becomes the Word of God if and when God uses it as an instrument of spiritual encounter with an individual.

b. Infallibility, Inerrancy, and Authority

We affirm that the Scripture, having been given by divine inspiration, is infallible—true, safe, and reliable in all the matters it addresses (John 17:17; Psalm 19:7) and is inerrant—free from all error, falsehood, fraud, or deceit (Hebrews 6:18; Titus 1:2). It is thus the supreme authority and norm for all matters of faith and practice (Matthew 4:4, 7, 10; Deuteronomy 6:6–9; John 16:12–13).

We deny that the Scripture receives its authority from the Church, tradition, or any other human source. It is the responsibility of every individual to ascertain the true intent and meaning of Scripture because proper application of the Scripture is binding on all generations. The truth of Scripture stands in judgment of men; never do men stand in judgment of Scripture.

c. Interpretation and Application

We affirm the literal, grammatical-historical interpretation of Scripture. Whereas there may be several applications of any given passage of Scripture, there is but one true interpretation which can be reached under the enlightenment of the Holy Spirit (1 Corinthians 2:7–15; 1 John 2:20).

We deny the legitimacy of any treatment of the text or any quest for sources lying behind it that leads to relativizing, dehistoricizing, or rejecting its claims to absolute, divine authority.[20]

Part of the reason why this doctrinal statement is so well written is because it tells the reader not only what they believe, but also what they don't believe. Notice the last statement: it purposefully states opposition to those who reject the authority of Scripture. This type of statement is a key characteristic that differentiates Moderate Fundamentalists from other Christian institutions (see Post-Conservative Evangelicals below).

The Divisions within the New Evangelicals, 1950s to Today

It is not surprising to many Evangelicals that today there are divisions among the Fundamentalists. One reason why Evangelicals moved away in

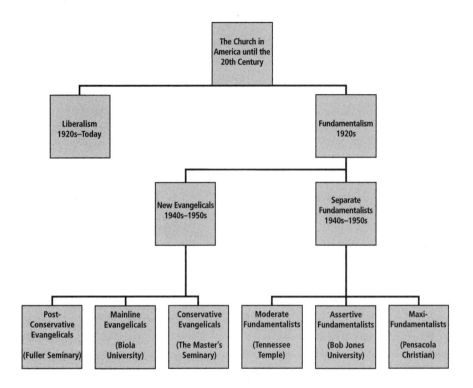

the first place was because of separatist tendencies among Fundamentalists. What is surprising to many Evangelicals, however, is that there has been about as much division among them as among those in the Fundamentalist camp. Indeed, there are at least three identifiable categories of Evangelicals that exist today. As mentioned before, the Conservative Evangelicals would be closest to the Moderate Fundamentalists. Next to them would be Mainline Evangelicals. And on the far left (but still to the right of the Liberals) would be Post-Conservative Evangelicals.

As you view the chart and read this outline, please keep in mind that this is merely a spectrum of theological groups. It is designed to assist you in identifying where your church is, positionally, compared with the position of your pastoral candidate. Some institutions mentioned may not like being placed in a box; they may prefer being placed somewhere between the lines. Indeed, some institutions have even drifted from box to box over the years. Again, perhaps your church has drifted without even realizing it. This is a good time for your church to look at where its theology has been, historically, and if or why it has drifted. If this process helps you to identify that your church has been drifting theologically, you can look for a pastor who will help you to get back to where you ought to be. It is important to keep in mind that the Bible is the standard by which one measures theological drifting. If a single church is helped by this chart and outline, it will be worth all the grief I am likely to experience from people who accuse me of causing division by placing people in boxes. That is not my intention at all.

Conservative Evangelicals

Whether The Master's Seminary would be in the category of "Conservative Evangelical" or "Moderate Fundamentalist" is debatable. This just emphasizes the point that it is not really fair to place any institution in a box. Though it is helpful in one sense to see the variations of doctrine among institutions, it can be damaging in another sense. In reality, the lines between the boxes are often blurry and may overlap (perhaps the overlapping links of a chain would be a better illustration).

The problem with putting an institution in the right category has to do with the institution's history as well as with its doctrinal beliefs. Historically, The Master's Seminary was originally an extension campus of Talbot Seminary (Biola University). It wasn't until 1986 that The Master's Seminary extended itself away from Talbot and became its own independent seminary. In 1973, George W. Dollar identified Talbot Seminary as a school right in the middle of the Fundamentalist movement.[21] Indeed, Talbot Seminary's roots are in Fundamentalism. Today, however, Talbot Seminary has drifted toward the left and is primarily in the same category as the Mainline Evangelicals. (For more on Talbot Seminary, see the next section on "Mainline Evangelicals.") In the Master's Seminary 2006–2008 Catalog there is no mention of Fundamentalism or Evangelicalism in the section entitled "History of the Seminary." Since The Master's Seminary is theologically more conservative than Talbot Seminary, I have placed it comfortably between Mainline Evangelicals and the Moderate Fundamentalists.

A key distinguishing mark of The Master's Seminary doctrinal statement is that it is detailed about what they do believe, but lacks a characteristic trait of a Moderate Fundamentalist statement of faith: it neglects to say what they don't believe. Below is a section from their "What We Believe" statement on the Holy Scriptures:

We teach that the Bible is God's written revelation to man, and thus the sixty-six books of the Bible given to us by the Holy Spirit constitute the plenary (inspired equally in all parts) Word of God (1 Corinthians 2:7–14; 2 Peter 1:20–21).

We teach that the Word of God is an objective, propositional revelation (1 Thessalonians 2:13; 1 Corinthians 2:13), verbally inspired in every word (2 Timothy 3:16), absolutely inerrant in the original documents, infallible and God-breathed. We teach the literal, grammatical-historical interpretation of Scripture which affirms the belief that the opening chapters of Genesis present creation in six literal days (Genesis 1:3; Exodus 31:17).

We teach that the Bible constitutes the only infallible rule of faith and practice (Matthew 5:18; 24:35; John 10:35; 16:12–13; 17:17; 1 Corinthians 2:13; 2 Timothy 3:15–17; Hebrews 4:12; 2 Peter 1:20–21).

We teach that God spoke in His written Word by a process of dual authorship. The Holy Spirit so superintended the human authors that, through their individual personalities and different styles of writing, they composed and recorded God's Word to man (2 Peter 1:20–21) without error in the whole or in part (Matthew 5:18; 2 Timothy 3:16).

We teach that, whereas there may be several applications of any given passage of Scripture, there is but only one true interpretation. The meaning of Scripture is to be found as one diligently applies the literal grammatical-historical method of interpretation under the enlightenment of the Holy Spirit (John 7:17; 16:12–15; 1 Corinthians 2:7–15; 1 John 2:20). It is the responsibility of believers to ascertain carefully the true intent and meaning of Scripture, recognizing that proper application is binding on all generations. Yet the truth of Scripture stands in judgment of man: never do men stand in judgment of it.[22]

Mainline Evangelicals

Universities, churches, and pastors that fall into the category of "Mainline Evangelical" are much broader in their acceptance of theological diversity than "Conservative Evangelicals." While Conservative Evangelicals might be more concerned about finer points of theology, Mainline Evangelicals have a greater concern for unity. Mainline Evangelicals are often interested in uniting the largest number of people for the greatest common cause. Unlike Separatist Fundamentalists, Evangelicals (especially Mainline Evangelicals) are concerned that Christians lay aside their differences and work together.

Billy Graham is the quintessential Mainline Evangelical. Though early on in his ministry he was clearly identified with the Fundamentalists, he later cut ties with them in order to have a broader ministry. As Marsden has recorded, "Billy Graham had decisively broken with the separatist fundamentalists, had made inroads into the major denominations, was immensely popular, and stood almost alone as a recognized evangelical leader."[23] In a bold move in 1948, Billy Graham attended the World Council of Churches Congress in Amsterdam. This showed, "according to [Billy Graham's] official biographer, John Pollock, that 'he would not hesitate to break those taboos of his circle in order to further the Gospel.' This was a very different view from that expressed by his fellow Evangelicals, Martyn Lloyd-Jones and Francis Schaeffer."[24] A historic moment when division between Fundamentalists and Evangelicals was clearly seen came in 1957. As one writer has noted,

In preparation for the New York Crusade, to be held in 1957, Billy Graham decided to aim for ecumenical cooperation. It meant that enquirers would be sent back to their own churches, whatever their theological complexion, and not referred only to fundamentalists or evangelical churches. Fundamentalism rallied its waning strength in protest. The decision caused a parting of the ways. Evangelicalism and fundamentalism separated.[25]

"Ecumenical cooperation" meant that Liberal churches, Catholic churches—in fact, just about any church that was willing to associate itself with Billy Graham—would receive referrals to follow up individuals who came forward at a crusade. On one occasion when Billy Graham was asked if he was in favor of the ordination of women, he responded, "I feel I belong to all the churches. I am equally at home in an Anglican or Baptist or a Brethren assembly or a Roman Catholic Church. I would identify with the customs and the culture and the theology of that particular church."[26]

Because many Evangelicals, like Billy Graham, were willing to associate themselves with a wide spectrum of Christians, even Catholics, the result was that Evangelicalism boomed. Evangelicalism had grown so popular in the latter part of the twentieth century that *Newsweek* magazine even declared 1976 to be "The Year of the Evangelical." The downside of this exponential growth was that, as more and more people associated themselves with Evangelicals, Evangelicalism became more difficult to define. Marsden concurs: "As evangelicals gained some of the national prestige they had once only dreamed of, the neo-evangelical leaders could no longer agree among themselves as to what an evangelical was."[27] It is for this reason that it is better to differentiate between Conservative Evangelicals, Mainline Evangelicals, and Post-Conservative Evangelicals.

A distinctive of Mainline Evangelicals is that they are willing to partner and associate with a broad spectrum of other evangelicals. Yet, at the same time, the Mainline Evangelical still has a high view of God's Word. Most Mainline Evangelicals still believe the Bible to be infallible and inerrant. Though they are willing to work with Post-Conservative Evangelicals (or even Liberals) who reject inerrancy, they themselves still hold on to doctrinal statements that include inerrancy.

Talbot School of Theology, the graduate school of Biola University, is a good example of a Mainline Evangelical training institution. It has a wide range of denominational acceptance, yet it still holds to a view of biblical inerrancy. Its doctrinal statement says,

Inasmuch as the University is interdenominational and yet theologically conservative, the Articles of Incorporation contain a doctrinal statement which is given below:

The Bible, consisting of all the books of the Old and New Testaments, is the Word of God, a supernaturally given revelation from God Himself, concerning Himself, His being, nature, character, will and purposes; and concerning man, his nature, need and duty and destiny. The Scriptures of the Old and New Testaments are without error or misstatement in their moral and spiritual teaching and record of historical facts. They are without error or defect of any kind.[28]

Notice the brevity of this statement of belief about the Scriptures (compared with statements of the Conservative Evangelicals and even the Moderate Fundamentalists). At the same time, Talbot is clear about inerrancy in reference to both "spiritual teaching" and "historical facts." The doctrinal statement also includes an explanatory note at the end. Several paragraphs were added at a later date, evidently to give clarification on certain present-day issues that had been raised. One note reads, "Where 'man' is used, referring to the human race, it includes both genders."[29]

Talbot School of Theology was founded in 1952 as Talbot Theological Seminary. Originally, the seminary was primarily dedicated to training pastors. The direction of the seminary changed, especially in the 1980s, when its name was changed to Talbot School of Theology. The name change fell in line with Biola's transition from a college to a university. Today, Talbot is one of many schools associated with Biola. Others include Cromwell School of Business, Rosemead School of Psychology, School of Arts and Sciences, School of Intercultural Studies, School of Professional Studies, and School of Philosophy. The consequence of this transition for Talbot is that, instead of focusing primarily on training pastors, it serves other schools in the university as well. Psychology students, philosophy students, and others can take their theology classes at Talbot.

This intentional shift in focus has helped to establish Talbot as a seminary that trains Mainline Evangelicals who serve in a variety of occupations (not just pastors). Training pastors is still one of Talbot's goals. Unlike in its early years, however, today both men and women are being trained for the pastorate by both male and female professors (this is another example of Talbot's drift from its Fundamentalist roots). The school, today, is clearly in line with Mainline Evangelicalism. According to its own statement of history and heritage, "Talbot School of Theology is one of the nation's leading evangelical seminaries and continues to grow with the needs of Christian leaders. Talbot has approximately 900 students, 52 full-time faculty members, and offers seven master's degrees and three doctoral degrees."[30]

Post-Conservative Evangelicals

There are many distinctions that characterize Post-Conservative Evangelicals, but chief among them is their denial that the Bible is inerrant. Post-Conservative Evangelicals are not Liberals, but many of their "children" resemble Liberals more than they do Evangelicals. A perfect example of a Post-Conservative seminary today is Fuller Theological Seminary in Pasadena, California.

I have already described Fuller Theological Seminary as a flagship seminary for Evangelicals in the 1940s and 1950s. Back then, the seminary actually held to a view of biblical inerrancy. But, as Evangelicals were losing their identity in a cloud caused by the ecumenical movement, Fuller drifted toward the left. As Erickson has noted,

The first strong indication of a real divergence within the camp of the New Evangelicalism appeared on what has come to be known as "Black Saturday," December 1, 1962. The Fuller faculty were holding their ten-year planning retreat, and Daniel Fuller, son of the founder, just returned from studying in Switzerland, was the dean-elect of the school. Urged by one of the school's administrators to speak out forcefully on matters if he was to establish his leadership, Fuller chose to address the issue of biblical inerrancy. He contended there were errors in the Bible that could not be accounted for as copyists' errors. He suggested instead that the Bible was fully truthful and free from all error when referring to revelational or doctrinal matters, matters pertaining to salvation, but that it was not inerrant in matters of science and history.[31]

Today, while Fuller Theological Seminary subscribes to the authority of Scripture, its doctrinal statement does not speak about the inerrancy of Scripture. Regarding the Word of God, Fuller's statement of faith says,

Scripture is an essential part and trustworthy record of this divine self-disclosure. All the books of the Old and New Testaments, given by divine inspiration, are the written word of God, the only infallible rule of faith and practice. They are to be interpreted according to their context and purpose and in reverent obedience to the Lord who speaks through them in living power.[32]

To say that the Bible is infallible is different from saying that it is inerrant. Inerrancy means that the original autographs of the Bible were completely accurate in their message, historicity, and scientific details. Those who hold to an inerrant view of Scripture believe that, though we might find errors in translation today, careful research of available copies can be made and an adequate explanation can be found for any apparent contradiction. Biblical infallibility simply means that God's Word is reliable when it comes to issues of faith and practice. One can believe that the Bible is reliable, for example, in all that it says about salvation. But someone who believes only in the infallibility of Scripture may believe that the biblical writers were wrong about details in history or scientific facts.

The proverbial Pandora's box is opened by theologians who contend that the Bible is infallible but not inerrant. Which texts are reliable? Who decides what can be trusted and what is wrong? Those who believe in inerrancy can say, "We believe the Bible, the whole Bible, and all that the Bible says." Those who deny inerrancy can only say, "We believe that the Bible's message is true when it speaks about what we should believe and how we should live, but some parts of the Bible are not accurate or true." Therefore, some could say that, though homosexuality is condemned by Scripture, science is teaching us that homosexuality is actually related to the genetic makeup of some people. Still another implication of the denial of inerrancy is that some might say, "Even though Jesus said, 'I am the way, and the truth, and the life; no one comes to the Father but through Me' (John 14:6), other religions may also offer valid paths to God." Some churches may be surprised that both these issues plague Post-Conservative institutions like Fuller. Homosexuality and the exclusivity of the gospel are debatable issues at Fuller.

Jack and Judith Balswick are a husband-and-wife combo who team-teach a course at Fuller entitled "Gender and Sexuality." They refer to their book, *Authentic Human Sexuality*, as "the culmination of our teaching over the last 15 years at Fuller."[33] Regarding homosexual unions, the Balswicks write,

We acknowledge that some gay Christians may choose to commit themselves to a lifelong, monogamous homosexual union, believing this is God's best for them. They believe that this reflects an authentic sexuality that is congruent for them and their view of Scripture. Even though we hold to the model of a heterosexual, lifelong, monogamous union, our compassion brings us to support all persons as they move in the direction of God's ideal for their lives.[34]

The editor of *World Magazine*, Joel Belz, commented on the content of the above quotation: "If that isn't an explicit example of relativism at work, I'm not sure I'd ever know one ... Whether careful or careless, the ambiguity in the Balswicks' conclusion is the last thing needed by a young professional trying to set her feet on a solid biblical and theological foundation."[35]

In 2003, Fuller Theological Seminary received a federal grant for $1 million to encourage cordial contact between Evangelicals and Muslims. Cordial contact, of course, is not a bad thing; all believers should be kind and cordial to non-Christians. The expectation, however, of this particular grant was that both parties would "recognize a mutual belief in one God."[36] The problem with that is that Muslims do not worship the God of the Bible. Their god is a different god. Scripture is clear that worship of any god besides Yahweh is incompatible with saving faith (Exod. 20:3; John 14:6). Unfortunately, the president of Fuller Seminary, Richard Mouw, does not believe that Scripture is as clear on this issue as I have just stated. "Mouw said the issue 'is tremendously complex' as to whether followers of the two faiths, as well as Judaism, worship the same God ..."[37]

Conclusions about Diversity in Doctrine
The benefit of the above spectrum is that your committee can easily see that there is a wide variety of theological camps among Christians today. You should be able to discuss these issues with your church leadership and

identify where you would place your own church among the spectrum of churches. You may also be able to determine if your church has drifted in its practical theology from its historical theological position. In other words, does your church really believe sound theology? If not, why not? Consider calling a pastor (or interim pastor) who will be able to bring you back in line with Scripture.

The problem with the spectrum, as I have explained, is that it may be difficult to determine where your pastoral candidate stands theologically. As important as it is for you to understand that a spectrum exists, you cannot simply show the candidate the spectrum and ask him to identify his position. Often, people drift in practice from where they think they are theologically. Another limitation is that you cannot merely look at the institution your candidate graduated from and assume that he is positioned theologically with that institution. Not every graduate from Fuller Seminary, for example, is theologically aligned with where Fuller Seminary stands today. *When* your candidate graduated from a particular institution is just as significant as what its doctrinal statement says today. If the candidate is older and has been out of seminary for a number of years, he may no longer be theologically aligned with his alma mater.

There are several steps you can take in order to try to identify the theological distance between your candidate and your church. I have already suggested that you give your candidate a detailed doctrinal statement like the one in Appendix A of this book. Ask him to read it and write out where he differs from the statement. Ask your church leaders to do the same and then compare responses.

A second step you can take is to ask your pastoral candidate to talk about his theological background. What kind of church did he grow up in? Why did he choose the institutions where he studied? Ask him to identify some other institutions that are more liberal or more conservative than his position. How does his theology line up with his alma mater's current position? Can he give you a written doctrinal statement that he agrees with? There are a number of other theological questions in Appendix B that you can ask your candidate.

There is a third step you can take to identify your candidate theologically. Ask him questions about his practical theology. Since many preachers are more conservative in their doctrinal statement than they are in practice, you need to investigate how this man applies his theology to real-life situations. The next chapter is devoted to helping you improve your understanding of practical theology and its importance.

Notes

1 These titles are adaptations from terms used in the book by **George W. Dollar,** *A History of Fundamentalism in America* (Greenville, SC: Bob Jones University Press, 1973). I was first introduced to these particular terms in some unpublished material by **Dr. Larry Pettegrew,** Professor of Theology at The Master's Seminary in California. Pettegrew has since published the terms in "Evangelicals, Paradigms, and the Emergent Approach," in *The Master's Seminary Journal*, 17/2 (Fall 2006), 159. I prefer these terms to Dollar's, since Dollar's are more than thirty years old and many of the institutions that he had categorized have since shifted.

2 As quoted by **Jamie Dean,** "Classroom Christianity," in *World Magazine*, 22/4 (Jan. 27, 2007), 35. Ehrman is also described as a "former evangelical."

3 **Millard J. Erickson,** *The Evangelical Left: Encountering Postconservative Evangelical Theology* (Grand Rapids, MI: Baker, 1997), 18.

4 Ibid.

5 **George M. Marsden,** *Understanding Fundamentalism and Evangelicalism* (Grand Rapids, MI: Eerdmans, 1991), 100.

6 **Erickson,** *The Evangelical Left*, 22.

7 Erickson has noted that Carl F. Henry has been credited with coining this term because he "used the term in three articles" (published in 1948), beginning with one published in *Christian Life and Times*: "The Vigor of the New Evangelicalism," 3/1 (Jan. 1948), 30–32 (**Erickson,** *The Evangelical Left*, 23).

8 **David O. Beale,** *In Pursuit of Purity: American Fundamentalism since 1850* (Greenville, SC: Unusual Publications, 1986), 317.

9 **Ned B. Stonehouse,** *J. Gresham Machen: A Biographical Memoir* (Grand Rapids, MI: Eerdmans, 1954), 337–338.

10 **Erickson,** *The Evangelical Left*, 23.

11 Ibid.

12 See the first note in this chapter regarding the origin of these terms.

13 For a detailed work on these divisions, consult **Dollar,** *History of Fundamentalism*.

14 Dollar, *History of Fundamentalism.*

15 "Pensacola Christian College Articles of Faith," at www.pcci.edu; accessed December 2010.

16 Dollar, *History of Fundamentalism.*

17 "International Testimony to an Infallible Bible," at www.itib.org; accessed February 2, 2007.

18 Rolland D. McCune, "The Self-Identity of Fundamentalism," in *Detroit Baptist Seminary Journal*, vol. 1 (1996), 10.

19 *Temple Baptist Seminary Catalog*, vol. 1 (Chattanooga, TN: Temple Baptist Seminary; 54th edn., 2006–2007), 28.

20 Ibid. 29–30. A digital copy of this catalog can be viewed at www.templebaptistseminary.edu; accessed February 19, 2007.

21 Dollar, *History of Fundamentalism*, 285.

22 John MacArthur, *The MacArthur Study Bible* (Nashville: Word, 1997), 2003–2008.

23 Marsden, *Understanding Fundamentalism and Evangelicalism*, 62.

24 Christopher Catherwood, *Five Evangelical Leaders* (Fearn: Christian Focus, 1994), 222.

25 Derek J. Tidball, *Who Are the Evangelicals?* (London: Marshall Pickering, 1994), 71.

26 David Frost, *Billy Graham in Conversation* (Oxford: Lion, 1998), 68; quoted in **Iain H. Murray,** *Evangelicalism Divided: A Record of Crucial Change in the Years 1950 to 2000* (Carlisle, PA: Banner of Truth, 2000), 69.

27 Marsden, *Understanding Fundamentalism and Evangelicalism*, 63.

28 "Doctrinal Statement," Talbot School of Theology, at www.talbot.edu; accessed December 2010.

29 This particular explanatory note cannot be found in the Biola University Doctrinal statement from 1985 to 1986. It is present in the current doctrinal statement. Obviously, this became an issue and clarification was made some time between the publishing of the two catalogs. This is a good example of the sensitivity Biola University has on issues that are big among mainline denominations.

30 "History and Heritage," Talbot School of Theology, at www.talbot.edu; accessed December 2010.

31 Erickson, *The Evangelical Left*, 25–26.

32 "Statement of Faith," Fuller Theological Seminary, November 24, 2010, at: www.fuller.edu.

33 Judith K. Balswick and **Jack O. Balswick,** *Authentic Human Sexuality: An Integrated Christian Approach* (Downers Grove, IL: InterVarsity Press, 1999), 102.

34 Ibid.

35 Joel Belz, "Relativism at Fuller," in *World Magazine*, 21/25 (July 1, 2006), 8. Belz's article focused on a female graduate of Fuller Seminary who owed $50,000 in school loans and was wondering how she benefited by getting her degree from Fuller. She was unhappy with the relativism she found in the classroom.

36 John Dart, "U.S. Funds Evangelical–Muslim Project," in *Christian Century*, 120/26 (Dec. 27, 2003), 11.

37 Ibid.

Where Is His Theology, in Practice?

People do not drift toward holiness. Apart from grace-driven effort, people do not gravitate toward godliness, prayer, obedience to Scripture, faith, and delight in the Lord. We drift toward compromise and call it tolerance; we drift toward disobedience and call it freedom; we drift toward superstition and call it faith. We cherish the indiscipline of lost self-control and call it relaxation; we slouch toward prayerlessness and delude ourselves into thinking we have escaped legalism; we slide toward godlessness and convince ourselves we have been liberated.

D. A. Carson, *For the Love of God*

Many pastors say that their theology is more conservative than it actually is in practice. Perhaps that is because people are idealistic, or possibly it is because one's theology tends to drift over time. Your pastoral candidate may not even realize that his theology has drifted. For this reason, it is important to ask your applicant detailed questions about his practical theology—that is, his theology as it is actually put into practice on a daily basis. All of our actions are related to issues of practical theology. It is not possible in this work to write about all the issues of practical theology that you may want to discuss with your candidate.[1] To help give you a better understanding of these issues, I have selected several pertinent subjects. Your candidate should be able to discuss how his theology relates to his views on the Bible, creation, the sovereignty of God, sin, music in the church, and spiritual gifts.

While specific questions related to these issues are found in Appendix B, my goal for this chapter is to prepare you for a dialogue with your candidate. All would agree that to merely ask your candidate questions from an appendix of a book is not a good way to examine his theology. The more you can dialogue on key issues for your church, the better.

The Authority of Scripture

As a pastor, I am often asked for counsel. Typically, I begin all of my counseling sessions with the same two questions: "Have you genuinely given your life to Christ as Lord?" and "Is God's Word your highest authority?" I ask the first question because I want to hear the person's testimony. Especially if these counselees are new to me, I want to hear from their own lips their "stories" about recognizing their own sin, repenting of that sin, and trusting in the work of Jesus Christ. I want to hear about the work of redemption that God did in their lives. I do this because I believe that, without God's work of spiritual renewal in their lives, no *significant* change can take place. I emphasize the word "significant" because what good is outward change if no spiritual change takes place within the heart? Using some accountability techniques, I may be able to help drug addicts to stay off drugs. They may even become model members of society. But what good is such behavioral change if, when they die, they still spend eternity suffering because they did not give their lives to Christ? Both types of change are important, but a change that will impact the eternal state of the individual is far more important.

The second question I ask my counselees is, "What is your greatest authority?" If they don't really submit themselves to the authority of Scripture, of what value is my counsel to them? Since my counsel is not based on personal experience or man's wisdom but on God's Word, I want to know if they are willing to submit to God's Word *before* I counsel them. If they do not view God's Word as the highest and final authority in their lives, counsel from God's Word will be just one option for them. They can take counsel from their hairdressers, their mechanics, and God's Word. If these all have the same weight of authority in their lives, they can pick and choose which option they want. But if God's Word is the ultimate and final authority for them, any passage that applies to their lives needs to be obeyed. Real change takes place in people's lives when they submit themselves to the Word of God. "For the word of God is living and powerful, and sharper than any two-edged sword, piercing even to the division of soul and spirit, and of joints and marrow, and is a discerner of the thoughts and intents of the heart" (Heb. 4:12, NKJV). When Peter wrote to first-century believers, he spoke of them being born again. He was talking about *significant* change. He said, "For you have been born again not of seed which is perishable but imperishable, that is, through the living and enduring word of God" (1 Peter 1:23).

Your pastor needs to have that kind of trust in the enduring Word of God. He doesn't merely preach the Word; he relies upon it to do a work of transformation in the lives of his people. He needs to believe that the Bible is sufficient to deal with any spiritual or emotional problem. That reliance upon God's Word for solutions to life's problems needs to permeate this man's life and speech. John MacArthur has noted, "Is the Bible really sufficient to meet every problem of human life? Of course it is. And anyone who says it's not, whether by explicit statement or by implicit action, calls God a liar and ignores or seriously undermines Paul's clear, self-explanatory instruction to Timothy:"[2]

But you must continue in the things which you have learned and been assured of, knowing from whom you have learned them, and that from childhood you have known the Holy Scriptures, which are able to make you wise for salvation through faith which is in Christ Jesus. All Scripture is given by inspiration of God, and is profitable for doctrine, for reproof, for correction, for instruction in righteousness, that the man of God may be complete, thoroughly equipped for every good work.

(2 Tim. 3:14–17, NKJV)

Creation

The issue of creation is not an issue of preference, but rather one of biblical authority. The first two chapters of Genesis teach that God created the world in six days. There is no biblical warrant to interpret those days as anything other than normal twenty-four-hour days. There was evening, there was morning: these were literal days.

The fact that so many Christians have capitulated to proponents of evolutionary theory is not only a sad commentary on the state of the church but it is also completely unnecessary. This is because theories that deny a six-literal-day creation account are not scientific. All scientific experiments are merely observations of repeatable events. Since the creation account is not repeatable, science cannot make an observation about it.

Some might ask, "But what about carbon dating and other scientific methods which tell us that the earth is far older than the Bible would allow?" The answer is that no scientific dating method can measure the age of the earth because the earth may have been created to look older than it really is. Imagine that you and I were able to travel back in time to the Garden of Eden. Let's say that we could get in a time machine that took us to the day when Adam was created. Suppose that we took some medical doctors along and we arrived just moments after Adam was formed out of dust. If you were to ask any of those doctors to give Adam a physical examination, how old would they say that Adam appeared to be? In his late teens? Perhaps early twenties or thirties? What if you were to tell them that Adam was only a day old? "No way!" would be their response. Adam wouldn't look anything like any one-day-old human they had ever examined before. That's because Adam was created to look older than he really was. There is no definitive way that science can ever determine the age of something created by God.

Creation is a miraculous work of God. Those who deny creation deny the clear, plain, ordinary understanding of Genesis 1–2. The frightening question regarding Christians who deny Genesis 1–2 is, where will they stop? Will they deny a worldwide flood (Gen. 6)? Will they deny the miracles of Jesus? Once you have decided that some portions of God's Word are not accurate, you have opened the door to removing any portion of Scripture that offends you. As MacArthur points out,

The starting point for Christianity is not Matthew 1:1 but Genesis 1:1. Tamper with the book of Genesis and you undermine the very foundation of Christianity. You cannot treat Genesis 1 as a fable or a mere poetic saga without severe implications to the rest of Scripture. The creation account is where God starts His account of history. It is impossible to alter the beginning without impacting the rest of the story—not to mention the ending. If Genesis 1 is not accurate, then there's no way to be certain that the rest of Scripture tells the truth. If the starting point is wrong, the Bible itself is built on a foundation of falsehood.[3]

The Sovereignty of God

The almighty God is absolutely and completely in control of everything.

This does not mean that humans are robots and are not permitted to exercise their wills; rather, it means that God, who knows the hearts and intentions of men and women, uses our actions to bring about His will. He orchestrates all things for His glory and our benefit. This is the clear teaching of Scripture.

Romans 8:28 says, "And we know that God causes all things to work together for good to those who love God, to those who are called according to His purpose." This means that in God's providence, he orchestrates *all* things—every event in life. Proverbs 21:1 tells us that all leaders are used by God: "The king's heart is like channels of water in the hand of the LORD; He turns it wherever He wishes." In Daniel 5:23, Daniel says to the pagan king, Belshazzar, "But the God in whose hand are your life-breath and all your ways, you have not glorified." Philippians 2:13 says, "It is God who is at work in you, both to will and to work for His good pleasure." Proverbs 16:4 says, "The LORD has made everything for its own purpose, even the wicked for the day of evil." These are just some of the clear passages in Scripture that your pastoral candidate will need to deal with if he denies that God is completely in control.

Historically, the sovereignty of God has been a foundational doctrine for many great preachers. The fact that God is ultimately in control during every calamity, every disaster, every sunny day, and every dark storm should be evident in the preaching of your pastor. For indeed, God's hand of providence is found in every action on this earth. No trial, no hardship, no suffering comes our way without the explicit decree and specific permission of God. As Charles Spurgeon said,

I believe that every particle of dust that dances on the sunbeam does not move an atom more or an atom less than God wishes—that every particle of spray that dashes against the steamboat has its orbit, as well as the sun in the heavens—that the chaff from the hand of the winnower is steered as the stars in their courses. The creeping of the aphid over the rosebud is as much fixed as the march of the devastating pestilence—the fall of … leaves from a poplar is as fully ordained as the tumbling of an avalanche.4

Some would object and call that fatalism. They would reduce it to the old saying "What will be, will be." But fatalism offers no hope to us who are in this world. Spurgeon challenged that notion when he asked,

What is fate? Fate is this—whatever is, must be. But there is a difference between that and Providence. Providence says, whatever God ordains, must be; but the wisdom of God never ordains anything without a purpose. Everything in this world is working for some great end. Fate does not say that ... There is all the difference between fate and Providence that there is between a man with good eyes and a blind man.[5]

This doctrine of God's sovereignty is important for your pastor to understand—not merely so that his thinking can be right, but so that his actions will be right. Your pastor will need to respond to numerous trials that occur in the lives of your church family members and it is essential that his theology be worked out in his mind so that he can offer the complete comfort of God's truth to those who are suffering.

Recently, I heard the testimony of a man whose family lost their ten-month-old baby. On January 6, 2007, this baby fell into an unattended bathtub. For twelve days the ten-month-old held on to his life, causing great agony in the hearts of family members. Several churches were praying for this child and his family. Less than a month after the baby died, his grandfather said, "It was difficult to deal with the emotions of an event like this, but it would have been unimaginably difficult if we would have had to deal with poor theology at the same time." I found it striking that this mature Christian man mentioned that he was helped through this trial not only by his relationship with Christ, but also by his theological understanding of who God is. In his testimony, he mentioned several Scripture passages that relate to the sovereignty of God and he described how they helped him. He later told me how a pastor friend of his had written him and shared that Charles Spurgeon had once said, "The sovereignty of God is the pillow that I lay my head on at night." Your pastor's understanding of who God is will be directly related to how he responds during times of trouble.

This is precisely what we learn about David in Psalm 34. Though there is uncertainty about the occasion when David wrote this particular psalm, it is clear from the first fourteen verses that he is exuberant in his praise to the

Lord at all times. Though David certainly went through many trials, he was always able to sing praise to the Lord. In Psalm 34:15–22, we learn that David's ability to praise at all times was related to his doctrinal understanding of God. God is a God who takes care of His own (vv. 15, 22). God is a God who takes care of the righteous, dealing with them in a different way from the wicked (vv. 16, 21). God is a God who provides security for His own (vv. 17, 20). God is a God who is involved personally in the present (vv. 18–19).[6] David's reaction to his personal trials flowed from his doctrinal understanding of God. This is significant for your search committee. Doctrine is important because it is the foundation for how we live our lives and counsel others.

Man's Responsibility for Sin

While it is true that God causes all things to work together for good, it is important to know that God never sins. He never acts in a sinful manner and He cannot be blamed for sin. All people are sinners and deserve to be held responsible for their sin. This is, after all, why we are in such desperate need of a Savior. In spite of this need, it has become increasingly popular for preachers to downplay the sinfulness of man. Many preachers rarely use the term "sin." Some of them prefer to soften the issue by saying that we are weak, dysfunctional, or have low self-esteem, or they use other psychological terms. Those who downplay sin are guilty of preaching an incomplete gospel (Rom. 1:18; 3:23; 6:23). Our congregations need to hear about the stain and guilt of sin. If they don't, they are less likely to see their need for Christ. Not only that, but if your pastor does not preach about the severity of sin, your people are likely to have a skewed view of God. They may see Him as someone who punishes unjustly, and who is ultimately responsible for sin.

Deep down, of course, we all know that God is not responsible for sin. This is still often a difficult issue for us to grasp. How can God ordain evil and still not be blamed for it? One passage that your pastor should be able to deal with is Isaiah 45:5–7:

I am the LORD, and there is no other;
Besides Me there is no God.

I will gird you, though you have not known Me;
That men may know from the rising to the setting of the sun
That there is no one besides Me.
I am the LORD, and there is no other,
The One forming light and creating darkness,
Causing well-being and creating calamity;
I am the LORD who does all these.

In this forty-fifth chapter of Isaiah, the prophet was speaking to Cyrus the Great, King of Persia. King Cyrus lived about 550 years before Christ, and although he was not a follower of God (nor did he acknowledge God as the true God) God used Cyrus to restore the Israelites to the promised land. According to God's plan, Cyrus set the Israelites free from their Babylonian captivity. Not only that, but at his own expense he also restored the temple in Jerusalem. He returned the stolen temple vessels that Nebuchadnezzar had stolen. This is truly a clear example of God using an unbeliever to accomplish His purposes.

But there are some puzzling words used to describe God in this section. In verse 7 of Isaiah 45, God says, "I make peace and create calamity" (NKJV). The word "calamity" is a translation of the Hebrew word *ra'ah* that means "evil, distress, misery, injury, or calamity." "Calamity" tends to give us the idea of natural disaster, but the King James Version actually says, "I make peace, and create evil: I the LORD do all these things." Many have asked, what does the Bible mean when it says of God "I create evil"? There is some debate as to what kind of evil Isaiah was talking about here. John Calvin said,

Fanatics torture this word *evil*, as if God were the author of evil, that is, sin; but it is very obvious how ridiculously they abuse this passage of the Prophet. This is sufficiently explained by the contrast … for he contrasts "peace" with "evil," that is, with afflictions, wars, and other adverse occurrences. If he contrasted "righteousness" with "evil," there would be some plausibility in their reasoning.[7]

According to Calvin, a key to understanding this passage is that the contrast here is between "peace" and "evil" rather than between "righteousness" and "evil." Calvin believed that the kind of evil that Isaiah is talking about here is affliction, war, and adversity—not sin. Wayne Grudem, on the other hand, said that "the contrast with 'peace' (*shalom*) in Isaiah 45:7 might argue that only 'calamity' is in view, but not necessarily so, for moral evil and wickedness is certainly also the opposite of the wholeness of God's 'shalom' or 'peace.'"[8]

I agree with Grudem that even if this passage were speaking mainly about "war," there is certainly a lot of wickedness in "war." It is also important to note that *ra'ah* is used dozens of times in the Old Testament to speak about wickedness and evil. Another key to the passage is understanding how the verbs are used. It is said of God in Isaiah 45:7, "I am … the One forming light and creating darkness, causing well-being and creating calamity." It is important to realize that the verb "create" doesn't necessarily demand responsibility. In some passages (e.g. Gen. 1:1) the verb "create" is obviously associated with a responsible action ("God created the heavens and the earth"), but the verb does not always require a responsible action. For example, if I told you that the sun "creates" darkness and cold, you would think I was crazy. The sun creates or produces light and heat. This is true, but equally true is the fact that, the further you are away from the sun's warmth, the colder and darker it is. Darkness is caused by the sun dropping below the horizon. Jonathan Edwards used this same illustration to explain the cause of sin: "If the sun were the proper cause of cold and darkness, it would be the fountain of these things, as it is the fountain of light and heat: and then something might be argued from the nature of cold and darkness, to a likeness of nature in the sun."[9] God is not responsible for producing evil any more than the sun is responsible for producing cold and darkness. Sin does not come from the positive activity or influence of the Most High God. On the contrary, sin arises when He orders things so that they may come to pass. He is not responsible for acts of sin that are committed any more than the sun is responsible for ice. But God uses the sinful acts of men and women, in His sovereign plan, to carry out His will, for His glory, and according to His good pleasure. Edwards explains:

God may hate a thing as it is in itself, and considered simply as evil, and yet … it may be

His will it should come to pass considering all consequences ... God doesn't will sin as sin or for the sake of anything evil; though it be His pleasure to so order things, that he permitting, sin will come to pass; for the sake of the great good that by his disposal shall be the consequence. His willing to order things that evil should come to pass, for the sake of the contrary good, is no argument that he doesn't hate evil, as evil; and if so, then it is no reason why He may not reasonably forbid evil as evil, and punish it as such.[10]

In other words, God has every right to punish men and women and hold them responsible for their sin, even though He can and does use their evil deeds to accomplish His righteous purpose. God permits evil according to His plan—He even establishes situations where evil is carried out. And man is fully responsible for his own sin because God never asks him to sin or makes him sin. When man sins, he never does anything that he isn't naturally inclined to do in the first place. God merely allows sinners to go the way they want to go when it will serve His purpose. As Romans 1:24 says, He "gave them up to uncleanness, in the lusts of their hearts." Unrepentant sinners will say, "We don't want anything to do with God or His ways." And so God lets them have the desire of their wicked hearts, but He uses their wicked actions for His divine purposes.

God permits evil things to happen to us, knowing that He will use them for His glory and our benefit. It is important that your pastor understand that truth; it is a foundation for how he will understand why God allows suffering. As such, it is a basic truth he should be able to explain when presenting the gospel. Man is responsible for his own sinful actions. Joseph's brothers understood that they were sinners when they were contemplating their future after their father died: "Perhaps Joseph will hate us, and may actually repay us for all the evil which we did to him" (Gen. 50:15, NKJV). After all, they hated him when he was younger. They plotted to kill him, but instead they beat him up and sold him as a slave. They lied to their father about him, saying that he had been attacked by a wild beast. Twenty-two years went by before their lie was exposed, and then Joseph forgave them. He loved them, and then totally forgave them. He invited them and their father to come and live with him. He provided for them and for an entire nation that would have starved if Joseph had not saved grain during the years of plenty. But when their father died, Joseph's brothers panicked. As Genesis 50:16–17 says,

So they sent a message to Joseph, saying, "Your father charged before he died, saying, 'Thus you shall say to Joseph, "Please forgive, I beg you, the transgression of your brothers and their sin, for they did you wrong."' And now, please forgive the transgression of the servants of the God of your father." And Joseph wept when they spoke to him.

Why did Joseph weep? Because his brothers thought that his forgiveness was not genuine. They feared his revenge, so they conceived a lie to try to win him over again. They tried to make peace with their brother by adding more lies. They feared him because they thought he would act just as they would have acted if they were in his place. For seventeen years they thought he was a hypocrite—living among them and faking forgiveness. So Joseph wept, and then he said to his brothers, "Do not be afraid, for am I in God's place? As for you, you meant evil against me, but God meant it for good in order to bring about this present result, to preserve many people alive" (vv. 19–20). Joseph understood that even when people sin against us, God can be praised because He takes their actions and uses them for good!

Of course, the ultimate example of God taking something intended for evil and using it for good is the crucifixion of Jesus Christ. Lawless men took the perfect Son of God and nailed Him to a cross. The people who looked on shouted, "Crucify Him, crucify Him!" Christ was murdered as a direct result of sinful acts by sinful men who hated God. The early Christians understood the principle that God holds people accountable for their sin, but, at the same time, they also understood that He uses people's sin for His purposes. We know they understood that because in Acts 4:27–28, they prayed to God, "For truly in this city there were gathered together against Your holy servant Jesus, whom You anointed, both Herod and Pontius Pilate, along with the Gentiles and the peoples of Israel, to do whatever Your hand and Your purpose predestined to occur." God predestined that Herod, Pilate, the Gentiles, and the Jews would gather together and murder Jesus Christ unjustly. God allowed it all to happen so that His plan of redemption could be carried out—for you. God forsook His Son, and wrath was laid upon Him—so that you could know what it is like to have your sins forgiven. If you have repented of your sins and trusted in Christ, you are forgiven. God's love for you is so great that He offered His only Son as a sacrifice when evil men crucified him. Some of those evil men later repented of their sin and were saved. Others perished in their sin and are being punished—for all of eternity. In it all, God is good, and unrepentant sinners are held responsible for their own sin.

When you interview a potential pastor for a position in your church, it is vital that he has a clear understanding of what God's Word teaches about sin. We live in a world in which injustice is common. When a family in your church wants to know why God has allowed them to experience great suffering, your pastor needs to have an answer that is satisfying and biblically accurate.

Styles of Music in Worship

Another issue that your pastor should be familiar with is music. The kind of music your church uses in its worship services can be a controversial point. It is important that you, as a committee, find out not only what your candidate's preference is, but *why* he holds his position on the issue. His preaching will affect your church's music program and, in turn, everyone who participates in it. It is better to investigate this issue before he is hired rather than after. Your pastor should be able to clearly differentiate between what is biblical in music ministry and what is not.

If you were to study the background of the English word "worship" you would find that it actually means "worthship." It refers to the worthiness of a person who receives special honor. Worship, then, is simply honor and adoration directed toward the God who is worthy to receive it. In both Hebrew and Greek, the word that is often translated in English as "worship" can also be translated "service." That is why some verses in different Bible versions use those words interchangeably. For example, in the New International Version, Romans 12:1 says, "This is your spiritual act of worship." In the New King James Version, however, the same verse is translated, "… which is your reasonable service." The two words "worship" and "service" are interchangeable because their biblical meaning is synonymous. Service is one way we can acknowledge God in a manner acceptable to Him; worship is another. Both involve acknowledging God in everything we do. For the Christian, everything we do should be worship—life is ministry. As Colossians 3:17 reminds us, "Whatever you do in word or deed, do all in the name of the Lord Jesus, giving thanks through Him to God the Father." So, in spite of the fact that many people use the term "worship" to refer only to worshipping God in song, "corporate worship" actually includes every aspect of the worship service—preaching, corporate prayer, the reading of Scripture, giving, even the benediction and the prayer of invocation. It is all "worship."

In musical worship, there are two extremes we should want to avoid. On the one hand, we need to avoid making worship an ecstatic experience in which our minds are removed from what we are doing and the worship service becomes solely an emotional experience. At the other end of the spectrum, worshipping God simply for tradition's sake is not God-honoring either. In Scripture, vain repetition is forbidden.[11] Avoiding those two extremes is becoming increasingly difficult for many churches as the world's influences are infiltrating the church and making demands.

Those who lead corporate worship services should understand the primary purposes of worship. Church worship should not focus on attracting (or enticing) people to come and hear the gospel. If you want a healthy church, you don't plan your music ministry with the objective of attracting people. There is a reason for this: the world is attracted to fleshly activities. Those who use a fleshly focus to attract people will have their churches filled with fleshly people. While it is the responsibility of the church to evangelize the world, we must not confuse the goal of corporate worship with the goal of evangelism. The primary purposes of a church service for believers are to glorify God and to edify one another (1 Cor. 14). While many unbelievers who visit Bible-believing churches will get saved, the service should be planned primarily for believers.

When believers gather for worship, the environment is unique because the Spirit of God indwells each believer. Emotion itself is not wrong, but it should be the natural outcome of biblical preaching and other expressions of biblical worship.[12] When the Word of God "richly dwells" in a Christian (Col. 3:16), his or her natural response should be spiritual behavior like singing, thankfulness, and mutual submission to one another.[13] My point here is that true worship is motivated by an understanding of God's truth. When a redeemed heart meditates on the words of a God-glorifying hymn, Bible verse, or prayer, that person should respond with genuine praise. Ecstatic experience that is produced through mindless manipulation is not the same as genuine praise. For example, the rush of feelings that one may experience at a secular music event is not related to godly worship. Church leaders need to understand this and avoid the temptation to imitate the world. Emotion that accompanies corporate worship in song should not be falsely produced through repetitive singing (like mantras) or any other fleshly gimmick.

A BIBLICAL MUSIC MINISTRY

Paul explains in Ephesians 5:19 that when the Spirit-filled life produces music in a healthy body of believers, there should be four dominant aspects to our singing: we should sing with other disciples, our singing should include diversity, we should sing with deep devotion, and our singing should have the right focus.

Singing Should Include Others

In Ephesians 5:19, Paul says, "speaking to *one another* ..."; so, singing to the Lord is to be done with fellow believers. Obviously, singing alone is also appropriate for believers. Likewise, it is not wrong for a believer to sing in front of unbelievers. But it would be wrong if a body of believers did not sing together. This is fascinating to me, because it seems as though some people think that God gave us music for evangelism. But the primary purpose of singing is not evangelism. As John MacArthur noted, "No music in the Bible is ever characterized as being or intended to be evangelistic."[14] I do not believe it is wrong to hold a music concert as an evangelistic outreach, but it is important to remember that the primary purpose of Christian singing is to express both individual and corporate worship—it is a celebration of life together in Jesus Christ.

Singing Should Include Diversity

A second characteristic of our singing that accompanies our worship is diversity. Because different generations and cultures prefer different genres of music, there is a danger that one generation's preferences will dominate your church's music program. In a church with an older congregation, that may mean that they sing only hymns. In a church with a predominately younger congregation, it may mean that they sing only praise choruses. Neither church includes diversity.

There are some who act as though the hymnbook should be pasted to the back covers of our Bibles. The way some believers talk, you might think that, if a hymn or song doesn't have four stanzas that can be played by pipe organ, it must be from the devil. But the truth is that the hymns we sing are not inspired by God. Even though many of them are filled with great and rich theology, we must admit that others have poor theology. It is likely that many great hymns, such as "Amazing Grace," will be sung in churches until Christ returns. Others are so difficult for today's congregations to sing that they are a hindrance to appropriate worship. If the church is still here in 200 years, we can be sure that many of those hymns will have faded into disuse. Consider the fact that the majority of the hymns we sing are less than 200 years old. None of them is a first-century hymn that the early church sang.

I am a lover of hymns. I grew up with them, and we continue to sing them every Sunday in our church. But hymns are not inspired. When they become a hindrance for effective worship, they should fall away. Today, many churches are projecting the words of their hymns onto large screens, instead of providing hymnals. This will make it much easier for the next generation to lose many great hymns—perhaps prematurely. Even so, the goal of a music ministry should not be to preserve hymns for generations that do not want them.

The current alternatives to hymns today do not offer much hope for the future. Many of the praise choruses we sing today are theologically and musically weak. Some people refer to praise choruses as "7–11s" (seven words repeated eleven times). Others have described a praise chorus as "one word, two chords and three hours." Sadly, some choruses do fit that description.[15] But, thankfully, not all praise choruses or contemporary worship songs are weak. Some of them are richly focused upon Jesus Christ and have an effective way of directing the attention of a congregation toward Christ. A remarkable worldwide proliferation of worship songs has emerged since the early 1970s, and much of it has had a positive influence on the church. I can walk into virtually any church in the Western world, start singing a few words of a chorus, and the congregation could join me because they are familiar with that song. Some of these choruses assist believers in Scripture memory since they put verses of God's Word to music. Even still, we need to keep in mind that Scripture portrays a pattern of diverse musical styles in the church.

In Ephesians 5:19, Paul mentions three different types of song: hymns, psalms, and spiritual songs. Of course, it needs to be mentioned that that verse says that we are to "speak" to one another with "songs," "singing and making melody with our heart." This begs the question of the author's intent. Should we speak to one another using the words of the Psalms? Should we sing to one another? Or are we supposed to hum a tune in our hearts silently while talking to one another?

This question is easily clarified once we have a proper understanding of the Greek word translated "speaking"—*laleo*. It is a word that probably developed from the sound a baby makes when learning to talk—"la, la, la." In its most basic sense, the word means "to make a sound." In Revelation 4:1, trumpets "speak" (*laleo*). In Revelation 10:4, thunder also "speaks." "Speaking" in the context of Ephesians 5 refers to any sound that is offered to God with a Spirit-filled heart. You could "speak" through singing. You could "speak" through humming. You could even "speak" with instruments. In fact, the word translated "making melody" literally means to "pluck using a stringed instrument" (like a harp). Over time, the word came to represent the playing of any instrumental music. So, whether you are singing, humming along, playing an instrument, or doing a combination of singing and playing—it all can be done as an expression of a Spirit-filled heart.

To return to the three types of songs mentioned in Ephesians 5:19: "psalms" primarily refers to Old Testament psalms put to music. The early church did most of its singing straight from the Psalms using various tunes that were familiar to the congregation. Many of the psalms have a superscription that instructs their readers regarding the tune to which they were to be sung:

Psalm 22:1: For the director of music. *To the tune of* "The Doe of the Morning." A psalm of David.

My God, my God, why have you forsaken me?
Why are you so far from saving me,
so far from the words of my groaning? ...

Psalm 69:1: For the director of music. *To the tune of* "Lilies." Of David.

Save me, O God,
for the waters have come up to my neck ...

(NIV; emphasis added)

"Hymns," in Ephesians 5:19, refers primarily to songs of praise which the early church probably distinguished for church use. Sometimes, when people are trying to plead their case that a church should sing only hymns, they quote this verse and say, "See, hymns are mentioned in the Bible." As mentioned above, these are not the same hymns that we sing today. Most of ours were not written until hundreds of years later. We have lost nearly all of the first-century hymns that used to be sung by the early church. Many biblical scholars[16] believe that various New Testament passages were used as hymns in the early church; one such passage may have been Colossians 1:15–20.

"Spiritual songs" were probably songs of testimony, a broad category that included any music that expressed truth. You and I might categorize different types of Christian music. Psalms: many churches have psalters which are hymnbooks containing the words of the Psalms. Hymns: we would say that "Holy, Holy, Holy" or "Immortal, Invisible" and others would fall into this category. And many people today would say that "spiritual songs" are similar to modern-day praise choruses—"Majesty," "As the Deer," and so on. Whether the New Testament writers would put our music in the same categories, we certainly don't know. One of the points of Ephesians 5:19, however, is that we should not categorize our music in an exclusive manner. Paul emphasized that there is room for diversity and that there are many different musical expressions that can exalt and be used to worship the Lord.

Singing Should Include Devotion

A third aspect that should accompany our worship is that singing should be done with devotion. Believers who are filled with the Spirit delight to sing the praise of Christ, and this praise comes not only from our lips, but also from our innermost being, our hearts. Ephesians 5:19 says, "... speaking to one another in psalms and hymns and spiritual songs, singing and making melody *with your heart* to the Lord." Of course, it makes sense that we would be rejoicing in our hearts because, according to Ephesians 3, that is where Christ's Spirit is. In Ephesians 3:16 Paul prays for his readers "to be strengthened with power through His Spirit in the inner man, so that Christ may dwell in your hearts through faith." Every Christian is "indwelt" by Christ at the moment of salvation (Rom. 8:9), so all Christians are indwelt by the Spirit; He resides in them, but, depending on our behavior, we may not be walking in a "Spirit-filled" manner. The word translated "to dwell" in Romans 8:9 means "to be at home." When our hearts are cleansed and we are controlled by His Spirit, Christ is "at home" in our innermost being. The questions we need to ask ourselves as we prepare for corporate worship are "Have I prepared for this time of corporate worship?" and "Will I be singing with my lips today, or will I also be singing from my heart?"

Often, when people attend church, they are out of harmony with God's Spirit because they have not prepared for church in the right way. Perhaps they rushed to church and their family was arguing on the way there. Other examples of being out of harmony with God's Spirit would be when you have been involved in some sin for which you have not repented, when you are holding on to a pet sin, or when you are planning to be disobedient. If any of these conditions apply, it will be impossible for you to worship God with any depth.

When we sing praises to our Lord, we rejoice in who He is and what He has done. If on the outside you are rejoicing in Christ but on the inside you are angry, bitter, or resentful toward Him or others, you practice hypocrisy. This type of singing never truly praises or pleases God. In Amos

8:10, God sent a message through His prophet to Israel because their hearts were not right with Him. God declared, "I will turn your religious feasts into mourning and all your singing into weeping" (Amos 8:10, NIV). In Amos 5:23–24 God declared, "Take away from Me the noise of your songs; I will not even listen to the sound of your harps. But let justice roll down like waters and righteousness like an ever-flowing stream." What He was saying to Israel was, "Stop your singing of praise to Me until your hearts are right!" Our worship needs to be deeply devotional.

Singing Should Include the Right Focus

For whom are we singing? Ephesians 5:19 says, "… speaking to one another in psalms and hymns and spiritual songs, singing and making melody with your heart *to the Lord.*" We do not sing so that we can draw attention to ourselves; we do not sing in order to entertain others; we sing in order to express praise and joy to God because of all He does according to His Word.

I will never forget the time I saw and heard a young man play a certain tremendous piece of music before a congregation of believers. It might have been the best rendition I had ever heard of the hymn "To God Be the Glory." The problem is that what I remember about that musical solo was not God; it was the young man playing. To my astonishment, after he was finished, he even walked to the front of the platform and took a bow. It was a stark reminder to me that we need to pay attention to the words we sing. Charles Spurgeon summed this up so appropriately when he said,

God's house is meant to be sacred unto Himself, but too often it is made an opera house, and Christians form an audience, not an adoring assembly. We come not together to amuse ourselves, to display our powers of melody, or our aptness in creating harmony. We come to pay our adoration at the footstool of the great King, to whom alone be glory forever, and ever.[17]

AN UNBIBLICAL MUSIC MINISTRY

There is a vast amount of worship music today that is sung in the name of Jesus in an unbiblical manner. With that in mind, let me summarize these abuses in seven categories. There are seven unbiblical practices that should be avoided in music ministries.

First of all, churches should avoid disorderly worship. First Corinthians 14:40 says, "All things must be done properly and in an orderly manner." This verse comes right at the end of a section specifically dealing with the order of church meetings. Most people are aware of churches that permit extreme disorder during their worship services. Stories of people shaking with convulsions or barking like dogs during a "worship service" are not uncommon. Entire congregations dancing to the point of frenzy is typical in many churches all over the world. But it is clear from Paul's first letter to the Corinthians that disorder and worship are incompatible.

A second unbiblical practice is worship that shows disrespect to God. Proper worship gives God the honor and adoration that God is worthy to receive. Anytime the worshippers focus on anything or anyone other than God, it is not giving Him the honor, respect, and awe that are His due. When Isaiah saw (and felt) the glory of the Lord, he trembled and said, "Woe is me, for I am ruined! Because I am a man of unclean lips, and I live among a people of unclean lips; for my eyes have seen the King, the LORD of hosts" (Isa. 6:5). When we read about the future worship of God in the Book of Revelation we learn that the four living creatures that John saw worshiping did not rest day or night, and they were continuously saying, "Holy, holy, holy is the Lord God, the Almighty, Who was and Who is and Who is to come" (4:8). We know that God has demanded reverent worship in times past, and that He will receive reverent worship in the future. Therefore, our worship today should give Him the utmost respect. Worship that is too casual has no place in the church. Worship is to express joy. Its purpose is not to amuse or entertain. The focus needs to be the honoring of God.

Another sign of unbiblical worship is that it offends other true worshippers. This is basic Christianity. Philippians 2:3–4 says, "Do nothing from selfishness or empty conceit, but with humility of mind regard one another as more important than yourselves; do not merely look out for your own personal interests, but also for the interests of others." In Mark 9:35 Jesus taught his disciples, "If anyone wants to be first, he shall be last of all and servant of all." Romans 14 and 1 Corinthians 10 teach this same truth. It is important that, during a worship service, those who have planned it and those who are leading it are sensitive to giving the entire body of Christ the opportunity to worship. This is one of the reasons why hymns and many of our praise choruses are such great tools for worship. The historic music of the church is so appropriate for worship because no other style of music is like it. It distinctly belongs to the church. This means that none of the worshippers are excluded, because everyone learns songs that do not belong to any particular generation outside of the church. When a church tries to take a certain genre of the world's music and "convert" it, by putting Christian words together with what some consider to be worldly music, one result is that it excludes others.[18] There is no way that your church can cater to the musical preferences of every age, ethnic group, and class in your congregation. But if you continue to emphasize the wonderful music that belongs to the church, everyone can partake.

Unbiblical (or false) worship may also cause division in the church. Paul speaks out against division quite strongly in 1 Corinthians. In chapter 11 he warns against a division with economic roots. The wealthier people were coming to the church love feasts early, gorging themselves, and leaving nothing for the poorer members of the body. Chapter 12 speaks out against those with certain spiritual gifts who made others without those spiritual gifts feel like second-class citizens.

Today, there is a great concern among many pastors about younger people not attending church. Great effort is made to try to reach those in their twenties and thirties. Unfortunately, much of that effort ends up excluding older Christians. When the church adapts all of its worship to the young, it ends up separating the young from the old. This is sad, because the body of Christ should be a united organism, made up of individuals from every class, culture, and generation. The church is a unique place. A five-year-old can be encouraged by an eighty-five-year-old. A sixteen-year-old can serve beside a fifty-five-year-old. They learn from each other, build up each other, and glorify God as His elect body of believers. Titus 2 speaks about multi-generational interaction as though it should be the norm for the church. We need to pattern our churches after biblical models, not mono-generational hotspots.

A fifth practice that true worshippers should avoid is hypocrisy. In

Mark 7:6 Jesus said to the Pharisees, "Rightly did Isaiah prophesy of you hypocrites, as it is written: 'This people honors Me with their lips, but their heart is far away from me.'" Jesus went on to rebuke them for legalistic practices like ceremonial cleansing and not taking care of their parents. Hypocritical practices, such as worshipping God with your lips but not your heart, should be avoided in the church. This would also include worshipping God with your fingers but not your heart. It has become common for some churches to hire musicians simply for their musical ability, disregarding their Christian character. (Some churches even hire unbelievers to lead worship.) Those who are involved in leading corporate worship need to have hearts wholly dedicated to Christ. A lower standard of musical ability is better than a lower standard of spiritual maturity among those who lead your congregation. A church with a "not-so-good" piano player can be growing more spiritually than a church with a full orchestra or praise band. The character of your leadership will have a lot to do with how your congregation responds to God's Word.

A sixth practice to be avoided in your church music is worldliness. First John 2:15 says, "Do not love the world or the things in the world. If anyone loves the world, the love of the Father is not in him." James 1:27 says, "Pure and undefiled religion in the sight of our God and the Father is this: to visit orphans and widows in their distress, and to keep oneself unstained by the world." James 4:4 says, "You adulteresses, do you not know that friendship with the world is hostility toward God? Therefore whoever wishes to be a friend of the world makes himself an enemy of God." This principle overlaps with several others I have mentioned above. Worldly music is not appropriate for corporate worship because it can offend your brothers or sisters (especially those who were caught up in the world prior to coming to Christ). When you go to one extreme, you also tend to divide the church. Some say, "But if we use the world's music, we may attract those in the world to the church." The result will be that your church is then filled with worldly people. There will be no difference between your church and the world.

Though my list is not comprehensive, a final practice that should be avoided in your church worship is sloppiness. Music ministry, like all other ministries, should be carried out with excellence. Again I refer to

1 Corinthians 10:31: "Whether, then, you eat or drink or whatever you do, do all to the glory of God." Psalm 33:3 says, "Sing to Him a new song; play skillfully with a shout of joy." Psalm 47:7 repeats the same principle: "For God is the King of all the earth; sing praises with a skillful psalm." Last-minute preparation, lack of practice time, and lack of concern for what you are doing are all ingredients for an ineffective music program. All of the above reflect a lack of concern for the One who deserves your greatest attention.

As you consider what is biblical in a music ministry, along with what is not, your pastor should also be in agreement and understand the controversies that can arise from different views.

Spiritual Gifts for Today

In many churches today, there is an overemphasis on spiritual gifts. Spiritual gifts are important, but in Scripture we find that they should not be the main focus of the church. In addition, some pastors put unnecessary pressure on their members to exercise gifts which are clearly not for everyone. My wife grew up in a church like this. She was told she needed to have the gift of tongues if she was really to be a Spirit-filled Christian. She was able to fake it as a child, but eventually she realized the futility behind that approach. (Her sister could never fake it, so she was made to feel like a second-class citizen in the church.) It is vital for your church that your pastor has a valid New Testament understanding of spiritual gifts.

There are several places in God's Word where spiritual gifts are listed and discussed. For the purposes of this chapter I have decided to deal with a passage in Paul's first letter to the Corinthians. In 1 Corinthians 12:27–31, Paul writes about various spiritual gifts and how they can be used to best foster spiritual growth in the church.

He begins with this statement in verse 27: "Now you are Christ's body." This statement is overwhelmingly significant because of three little letters—"a," "r," and "e": the word "are" right in the middle of this statement. Paul didn't say, "You *will be* the body of Christ." Nor did he say, "You *should be* the body of Christ." But, under the inspiration of the Holy Spirit, Paul was able to write, "You *ARE* the body of Christ." This little verb is indicative, present active, and in the second-person plural—

which is significant because it indicates something about his readers. The present tense is amazing because that described their condition at the time when Paul was writing to them. The second-person plural is significant because it means that he was speaking to all of them. Paul said, "You all, the Corinthian church, ARE the body of Christ." He said this even though the Corinthian church was torn by internal strife. This church was known for its jealousy and bitterness. The Corinthian believers were so full of self-indulgence that some people would go hungry at their love feasts because others were coming early, eating all the food, and then getting drunk on the communion wine (1 Cor. 11:21). And yet Paul could say to them, "You all ARE the body of Christ."

He could say that because, from God's perspective, those who have been cleansed by Christ's blood are saints. Paul even addressed them as "saints" in only the second verse of the same book. They were so associated with Jesus Christ that it was said of them that they were Christ's *body*. If they were not the very body of Christ, it would have been impossible for them to grow.

This is not the only significant lesson we learn from this statement of Paul's. There is something about the construction of this sentence in the original language that is qualitative. In other words, Paul did not mean that the church in Corinth was the body of Christ exclusively. If it were, how then could Paul have been part of Christ's body too? Nor did he mean that the church in Corinth was a miniature body of Christ, Christ having many bodies, the church in Corinth being just one of them. If that were true, how could 1 Corinthians 12:13 say that we were all baptized into *one body*? But there was something about the Corinthian church that completely characterized the body of Christ. It possessed the qualities necessary to be an actual representation of Christ's body on earth.

Commentators agree that "it is not that each church is a separate body, but that each church as a local group possesses the quality of the whole."[19] You see, God, in His sovereignty, has equipped every local church with qualities that are essential to make it a visible portrayal of the body at large. Each church is indeed a representation of the body of Christ. As another commentator confirms, "Each local congregation is a microcosm of the entire church, so that everyone who observes the congregation's various functions knows that this body is the church in action."[20]

As the body of Christ, you are the beneficiaries of God's "gifting." In 1 Corinthians 12:28–30 we have a list of individuals and gifts that the Lord has given to His church. In this list, Paul arranges the gifts in descending value. This was intended to be a general list, not a complete list. However, we should note that Paul's ranking (or order) here is consistent with that in his list in Ephesians 4:11.

If we follow Paul's line of reasoning in 1 Corinthians 12, we may be surprised to note that he ranks certain gifts. He says, "And God has appointed in the church, first apostles, second prophets, third teachers, then miracles, then gifts of healings, helps, administrations, various kinds of tongues." Some might ask, "How can he do that when he has just emphasized the importance of equality?" For in verse 21 he said, "And the eye cannot say to the hand, 'I have no need of you'; or again the head to the feet, 'I have no need of you.'" His point in that verse is that every member, and every gift, is vital for the body to function properly. However, even though every member and every gift is important, he doesn't mean that the church should place equal emphasis on each one.

Take, for example, your church service on a Sunday morning. Many gifts are used. The gift of helps is demonstrated when people come early and unlock the doors, straighten the chairs, test the sound, and so forth. The gift of administration is demonstrated as some organize the service and select certain individuals for certain tasks. The entire service is coordinated to bring the greatest glory to God. The gift of teaching is practiced by some members. It is practiced in the Sunday school rooms. It may be practiced by other church leaders in various classes. All these gifts are equally and vitally important for the proper functioning of the church. We should never think that someone who has the gift of teaching, for example, is more important than someone who has the gift of helps. A body that can teach but not respond with service is dysfunctional. All of us are expected to serve, but some have been especially gifted with the gift of helps. Those people are vitally important. But that doesn't mean that we should place equal emphasis upon every person or gift. We don't say that

everyone should have equal time to exercise his or her gift. It would be ridiculous to have a rigid schedule such as:
- 15 minutes to set up
- 15 minutes of singing
- 15 minutes of prayer
- 15 minutes of announcements
- 15 minutes for the sermon

We rightly emphasize the teaching of God's Word when we meet together on the Lord's Day. Everything should center around (and flow from) a proper understanding of God's Word. That is why the gift of teaching is positioned higher on Paul's list than many other gifts. It builds up the body more than many other gifts, and therefore should receive more emphasis. Is someone with the gift of teaching more important than someone else in the body? Certainly not. That is what Paul has been saying. It is fruitless for every member to pursue the same gift. And, in Corinth, we know that the gift everyone wanted to have (and practice) was the gift of tongues.[21] But where does Paul place tongues on his list of gifts? He places it last (v. 28). Consider the following details about Paul's priority list of eight gifts that were important for the first-century church in Corinth.

APOSTLES

Every true church relies on the gifts and responsibilities that the apostles had. When the Bible speaks of apostles, the primary reference is to the twelve disciples (including Matthias) who had seen Christ rise. Later, Paul was accepted as an apostle with all the authority that the early church recognized in the other twelve. John MacArthur has noted that these early apostles were given three basic responsibilities: "1) to lay the foundation of the church ([Eph.] 2:20); 2) to receive, declare and write God's Word (3:5; Ac 11:28; 21:10,11); and 3) to give confirmation of that Word through signs, wonders, and miracles (2 Co 12:12; cf. Ac 8:6,7; Heb 2:3,4)."[22] MacArthur also notes,

The term "apostle" is used in more general ways of other men in the early church, such as Barnabas (Acts 14:4), Silas, Timothy (1 Thess. 2:6), and others (Rom. 16:7; Phil. 2:25). They are called "apostles of the churches" (2 Cor. 8:23), rather than "Apostles of

Jesus Christ" like the Thirteen. They were not self-perpetuating, nor was any apostle who died replaced.[23]

PROPHETS

Prophets in the New Testament fulfilled a specific role for churches of that era. Since the canon of Scripture was not yet complete, God provided prophets for the early church so that they could help dispense his Word to those who followed Christ. When the canon of Scripture was completed, this gift was no longer necessary for the church, and prophets ceased to exist. Again, MacArthur's summary of this office is excellent. He notes that prophets in the New Testament were

... not ordinary believers who had the gift of prophecy but specially commissioned men in the early church. The office of prophet seems to have been exclusively for work within a local congregation. They were not "sent ones" as were the apostles (see Acts 13:1), but, as with the Apostles, their office ceased with the completion of the New Testament. They sometimes spoke practical direct revelation for the church from God (Acts 11:21–28) or expounded revelation already given (implied in Acts 13:1). They were not used for the reception of Scripture. Their messages were to be judged by other prophets for validity (1 Cor. 14:32) and had to conform to the teaching of the apostles (1 Cor. 14:37). Those two offices were replaced by evangelists and teaching pastors.[24]

TEACHERS

Ephesians 4:11 combines this gift with that of pastor. This doesn't necessarily mean that everyone with the gift of teaching should be a pastor, but every pastor should have the gift of teaching. The apostles and prophets have laid the foundation for the church. They have delivered to us the very Word of God. But until the Lord takes His church to be with Him, the church will always need teachers. And God will always "appoint" these in the church.[25]

GIFT OF MIRACLES

Miracles are supernatural works of God that cannot be explained by any other means. In the first-century church, the gift of miracles often accompanied the preaching of God's Word so that the message could be verified. Ever since the New Testament canon was completed there has been a different way of verifying someone's message: we compare it with the Bible. This is not to say that it is impossible for miracles to happen today. On the contrary, God is capable of miracles and He does perform them. The *gift* of miracles, however, is not in existence today. In fact, those who claim to have this gift today are often associated with poor theology. Since a purpose of this New Testament gift was to confirm God's message, that seems strange.

GIFT OF HEALINGS

Of course, in the Corinthian church these gifts were important because (as mentioned above) they confirmed the message that was taught. Mark 16:20 mentions the confirmatory purpose of such gifts: "And they went out and preached everywhere, while the Lord worked with them, and confirmed the word by the signs that followed." Again, God does still heal today. The *gift* of healings, however, has ceased. We simply do not see individuals who are able to heal people as Jesus did—instantaneously and completely.

GIFT OF HELPS

Romans 12:7 calls this the gift of "service." The word in 1 Corinthians 12:28 that is translated as "helps" is especially beautiful as it literally means "laying a hold of." It means "to take the burden off someone else and place it on yourself." This is what someone does who has this gift. Paul used the same word to encourage the Ephesian elders in Acts 20:35. This is an important spiritual gift for today.

GIFT OF ADMINISTRATION

As mentioned in an earlier chapter, the gift of administration is not the ability to run a church office efficiently. Someone with the spiritual gift of administration may also have the natural gift of being able to run an office efficiently, but the spiritual gift of administration (like all spiritual gifts) is something supernatural. It is something that only someone indwelled with the Holy Spirit can accomplish. This word "administrations" in the Greek literally means "to steer or pilot a ship." So the gift obviously has something to do with leadership. It is the Spirit-gifted ability to organize and coordinate the resources and individuals entrusted to a certain congregation in a way that glorifies God the most.

GIFT OF TONGUES

The ability to speak in tongues was a first-century gift that enabled a believer to proclaim God's truth in a foreign language that he or she had never studied or been taught. In 1 Corinthians 13 Paul foretold that this gift would cease to exist. Throughout church history this gift has not been present since those early years of the church. The "gift of tongues" that the Pentecostals and Charismatics have claimed to possess since the early 1900s is not even the same "gift": it is not proclamation through a foreign tongue and it is rarely attempted in an orderly manner (with interpretation). In any case, in Paul's list of gifs for the early church, Paul ranked this one last.

God has gifted His church in such a diverse way that every local church is equipped with members who have all been selected by God to carry out His work His way. We know that no one in the church in Corinth was without a gift because in 1 Corinthians 12:7 it says that "each one" had been given a gift. And we know that no gift was missing in Corinth because Paul opened that letter with the words "you are not lacking in any gift" (1:7). We know that not everyone was supposed to have all the gifts or the same gifts because Paul asked them in 12:29–30, "All are not apostles, are they? All are not prophets, are they? All are not teachers, are they? All are not workers of miracles, are they? All do not have gifts of healings, do they? All do not speak with tongues, do they? All do not interpret, do they?" Each question is worded in such a way that it naturally expects a negative answer.

Nowhere in the Bible are individuals instructed to seek certain gifts. God distributes them as He wills. The problem in Corinth was not that the church didn't have the gifts it needed, but rather that certain members weren't using the gifts they had. If people had been using the gift of administration, the church would not have been leaderless. Furthermore, all the members of the church would not have been seeking the showy gifts, like tongues (by "showy," I simply mean "more visible" and perhaps "more visibly impressive"). If some had been exercising the gift of helps, others wouldn't have been excluded from their love feasts. The church would have been growing instead of bickering. There would have been genuine love instead of hatred. Ultimately, the church would have looked here on earth just like it looked from heaven: as the very body of Christ. This should be our goal.

Before I conclude, I need to deal with a phrase in 1 Corinthians 12:31. Paul says, "But earnestly desire the greater gifts." After reading this, you might say, "I thought that you said that the Bible never tells us to seek certain gifts?" You might even go so far as to say that this verse teaches us that we should seek a particular gift (such as tongues). It is clear from the context of this verse, however, that it cannot mean that we are to seek showy gifts. One of Paul's main points in 1 Corinthians 12 has been that God distributes gifts according to His own will and pleasure. Verse 11 tells us that the Holy Spirit distributes "to each one individually just as He wills." Verse 18 says that "God has placed the members, each one of them, in the body, just as He desired." In verse 28 we learn that God has appointed these gifts in the church. Besides, even if Paul was saying that individuals should seek the showy gifts, tongues would be at the bottom of the list of gifts to seek after. But Paul is not saying that individuals should seek certain gifts.

We know this not only from the context, but also from the grammar of the verse. The verb translated "earnestly desire" is again in the second-person plural. In other words, Paul says, "You all—not individually, but you as a whole, the church—desire the greater [best] gifts." Paul has been quite careful to distinguish between individual members and the body as a whole. When he speaks about the role of the individual, he uses words like "each one of them" and "individually" (vv. 11, 18, 27). And it is clear from this passage as a whole that Paul is rebuking the Corinthians for individually running after the showy gifts.

He encourages them as a whole to place greater emphasis on gifts that are of the greatest benefit to the church. Which gifts are these? First, apostleship, second, prophecy, and, third, teaching. Perhaps one of the best ways to bring clarity to verse 31 is to consider how a church could obtain the higher gifts, like the gift of apostleship. A requirement for being an apostle was that you had to have seen and spent time with the incarnate Lord Jesus. It just doesn't make sense that Paul would have encouraged individuals in Corinth to become apostles when it is likely that the Corinthian believers could never do it—they couldn't meet the requirements. But a congregation during the first century could earnestly seek an apostle, like Paul, who could come to reveal and teach them God's Word. If they couldn't get an apostle, then they could pray that the Lord would add to their congregation more prophets—those who had the supernatural gift of speaking forth God's Word and revealing it. In our day, since the message of God for His people has been fully revealed in His Holy Scripture, it follows that at the top of our list of gifts to seek should be that of teaching. How do we do that? By "earnestly desiring" teachers. The words "earnestly desire" mean "to be zealous for." Therefore, churches today should be zealous to acquire the best teachers available to feed their flocks.

If a church today is going to emphasize a certain gift, let it be the gift of teaching. But, at the same time, do not elevate teachers and say that they are more important than others. Do not underestimate the importance of gifts that appear to be weaker. First Corinthians 12:22 says that "it is much truer that … [they] are necessary." Rather emphasize gifts that will bring the greatest benefit to the body as a whole. This brings us back to your search for a pastor.

Closing Remarks on Practical Theology
In this chapter I have attempted to discuss some key theological differences so that you can better understand what you need to be asking your pastoral candidate. Appendix B contains an extensive list of interview questions you can ask your candidate. Hopefully, issues such as the authority of Scripture, creation, the sovereignty of God, man's responsibility for sin, musical worship, and spiritual gifts will spark discussions with him. These discussions should flow into many other areas of practical theology that will help you to identify your candidate as a good match for your church. He should be the most biblical candidate available. If there are red flags in areas of practical theology, you should pay attention to them. When you

see these red flags, slow down. Perhaps it is time to continue your search by looking at other candidates. Otherwise, proceed with caution.

Notes

1 An excellent book that deals with these issues (and many more) has been written by faculty members from The Master's College and edited by **John MacArthur:** *Think Biblically! Recovering a Christian Worldview* (Wheaton, IL: Crossway, 2003). I highly recommend this book for committee members who desire to have a better grasp on issues relating to practical theology. It will be an immense help for you in selecting the right pastor.

2 **MacArthur,** *Think Biblically!*, 34–35.

3 Ibid. 82–83.

4 **C. H. Spurgeon,** "God's Providence," a sermon on Ezekiel 1:15–19, in the *Metropolitan Tabernacle Pulpit*, 54/3114 (October 15, 1908; repr. Pasadena, TX: Pilgrim Publications, 1978), 493.

5 Ibid.

6 These four points about God are observations noted in the unpublished sermon notes of Dr. Trevor Craigen, Associate Professor of Theology at The Master's Seminary (date not known).

7 **John Calvin,** *Commentary on the Book of the Prophet Isaiah*, vol. 8, *Calvin's Commentaries*, trans. by **William Pringle** (Grand Rapids, MI: Baker, 2005), 403.

8 **Wayne Grudem,** *Systematic Theology* (Grand Rapids, MI: Zondervan: 1994), 326.

9 **Jonathan Edwards,** *The Works of Jonathan Edwards*, vol. 1 (Carlisle, PA: Banner of Truth, 1990), 77.

10 Ibid. 79.

11 In Matthew 6:7, this principle is applied to prayer; the same warning would apply to any act of worship.

12 Prayer, giving, the reading of Scripture, as well as the singing of psalms, hymns, and spiritual songs—these are all examples of biblical worship that should motivate believers to rejoice in praise.

13 "Dwells" means "to be at home"; in Colossians 3:16, Paul calls upon believers to let the Word take up residence and be at home in their lives. The idea here is that the truths of Scripture then permeate every area of our lives. In fact, to "let the word of Christ richly dwell within you" is identical to being "filled with the Spirit" (Eph. 5:18–19). We know this because Colossians 3:16–4:1 is a parallel passage to Ephesians 5:19–6:8. The result of being filled with the Spirit is the same as the result of letting the Word of Christ richly dwell within

you. In his commentary on Colossians, John MacArthur puts it this way: "To be filled with the Spirit is to be controlled by His Word. To have the Word dwelling richly is to be controlled by His Spirit. Since the Holy Spirit is the author and the power of the Word, the expressions are interchangeable" (*Colossians and Philemon* [MacArthur New Testament Commentary; Chicago: Moody, 1992], 159).

14 **John MacArthur,** *Ephesians* (MacArthur New Testament Commentary; Chicago: Moody, 1986), 257. A possible exception to this could be Psalm 40:3. Nonetheless, Scripture demonstrates that evangelism is not the primary purpose of music.

15 In 1975 a praise chorus entitled "Halleluiah" was copyrighted. It had only two chords. I am amazed that anyone who "wrote" this song (consisting of one word) would assign his or her name to it, much less go to the effort to copyright it and try to seek royalties.

16 For example, **Peter T. O'Brien,** *Colossians and Philemon* (Word Biblical Commentary, vol. 44; Nashville: Thomas Nelson, 1982), 25.

17 Cited in **Tom Carter,** *Spurgeon At His Best* (Grand Rapids, MI: Baker, 1988), 177.

18 An urban legend leads people to believe that many hymns used popular tunes of their day, but this is not true. A few exceptions might be found, but even if many hymns did use contemporary secular tunes, they would still emphasize my point. What was once popular in society no longer remains popular. Some of remnants of popular music exist in tunes that have joined the vast compilation of music that is distinctly Christian. I am not for the preservation of old music just for the sake of preservation, but a distinct sound for the church is beneficial. Popular secular genres have more minuses for the church than pluses. For those interested in reading more on this subject, I recommend **Don Hustad,** *Jubilate 2* (Carol Stream, IL: Hope Publishing, 1993).

19 **Robert L. Thomas,** *Understanding Spiritual Gifts: A Verse-by-Verse Study of 1 Corinthians 12–14* (Chicago: Moody, 1978), 74.

20 **Simon J. Kistemaker,** *Exposition of the First Epistle to the Corinthians* (New Testament Commentary; Grand Rapids, MI: Baker, 1993), 440.

21 Chapter 14 of 1 Corinthians deals extensively with that problem.

22 **John MacArthur,** *The MacArthur Study Bible* (Nashville: Word, 1997), 1809.

23 Ibid.

24 Ibid.

25 Note that the word translated "appointed" in 1 Corinthians 12:28 is the same word that is translated "placed" in verse 18.

How to Find Your Pastor

Where are such men of God today? Where are the preachers like Calvin, who will preach the Word with unwavering commitment? Where are the pastors who believe that God is uniquely with them as they mount their pulpits for the exposition of His Word? Where are the shepherds who have prioritized the preaching of the Word in public worship? Where are the expositors who will preach entire books of the Bible consecutively month after month and year after year?

Steven J. Lawson, *The Expository Genius of John Calvin*

One of the most crucial times for any church is when it is searching for a new pastor. Unfortunately, the time when a church needs leadership and direction the most is often the time when it has them the least. Wesley E. Johnson has commented on the significance of this time for a church: "Any local church has episodes in its history that may alter both its life and its future. One such event is a change in pastoral leadership. Because of the position and influence of the pastor within a congregation, the calling of a man to shepherd the flock becomes an all-important decision."[1]

In spite of the great need for careful, well-informed decision-making at this time, many churches have very little direction. It is a time when members turn back to constitutions and other church documents for guidance. These helps were usually written decades before the search and are often cumbersome to read and apply. Even when a church's protocol is clear, the members doing the search often feel frustrated. Consider the following words, written by an elder of a church with 450 members to a seminary placement office:

We are currently forming a search committee to fill two staff positions in our church: (1) a primary Teaching, Preaching Elder (Pastor) and (2) an Administrative Elder of Ministry. Our church government is in the process of changing from a congregational structure to a Council of Elders. I'm writing you in the hope that you might be able to give me some direction or guidance in the following areas:

1. We need help in writing a Job Description for these two positions ...

2. How do we go about looking for a candidate? Where to look? How to look?

3. A sample Job Application

4. Where to look for candidates? How to interview them?

5. What does a Search Committee process look like?[2]

The writer went on to confess, "This process is new to us. We need help and we don't know where to start." Instead of signing his letter with "Sincerely" or "Cordially," he simply put the word "Needy" before his name. The Seminary Placement Administrator told me that this type of letter was common.

Although there is no flawless, universal system for finding the right pastor, there are certain reliable principles to assist every church in its pastoral search. Because every church is different, I cannot recommend a single, universal search model for each church to use. This chapter will evaluate the pros and cons of four contemporary search models. I will describe each model, mentioning some of their weaknesses. My intention is not to discourage those using these models, but to encourage those searching for a pastor to use the best decision-making procedures and principles for their particular situation. After consideration of the "committee model," the "elder model," the "trial-period model," and the "home-grown model," beneficial principles will be summarized. The more a church can utilize the helpful principles from these various models, the easier it will be for it to find the right man for their church.

The Committee Model
By far the most common method espoused in books and papers on this subject is the "committee model." Although the particular way this model of selection is used in churches varies, its basic elements are usually the same. Typically, the process begins with the selection of a committee that is representative of the church. Usually the church will select one elder, at

least one woman, an older person, a parent, and someone from the youth ministry. Sometimes the representative from the youth ministry will be a teenager. The idea, which is often unspoken, is that everyone in the church will have someone on the committee to whom he or she can relate, and everyone on the committee represents the perspective of his or her constituents.

The committee will then appoint a chairperson, vice-chair, secretary, and treasurer. This may leave only one person without an official position on the committee since most committees tend to number five or seven people. Occasionally a committee will consist of nine people, but it is seldom larger than this. The committee's first task is usually to identify what kind of pastor the church is looking for. It then begins to seek résumés. A survey may be sent out to the members of the church, asking for suggestions on what pastoral qualities they feel would be of primary interest. How old should he be? Must he be married and have children? How much and what type of education should he have? How important is his doctrinal position? How much can we afford to pay him? These are all questions that might be on the survey. Once applications are received, a filtering process is developed. Eventually, a handful of potential candidates are contacted by phone. Committee members listen to recordings of sermons. References may be called. Perhaps each person on the committee will interview one candidate and then present his or her findings to the rest of the committee.

After six to twelve months of searching,[3] the leading applicant will be asked to interview formally for the position. If he does well in the interview, he may be asked to come and preach in a church service. While some churches may have several applicants come and preach at their Sunday services, many churches refrain from doing that because it can become a popularity contest among members of the congregation. Even if they may not be aware that the guest preacher is a potential candidate, some members of the church may express disappointment over the final choice of the committee (especially when they later discover who else had been on the list of potentials).

If the leading applicant does well on the Sunday he preaches, he may then be presented to the congregation as a candidate. Only after the committee recommends him to be considered for the position is he officially called a "candidate." Usually the church will learn about the leading candidate and will either vote or have an opportunity to give some sort of written feedback concerning the candidate. Depending on how the church operates, if the candidate receives a majority of votes (usually at least 70 percent), then a "call" will be made. This officially invites him to be the next pastor of the church. He can then accept the call or refuse it, depending on whether he believes that the church is a right "fit" for him. If he accepts the call, plans are made for his move to the city and church. If he doesn't accept, or if the congregation does not vote to call him, the committee is forced to go back and look at other leading candidates. Another possibility is that it will notify all applicants that they were not selected for the position. Then the committee starts the process of looking for new applicants all over again. This could mean another year or two of searching.

This committee model may be the most common, but it can also be the most problematic. It frequently has the wrong people, and uses the wrong criteria and the wrong examination process. The committee frequently makes the wrong presentation to the wrong decision-makers, and hopes to end up with the man that is God's best choice. Sometimes the right man is selected, but far too often this process ends in failure. Here are some of the reasons why.

THE WRONG PEOPLE

The main reason why the committee model is destined for failure in so many cases is because it has the wrong people on the committee. Pastoral search committees should not be made up of representative members. The reason is that the democratic method of government is not the best method for making spiritual decisions. Choosing a pastor is a spiritual decision. Therefore, only the most spiritually mature members of the congregation should be involved in the selection process. God has designed the church to be a nurturing family in which older, more mature believers disciple younger, less mature believers (Titus 2). The search committee is not the place for that discipleship to occur. While every member of the body should be involved in the overall process, not every member is qualified to be on a search committee. If the members of a committee are selected primarily because of their availability, or because they represented a certain social group in the church, rather than because of their spiritual maturity, it is quite likely that the wrong people will be attempting to make this very important decision.

THE WRONG CRITERIA

I have read numerous surveys that have been prepared for members of the congregation. Their purpose is to assist the search committee in what to look for in a pastor. Many questions are simply irrelevant for a committee truly concerned about the biblical characteristics and qualities among their pastoral candidates. Often, these surveys (from both conservative and non-conservative churches) are concerned more with superficial demographics than spiritual qualifications.

One of the most common questions asked near the beginning of a church member survey is, "What age would you prefer the new pastor to be? Under 36? 36–45? 46–55? Or over 56?" This question is common on church surveys in spite of the fact that it is illegal in the United States to ask any potential church employee how old he or she is. It is considered discriminatory to make a decision about hiring an employee based on his or her age. Regardless of that legal detail, it is simply not one of the most important questions for a search committee to debate. Choosing the right man using biblical criteria is a far higher priority than choosing a man in the right age category.

Another question often asked at the top of a church member survey is, "What level of seminary degree would you prefer him to have? M.Div? Th.M? Or doctorate?" Again, this is a poor way to determine whether or not a man is spiritually qualified for the position. While seminary training is important, the level of his degree may be somewhat irrelevant to being the best spiritually qualified person for the job. I have known several pastors who have no formal seminary training but are better read, better qualified, and better suited for pastoral ministry than many men with doctorates in theology. While it would not be typical for your best candidate to be someone without seminary training, the level of degree earned should not be among your first considerations. It is a wrong move for a committee that receives 100 applications to begin by looking only at those with the highest degrees.

Usually, *where* the man studied is a better indicator of his doctrinal influence than *what* degree he earned. I recently spoke to a former member of a pulpit committee who later discovered that his committee had made the wrong choice. He said, "I never thought about how much this guy was influenced by both his undergraduate and seminary training institutions."

Other poor examples of questions asked on actual church surveys are: "I prefer that our new pastor be theologically: (a) Liberal; (b) Moderate/Conservative; (c) Fundamentalist/Conservative; (d) Fundamentalist; (e) No Preference"; "I prefer the new pastor be viewed as (indicate the three that are most important): (a) Administrator; (b) Theologian; (c) Preacher; (d) Evangelist; (e) Counselor; (f) Teacher; (g) Prophet; (h) Pastor; (i) Other."[4] These are poor questions because they use vague terms that should be defined for most church members taking the survey. Worse than that, however, is that they rely upon the personal preferences of church members to determine what the next pastor will be like. Nowhere in the Bible is it said that church members should specify standards for church leadership. These standards are set by Scripture, not pulpit committees. When a committee begins its search for a pastor using the wrong criteria, it is highly unlikely that it will make the right decision.

THE WRONG EXAMINATION PROCESS

Examining someone for a public position should not be confined to a process that is largely private. While much of the examination process needs to remain behind closed doors, some of it needs to involve others. When committee members feel that they have failed, one common regret is that they didn't really get to know the candidate well enough. Either his preaching wasn't as good as they thought, or his temperament wasn't as calm as they thought, or his character wasn't as moral as they thought. All in all, they just didn't examine him properly.

Theologically, many search committees are simply not equipped to ask the right questions. Even if they are prepared with good initial questions, they may be lacking the best follow-up questions. This problem can be helped by making sure that the most spiritually mature members are on your search committee. You may also ask a pastor of a sister church to attend the interviews so that he can help you to assess the applicant's theology.

Perhaps the most surprising confession from many weak search committees is that they simply did not spend sufficient time checking out the references of the candidate. Even when they did check out his references, they later found that they should have asked for secondary references. When your church application form asks for referrals, it is obvious that most applicants will provide names of people who will give them glowing recommendations. You should not rely merely on written recommendations, but you should also speak to every person listed as a reference. You should also ask that the primary reference give you the names and telephone numbers of others who may be able to give objective evaluations, such as other pastors who previously worked with the candidate. Then those people should be contacted too.

THE WRONG PRESENTATION

In many career fields, hiring involves a lengthy interview behind closed doors. The man being interviewed has shined his shoes, put on his best suit, and is on his best behavior. This is to be expected. When a pastor is interviewed, however, committees often fail when it comes to the way that they present him to the congregation. Typically, when a search committee is satisfied with an applicant, he is presented as a leading candidate to the church and what seems like a popularity contest follows.

The committee will plan a weekend when the pastor can bring his wife and visit. Frequently, the pastor will be encouraged to find a babysitter for his children for the weekend so that he and his wife can keep up a busy candidating schedule on the two-day visit. A social event might be planned for the Saturday, and the evening might culminate with a dinner to which key church families are invited. On Sunday morning the man will preach and be introduced to the congregation as the candidate presented to them by the search committee. Another social event might be planned for Sunday afternoon and at some point there may be a time for questions and answers. Perhaps at the Sunday evening service the pastor will be asked pre-screened questions that have been submitted earlier in the day by members of the church.

So far, there is nothing inherently wrong. It wouldn't necessarily be wrong for the candidate to leave his children with family or friends for the weekend, although it may be to the committee's advantage to see how the applicant and his wife interact with their children. There is nothing wrong with social times, meals, sermons, and times for questions. But it would be wrong if the evaluation process and presentation of the candidate stopped there. Too many churches invite a candidate for one weekend, perhaps two, and then they put it to the vote of the congregation. This decision, however, is far too important for such a casual evaluation and presentation.

THE WRONG DECISION-MAKERS
In many churches, a congregational vote is taken immediately following a candidate's visit. While input from the church body is extremely important, a congregational vote by that body can result in the wrong decision. One reason is that the congregation have not been privy to the interview process. They have not spoken to the candidate's primary and secondary references, and, with just a weekend visit, they have not begun to really know the man.

How can the church body possibly make a wise decision when the wrong group of people use the wrong criteria and the wrong evaluation process? Even if only one of the above processes is found to be at fault, how can the right decision possibly be made? A congregational vote is simply not the best way to make a biblical decision. In rare instances, when a congregation has been well taught and well prepared for such a decision, a vote might end up with the best candidate. But all too often, the congregation is not properly informed. Another problem exists: the congregation may simply be too diverse, theologically, to make a wise decision.

In Chapter 4, I discussed the broad and diverse spectrum of theology held by both Evangelicals and Fundamentalists. I also challenged churches that are looking for a new pastor to examine their doctrinal positions, to see how they might have drifted during the tenure of their previous pastors. Suppose that your church leaders recognized a steady drift toward Post-Conservatism. As a result, your leadership may have decided to consider only candidates who are more conservative than your previous pastor. If that were the case, many in your church might not want a more conservative pastor (some of them might even threaten to leave the church over the issue). Obviously, a vote would not be the best decision-making process in this situation. Therefore, having a solid church leadership involved in the decision would be ideal. Your church leadership should have a firm understanding of what Scripture requires of a pastor and also be in touch with where the members of your congregation are, positionally. It is for this reason that some churches have preferred to implement an "elder model" of pastoral selection.

The Elder Model

In Mark Dever's book *Nine Marks of a Healthy Church*, one of his essential ingredients is a biblical leadership. According to Dever, in order for your church's leadership to meet biblical qualifications, you should have a plurality of elders who are shepherding the congregation. He says,

The Bible clearly models a plurality of elders in each local church. Though it never suggests a specific number of elders for a particular congregation, the New Testament refers to "elders" in the plural in local churches (e.g., Acts 14:23; 16:4; 20:17; 21:18; Titus 1:5; James 5:14). When you read through Acts and the Epistles, there is always more than one elder being talked about.[5]

Because your church should be equipped with a group of qualified men who work together as overseers, there should be little need for a separate pastoral search committee.

As previously mentioned, the decision to call your next pastor is a spiritual matter. Therefore, it is natural that the spiritual leaders in your church should be the ones most involved in that decision. No godly group of leaders makes decisions autocratically, from the top down, without any interaction with the entire congregation. It is obvious that an eldership should listen to members of the congregation before choosing a candidate.

They must also seek God's choice by the process of fervent prayer. But the elder board that hands over the entire pastoral selection process to another group within the church, or one that relies completely upon a congregational vote, or neglects prayer, neglects its spiritual responsibility. This is simply too important a decision for those who know the Bible the best not to be involved.

The "elder model" of pastoral selection may involve a search committee to do some of the groundwork. Ultimately, though, the elders are highly involved with the process of interviewing and examining the candidates. The more this group of spiritually mature leaders can be drawn into this process, the better the result will be for the church. In spite of the ideal nature of this model, however, not every church is able to follow it. Here are some reasons why.

NOT EVERY CHURCH HAS ELDERS

It may be that your church does not have elders, either because of your denominational tradition or perhaps because your church is small and your previous pastor did not take the time to train up qualified elders. If tradition is keeping your church from establishing elders, then now is a good time for your church to seriously consider key biblical passages on eldership. Some of them are: Hebrews 13:17; Acts 20:28; 1 Peter 5:2; 1 Timothy 3:1–7; Titus 1:5–9. In his excellent book designed to assist churches in their efforts to establish qualified elders, Alexander Strauch writes about a church he attended as a young man, where he first saw eldership modeled biblically:

The elders of this church took seriously the New Testament commands for elders to be biblically qualified and to actively shepherd the flock of God. They provided strong leadership, loving pastoral care and discipline, sound Bible teaching, and humble, sacrificial examples of Christian living. As a result, they were highly esteemed by the church. The inspiring example of these men first awakened in me a positive interest in the subject of church eldership.[6]

What church wouldn't want spiritually mature men who are willing to serve their brothers and sisters with pastoral care and biblical shepherding? This is truly the model of church government toward which every church should be striving.

If the problem with your church is that it lacks qualified men, you are in a difficult position. Your previous pastor, who was acting as a qualified elder among you, quite likely is no longer available to assist you in your current search. It may therefore be in the best interests of your church to seek help from other churches. To continue searching for a pastor using a committee that is not qualified or that is not prepared to establish a new pastor/elder may prevent you from finding the right man. If that is the case, find another church that is theologically sound and ask its elders to assist you to find a new pastor. Submit yourself to the leadership of a good church and consider the candidates that it recommends. Your church is simply not in a position to make the wisest decision regarding a new pastor at this time.

NOT ALL ELDERS SHOULD BE ELDERS

Another reason why some churches may not like the idea of their elders choosing their next pastor is because their elders may not be qualified. A church member in my church used to be a deacon in another church. The reason why he left that church is that he was discussing the gospel with one of his church elders and it became clear to him that his elder wasn't exactly sure what the gospel was! When he approached his pastor with the concern that one of the elders might not be a genuinely committed Christian, the pastor rebuked him! The pastor explained that, since the elder was baptized as an infant, he was a "child of the covenant" and therefore he must be saved. The inadequacy of that response caused great concern in that deacon and eventually he left that church and came to ours. Alexander Strauch tells a similar story from his own experience:

My first encounter with church elders occurred when I was a young teenager preparing for confirmation. During confirmation classes I told the minister about my conversion to Christ, which had taken place the previous summer at Bible camp. He was so intrigued by my youthful, exuberant testimony of Christ that he asked me to share my story with the church elders. So I met with the elders and told them about my new relationship with Jesus Christ. They sat speechless, looking totally puzzled. I was saddened by their response because I realized that they didn't understand what I was saying. That experience left me with little confidence in the elders or the church.7

If your church is in a similar position—your leadership is simply not qualified—your search committee should be pursuing counsel and direction from a qualified group of church leaders. Like a church that doesn't have any elders, a church without qualified leadership needs to approach spiritually qualified leaders from another church to assist it in searching for a new pastor.

I am not suggesting that you, as a search committee, look for assistance from another church in a secret or underhand manner. Since many church constitutions place the responsibility of finding pastoral candidates onto a search committee, you should discuss your pursuit of assistance with your acting elders. Once your church has established a biblically qualified group of church leaders, a proposal should be made for a change in your constitution. Ideally, your church constitution should place the burden of candidate selection upon the elders or a sub-committee of elders, depending on the number of men serving your church elder board. Many church constitutions also require a three-quarters majority approval by the members of the congregation on the call of the candidate. There is nothing wrong with that, but any candidate presented to the congregation should be a man with sound theology and teaching ability, and should meet all the biblical character standards required of pastors.

The Trial-Period Model

A model that is not as common today as it was in times past is the "trial-period model." This requires the candidate to commit to an assessment period of at least three months. The idea is that this time can be an examination period for both the church and the candidate. At the end of the period, either of them can decide that the match is not right. While this model has its own set of weaknesses, it may be ideal for your church—especially if you are looking for a pastor who will stay with you for decades.

Paul V. Harrison has written an article in the *Journal of the Evangelical Theological Society* about the high turnover rate among pastors. In this article, Harrison examines the high percentage (71 percent) of New England pastors from the mid-1700s who "labored their entire pastoral career at the very church where they were ordained."[8] A major contributing factor to the long pastoral tenures in those days was the unpopularity and unacceptability of calling a pastor who was already serving in another church. Another contributing factor, however, was that it was common for pastors to enter into a trial-period agreement before accepting a call to a particular church. As Harrison notes, "When churches called pastors, they usually had them serve an extended time on probation. Three months was the minimum, but a year was not uncommon. During this time, both the candidate and the church examined each other closely."[9]

Though this is not the usual practice today, it has not been completely abandoned. I entered into a trial-period agreement in the 1990s when I began my current pastorate. My circumstances were somewhat unique. I was a single missionary looking at a church in South Africa. The church had originally invited me to come for six months to serve as an interim pastor while it was between pastors. When its leading applicant withdrew from the running (even before I had arrived), it asked me if I would consider applying for the position. Since I was already interested in pastoring overseas, I agreed. The church suggested that I come for a six-month trial period, at the end of which, if either party was not completely happy, we could part amicably. Though I agreed to the six-month trial period, I moved from Southern California to South Africa with the intention of staying at least five to ten years. I was willing to spend my lifetime there, but communicated to them my desire to help strengthen churches in Africa. When I moved, most of my possessions were either sold or shipped over to Africa in a crate. Whether the position was open for me for six months or sixty years, it made no difference for me in the way I prepared to go.

As it turned out, I met my wife in that church shortly after I arrived and we were married in Johannesburg about a year and a half later. So I have personally experienced a trial period with a church. The result was an official call to the church and a wholehearted acceptance. Both parties had a better idea of the commitment being made.

Another pastor friend of mine also entered into a trial-period agreement. His arrangement, however, did not result in an appointment. This colleague's trial period was not international but involved a move from the West Coast to the East Coast. Before moving his family 3,000 miles across the country, he was invited to bring them for a five-week trial. They accepted and the hosting church rented a home for them. During this time, he was able to teach at the church several times per week. They had meals with families in the church and one of the key families even went on a five-day vacation with them. The amount of time that this pastoral candidate was able to spend with his potential congregation was phenomenal.

During those five weeks, he had two primary goals. First, he wanted to find out if the people really saw Scripture as their highest authority. Second, he wanted to see if the people had a teachable attitude. At the end of the five weeks, he and his family returned to California to make a decision about a long-term commitment. He met with the elders of the church where he had been an associate pastor and asked for their counsel. After serious prayer and consideration, he phoned one of the church leaders to discuss some concerns that he had about the church. There had been some internal strife among members that was evident. His biggest red flag was that some of the leaders seemed to be more concerned about the appearance of a healthy church than with the application of God's Word in areas that they knew needed to change. Therefore, after this five-week trial period, this pastoral candidate declined the call. Within a year, the very concerns he witnessed during those five weeks caused a split in that church and it was later revealed that some of the leaders had been involved in immoral behavior! When I asked him whether or not his trial period had been a positive experience, his answer was, "Without a doubt, yes." He felt as though he had been rescued from a situation that might have been devastating if he had committed prematurely to that church.

Overall, his experience was positive. It was a growing and learning time for him. He and his family did enjoy some sweet times of fellowship with believers during their trial period. When the problems in the church did become evident to all, he was able to recommend help from another biblically minded church in the area. For him, it was all about the body of

Christ working together to find the best fit for each congregation. Even though the trial period did not result in a long-term position for him, he now strongly advises any church or pastor that has the option of a trial period to take advantage of its benefits.

Much can be learned from this model of candidating. One obvious principle, beneficial for both candidates and churches, is that the more time you have to look over each other, the better. If a church has a high view of God's Word and has nothing to hide about its desire to be taught, it can only benefit from an in-depth time of examination with its candidate (see end of chapter for more on this point). It is also important, however, to recognize some of the weaknesses of the trial-period model.

IT IS IMPRACTICAL

When I have discussed this model with other pastors, one of the first objections raised is that it is not practical. How do I move my family across the country with the promise of a temporary position? What about my children and their schooling? Who will pay the moving expenses? What if it doesn't work out—how long will the church support us? These are all questions that contribute to the fact that this model is not as popular today as it was two hundred years ago.

While some might argue that there are ways to make this type of venture more practical (temporary housing, homeschooling, prearranged financial agreements, etc.), let me simply admit that this model is not for everyone. Some churches cannot afford it. Some pastors are in current positions in which a trial period at another church is simply not feasible. The bottom line is that for many churches and pastors it is just not a viable option. But for those who have the option of a trial period, it is to their advantage. It is a luxury not everyone can afford, but it can work to benefit all the parties involved. Either the call is confirmed after the trial period and all parties know what they are getting into, or the call is left unconfirmed and at least one of the parties feels that it has been rescued. In God's providence, this arrangement—though impractical for many—could be a blessing for your church.

IT IS UNCOMFORTABLE

No one likes living in a glass house. Part of being a pastor means that the man and his family are likely to be unduly scrutinized by some immature Christians in the congregation. The added pressure of being in a "trial period" can make it an even more uncomfortable experience for some pastors. In Donald M. Scott's book about New England ministry from 1750 to 1850, he admits that some of the young men going through a trial period were under quite a bit of pressure:

> As one young candidate confided in his fiancée, "the people watch me as narrowly as a mouse is watched by a cat." Indeed, the diaries, letters, and journals of young preachers seeking a settlement are filled with anxieties about how the people were responding to them and to their preaching, and whether, if the signals were unclear, this meant hostility to their candidacy, or, even worse, was a sign of their own spiritual unworthiness for the office. [10]

It is true: a trial period can become uncomfortable for both parties. But personal comfort should never be the goal of a Christian leader. I am in no way suggesting that churches should intentionally set undue hardship on a pastor just to see how he handles pressure. But a trial period can be enormously advantageous for the examination of a pastor, especially if he is young.

IT CAN BECOME PROLONGED

A third problem for the trial-period model is that it can go on longer than necessary. As mentioned before, a trial period may be considered by some to be a luxury. It can be a luxury for the church because they have a man in the pulpit, caring for their people, and they haven't been forced to make a long-term commitment. It can be a luxury for the pastor because he has a job, but can pull out at anytime if it becomes too uncomfortable for him. To make a wise decision, it is possible that these "luxuries" must be afforded. But at the same time, the trial period can also be abused.

For example, it would be wrong for the pastor to use his temporary status to try to control people ("You had better treat me right, or I am out of here …"). Likewise, the church needs to be careful not to take advantage of the pastoral candidate. One way abuse can be avoided is for both parties to make certain that the arrangement terms are clear to all concerned and that the congregation understands them.

I mentioned earlier that I met my wife during the first six months of my pastorate. Our dating relationship caused no small amount of interest among the church members. They were simply not used to having one of the members of the church dating the pastor. None of us was sure how this dating relationship would end up. Because of that, the leaders, who originally invited me to come for a trial period of six months, wanted to extend the trial period. At my six-month review, the men asked me if I would be willing to enter into another six-month trial period. I declined their invitation.

They had spent six months getting to know me. I had been in their homes. They had sat under my teaching for six months. They had had the opportunity to scrutinize me more closely than most other candidates examined by other churches. In addition, from the beginning of my arrival they had announced to the congregation that I was coming on a six-month trial visit, at the end of which either party could decide that it was not a good match. In my opinion, agreeing to a second trial period would have sent the wrong message to the church. Either I was the man to serve their congregation, or I was not. At some stage they would have to make their decision by *faith*. I emphasize the importance of making a decision by faith because, eventually, all call committees must use the information God has revealed to them and make a decision. There is no perfect pastor, and the church that waits for one will never find him. Finding the right man for your congregation is never easy, but finding the perfect one is impossible.

In my case, I gave the leaders of the church two options at the end of the six-month trial period. If I was the man for the job, they should hire me and communicate that to the congregation. If I wasn't the man for the job, I was still willing to stay as long as they requested so that I could help to shepherd their congregation until they found the right man for the position. Either way, I was fine with whatever decision they made. It was my desire to stay and serve as their pastor, but I was confident that God's hand was intricately involved. If they had asked me to leave that day, I would have accepted it as God's direction. After all, He is sovereign over all things. At the same time, it is important for call committees to be able to make decisions at the appropriate times and not prolong the process when an agreed trial period has been established. When I presented those two options to the leaders of the church, they didn't even ask me to go outside so that they could discuss it. Immediately, someone said that he believed I was the man for their church and the others all agreed. That month I began serving the congregation as the official pastor-teacher, and for more than seven years it has been a glorious pastorate for me. The people have been responsive to the Word of God, and it has been a place of fertile ground where I have been able to grow as a young pastor.

The Home-Grown Model

A fourth model your church should consider is to produce your own pastor from within your own congregation. Since you are reading a manual for pulpit committees, it is likely that you are in need of a pastor immediately. Taking the time to "grow your own pastor" may not be a viable option for you at this time. On the other hand, if you consider the time it takes for the average church to find a pastor, you may do well to "grow your own."

Though a pastoral search can take less than eighteen months, in many churches it can take two to three years. If you factor in the high rate of pastoral turnover (the average American pastor stays in his church for only three or four years[11]), in any given decade, some churches can spend more time without a pastor than with one. This is why growing your own pastor can be a real blessing for your congregation.

This process would require your church leadership to identify one of its current leaders or faithful members who has the desire, gifting, and moral qualifications to serve as a future pastor. This person also needs to be above reproach (1 Tim. 3:1–7; Titus 1:5–9). Once the person is identified, and if he is willing, he can be recommended to the congregation, even though he may still need training.

Ray Meringer, Director of Admissions at The Master's Seminary, has said that it has become increasingly common for churches to send members of their churches to seminary for the three-year M.Div. program so that they can be trained to serve as their pastors. Such men and their families are generally supported by their home churches for the eight-month period they spend each year in Southern California, where the future pastors are attending class. During the Christmas break and the summer vacation, the men and their families return to their churches to minister to their home congregations. The result is that, after three years, the seminary students (and future pastors) have been with their congregations for a total of twelve months. But they have had to have other men fill the pulpits for the remaining twenty-four months. Two years of pulpit supply is not that much longer than many churches face during their search for the right man.

It could be that the right man is already in your congregation; he just needs more of the right training. Since this man is originally from your area, and since he already has close bonds with the members of the congregation, it is more likely that he will settle well into a lengthy period of ministry than someone who has had no history with you. This is an option that many pulpit committees do not consider. In many cases it would be better for them for the long term if they seriously began their search from within their own congregations.

One of the most striking examples of this search model occurred with G. Campbell Morgan and D. Martyn Lloyd-Jones. Before Lloyd-Jones was actually saved he often attended Westminster Chapel, because he was drawn to the preaching ministry of Campbell Morgan. He preferred the services at Westminster Chapel more than those of his own denomination (even though he had been quite involved with Sunday school and youth ministries).[12] He continued to attend services at Westminster Chapel when he was able, even after Campbell Morgan left for the U.S. in 1917. Between 1923 and 1925 (more than six years after Lloyd-Jones had started frequenting services at Westminster Chapel), he was converted under the ministry of John Hutton.

Martyn was so gripped by his [Hutton's] preaching that he began attending the morning services whenever he could. For the first time in his life Martyn was made aware of the power of God to change lives and sensed a spiritual reality he did not find at his own chapel ... Martyn began to see that the problem with human beings was neither medical nor intellectual, but moral and spiritual. At the same time he was beginning to sense his own spiritual need: "My trouble was not only that I did things that were wrong, but that I myself was wrong at the very centre of my being."[13]

Lloyd-Jones was later married and began his preaching ministry in Wales. In 1938, however, he received a letter from Campbell Morgan, who had returned to the U.K., suggesting the possibility that they share the preaching at Westminster Chapel for six months. Martyn Lloyd-Jones agreed and he served, not as an "assistant pastor," but together with Morgan as an "associate pastor."[14] They typically alternated sermons, sharing the preaching equally until 1943, when Campbell Morgan became physically unable to carry on with his pastoral responsibilities.[15]

The foresight that Campbell Morgan had to bring on Lloyd-Jones was brilliant. If only more pastors would have the same prudence to hire true "associates" rather than "assistants," the transition time between pastors would not be so difficult. Larger churches, especially, should raise up men who are not just "waiting in the wings" to take over the preaching responsibility. Of course, this model is not for every church and it also has some drawbacks.

ADDED EXPENSE

Supporting a full-time pastor is a big challenge for some churches. The additional expense incurred to support a future pastor while in seminary may prove to be prohibitive. Seminarians carry the costs of travel, accommodation, tuition, and books, in addition to normal living costs. It may not be feasible for a church to commit to such an endeavor, while providing honoraria for visiting speakers at the same time. It takes a special congregation, one committed to the entire training process, to have the necessary patience to receive its pastor when he has completed his studies. If your congregation is small, and the members are not sufficiently committed to seeing the process through, then the home-grown model might not be the one for your church.

In spite of the economic difficulties, however, this model should not be quickly discarded. Finances should never be the primary factor in a spiritual decision. God is able to provide for those He directs into ministry, and stories of amazing provision abounded among the men I studied with.

If your leadership will first consider the prospects among men in your congregation, finances can be considered at a later stage. As was the case for Westminster Chapel and Lloyd-Jones, your ideal candidate may be someone known by your congregation, either because he is now, or used to be, a member of your church.

SEMINARY ISN'T ENOUGH FOR EVERYONE

Another potential weakness of the home-grown model is the false expectation that seminary is all your man needs to prepare him for ministry. Not every seminarian is ready to pastor straight out of seminary. I was twenty-six years old when I graduated from seminary and I waited three years before entering my first pastorate. I simply was not ready. Even after I did begin my first pastorate, it took me at least a hundred sermons before I felt I could communicate the Word clearly, passionately, and accurately.

A few years ago, our church hired an associate pastor who had just graduated from seminary. In my opinion, he was a much better preacher than I had been shortly after my graduation. I was very thankful to be able to hire such a mature graduate. He has consistently demonstrated a well-formed understanding of what preaching and pastoring are all about. This is not the case with every graduate, and it is important that your church not set up false expectations—especially if it is used to itinerant preaching.

Preachers who are invited to preach once at a church without a pastor typically re-preach one of their best sermons. These "sugar-sticks" can be sweet to the soul, and can be a great encouragement to a congregation. But, like most sweet things, an occasional serving adds flavor to your life but does not affect your health. If your congregation gets used to a steady diet of "sugar-stick" sermons, you can expect an adjustment when your pastor comes to preach the meat of the Word. It is far more difficult to preach week after week to the same congregation than it is to take one of your best sermons and preach it once to an eager crowd.

If your preacher is "home-grown," he will need time to mature, and you may find yourself with a recipe for discontentment at an early stage. This is why your congregation will need to commit to this process for a long duration.

A smaller church may not be able to sustain such a commitment. Larger churches, however, should already be doing this. As part of the natural discipleship process that takes place in your church, some of your men should desire to be trained better in the teaching ministry. Therefore, larger churches should always have men from the congregation that they currently support away at seminary (this should be part of your philosophy of ministry). If you are always training men for church leadership, then, when you are without a pastor, you will always have somebody "waiting in the wings." Prepare your congregation for such transitions and teach them that patience is part of the process.

Conclusions for Committees

In this chapter I have evaluated four different models of pastoral selection and confirmed that there is no single perfect model for every church. Since your church is unique, you may find that a combination of two or more of the models will suit you best. It is important that you recognize the weaknesses of each model and try to identify the strengths that will help you the most in your search. Below is a summary of principles that it will be extremely helpful for you to keep in mind during the search process.

LONGER IS BETTER

You may not be able to invite your candidate for a trial period, but I hope that you see the importance of spending time with him before he is called to be your pastor. A few meetings behind closed doors and one time behind the pulpit simply does not provide a sufficient perspective for you to make this critical decision with wisdom. The more time you can spend with the man, the better. Send him on a three-day road trip with your elders. I am tempted to suggest that you send them in a car that is not mechanically sound! Of course, that wouldn't be very godly, but the idea is that you want to spend enough time with him so that you can see how he handles pressure situations. If he is married and has children, ask him to bring his family with him whenever he visits. Have people in your church spend time with them while he is interviewing.

FAMILY MATTERS

Pastors become the leaders of church families. For this reason, it is important to get to know the pastor's family before he is hired. Do you want your church to respond to his spiritual leadership as his family does? If he has grown children, it would be appropriate to contact them and ask them if they would recommend their father for the pastoral position at your church. Asking that question to younger children may not be appropriate as it might put them under too much pressure, but believing children who are grown and out of the home could make contributions that would be especially valuable for your committee's search. As I have interviewed the grown children of pastors who have disqualified themselves for ministry, several have said, "I wish the committee that hired my father had asked me for a recommendation before they hired him." In those cases, they would not have recommended their fathers for such a position.

The pastor's wife is also a key figure in the life of your church. While it is not appropriate to expect her to play the piano, teach Sunday school, and organize the church social events, this doesn't mean that she should be ignored in the candidating process. Meaningful conversations with her are important. Is she given to hospitality? How does she feel about people dropping by unexpectedly? As a fellow believer, where do her gifts lie, and where does she enjoy serving among the body? How does she handle situations when her husband is criticized? Has she learned how to direct people to her husband when they try to criticize him through her? What is her attitude toward pastoral ministry? These are all issues that should be discussed with her in detail. She will be partnering with him in ministry in many ways; therefore, you need to find opportunities when you can get to know her before her husband is hired.

DIG DEEPER

Listen to as many of your candidate's sermon tapes as you can get your hands on. Call his references and ask for more references. When you speak to the secondary references, ask for more. Ideally, you should be able to find a common friend—someone who knows your church and who knows your candidate. Experiments in the past have suggested that everyone in the world is connected by no more than six degrees of separation: that you can trace a link between yourself and anyone else in the world that involves no more than six people—he or she is a friend of a friend of a friend of a friend of a friend.[16] If that is true in the world at large, the degrees of separation between the people in your church and a pastoral candidate for your church are likely to be fewer than three. There must be someone who knows your candidate and also knows your church. If there is not, there must be someone who knows your candidate, and knows someone who knows your church. Try to find links between seminary professors, former churches, and so forth. Everyone would agree that this can become a waste of time if no clear connection seems obvious early on. But if you never look for a connection, you are not looking deep enough.

COMPARE APPLES WITH APPLES

If you want a preacher who can feed your flock with the Word consistently, week after week, inviting him to come and preach one of his best "sugar-stick" sermons is not going to give you or your congregation a fair look at his preaching ability. You may allow him to preach a sermon of his choice the first time he comes. But after that, assign him a text on a Monday and have him preach it six days later, on the following Sunday. Assign him at least one Old Testament text before calling him to be your pastor. When you assign him a text, ask him if he has preached from that passage before. Explain to him that you want your congregation to evaluate him on the kind of preparation he can do during an average week.

FIND QUALIFIED DECISION-MAKERS

In this book, I have tried to help prepare committees that are already formed so that they can ask better questions, understand answers better, and ultimately make better decisions. Making the best decision, however, should involve the most spiritually mature people in your congregation. Perhaps this book has caused you to rethink the common search committee model. As a result, you may have decided to disband your current committee and regroup with members who are not necessarily representative of the church body but who are the most spiritually mature and discerning leaders in your church. That would be prudent. For those committees that are content with their composition, but see changes that need to be made in their constitution for future searches, now may be a good time to initiate those changes.

DON'T EXPECT THE UNATTAINABLE

In this book, I have described a candidate who is an excellent expositor of God's Word. In addition to his preaching ability, he is a shepherd who cares for and tends the needs of his flock. He is above reproach when it comes to the biblical qualifications of an elder (1 Tim. 3:1–7; Titus 1:5–9). His doctrine is theologically sound, both in theory and in practice. He is available for your congregation. Some may read the above sentences with disappointment and say, "No such person exists." Others might believe that such a person does exist, and their expectations may be too high. The latter group tends to eliminate potential candidates prematurely.

Such a person does exist for your congregation, but you need to be careful that your expectations are not too high. There is no perfect pastor. Every pastor has personality flaws and areas of spiritual maturity that need growth. There should be no habitual sin that dominates his life, but he is a sinner, and, like all Christians, he wrestles against his fleshly nature. Your pastor needs to be a spiritual leader, but he will not be faultless. You can expect him to be available to visit and counsel with members of the congregation, but he also needs to guard his time with his family. You can expect him to have the tools he needs to study God's Word, but you cannot expect him to expound deep truths from the Word without study. You can expect that he will be the kind of man who is quick to ask for forgiveness when he fails, but don't expect him to never fail.

You cannot expect him to come knocking on your door the first Sunday you announce that you are looking for candidates. But, if you commit your need to prayer and use wise principles of searching and evaluation, you can expect that, in God's time, He will bring the right man to your congregation. You can know for sure that God cares about His church and promises to build it, sustain it, and preserve it (Matt. 16:18). Your job now is to be looking for God's man, according to God's time, with God's standards, in a godly manner.

Notes

1 **Wesley E. Johnson,** *The Right Pastor: Seeking God's Man for Your Church* (Schaumburg, IL: Regular Baptist Press, 2001), 7.
2 This is an excerpt from an actual letter that was shared with me during my time of research.
3 According to one source, the average search process ranges from eight to eighteen months; *The Search: Helpful Hints for a Successful Pastoral Search Process* (Dallas: The Dallas Theological Seminary Placement Office), 3. For a copy of this fifteen-page booklet, write to Dallas Theological Seminary at 3909 Swiss Ave., Dallas, TX 75204, or email them at placement@dts.edu.
4 "Pastoral Search Survey," 1999–2003, Mainstream Oklahoma Baptists, at: www.mainstreambaptists.org/mob/pastor_survey.htm; accessed January 2011.
5 **Mark Dever,** *Nine Marks of a Healthy Church* (Wheaton, IL: Crossway, 2004), 229–230.
6 **Alexander Strauch,** *Biblical Eldership: An Urgent Call to Restore Biblical Church Leadership* (Littleton, CO: Lewis & Roth, 1995), 9.
7 Ibid.
8 **Paul V. Harrison,** "Pastoral Turnover and the Call to Preach," in *Journal of the Evangelical Theological Society,* 44/1 (March 2001), 91.
9 Ibid. 92.
10 **Donald M. Scott,** *From Office to Profession: The Transformation of the New England Ministry, 1750–1850* (Philadelphia: University of Pennsylvania Press, 1978), 4.
11 **Harrison,** "Pastoral Turnover," 87.
12 **Philip H. Eveson,** *Travel with Martyn Lloyd-Jones: In the Footsteps of the Distinguished Welsh Evangelist, Pastor and Theologian* (Leominster: Day One, 2004), 49.
13 Ibid. 50.
14 Ibid. 77.
15 **Jill Morgan,** *A Man of the Word: Life of G. Campbell Morgan* (London: Pickering & Inglis, 1951), 315.
16 Articles about this phenomenon abound in encyclopedias and on the Internet, e.g., "Six Degrees of Separation" at: en.wikipedia.org (accessed Jan. 2011). Other articles on the same issue are associated with Milgram's small world experiment.

Doctrinal Statement from Grace Community Church, Sun Valley, California

What We Teach

THE HOLY SCRIPTURES

We teach that the Bible is God's written revelation to man, and thus the sixty-six books of the Bible given to us by the Holy Spirit constitute the plenary (inspired equally in all parts) Word of God (1 Corinthians 2:7–14; 2 Peter 1:20–21).

We teach that the Word of God is an objective, propositional revelation (1 Thessalonians 2:13; 1 Corinthians 2:13), verbally inspired in every word (2 Timothy 3:16), absolutely inerrant in the original documents, infallible, and God-breathed. We teach the literal, grammatical-historical interpretation of Scripture which affirms the belief that the opening chapters of Genesis present creation in six literal days (Genesis 1:3; Exodus 31:17).

We teach that the Bible constitutes the only infallible rule of faith and practice (Matthew 5:18; 24:35; John 10:35; 16:12–13; 17:17; 1 Corinthians 2:13; 2 Timothy 3:15–17; Hebrews 4:12; 2 Peter 1:20–21).

We teach that God spoke in His written Word by a process of dual authorship. The Holy Spirit so superintended the human authors that, through their individual personalities and different styles of writing, they composed and recorded God's Word to man (2 Peter 1:20–21) without error in the whole or in the part (Matthew 5:18; 2 Timothy 3:16).

We teach that, whereas there may be several applications of any given passage of Scripture, there is but one true interpretation. The meaning of Scripture is to be found as one diligently applies the literal grammatical-historical method of interpretation under the enlightenment of the Holy Spirit (John 7:17; 16:12–15; 1 Corinthians 2:7–15; 1 John 2:20). It is the responsibility of believers to ascertain carefully the true intent and meaning of Scripture, recognizing that proper application is binding on all generations. Yet the truth of Scripture stands in judgment of men; never do men stand in judgment of it.

GOD

We teach that there is but one living and true God (Deuteronomy 6:4; Isaiah 45:5–7; 1 Corinthians 8:4), an infinite, all-knowing Spirit (John 4:24), perfect in all His attributes, one in essence, eternally existing in three persons—Father, Son, and Holy Spirit (Matthew 28:19; 2 Corinthians 13:14)—each equally deserving worship and obedience.

God the Father

We teach that God the Father, the first Person of the Trinity, orders and disposes all things according to His own purpose and grace (Psalm 145:8–9; 1 Corinthians 8:6). He is the Creator of all things (Genesis 1:1–31; Ephesians 3:9). As the only absolute and omnipotent Ruler in the universe, He is sovereign in creation, providence, and redemption (Psalm 103:19; Romans 11:36). His fatherhood involves both His designation within the Trinity and His relationship with mankind. As Creator He is Father to all men (Ephesians 4:6), but He is spiritual Father only to believers (Romans 8:14; 2 Corinthians 6:18). He has decreed for His own glory all things that come to pass (Ephesians 1:11). He continually upholds, directs, and governs all creatures and events (1 Chronicles 29:11). In His sovereignty He is neither the author nor approver of sin (Habakkuk 1:13; John 8:38–47), nor does He abridge the accountability of moral, intelligent creatures (1 Peter 1:17). He has graciously chosen from eternity past those whom He would have as His own (Ephesians 1:4–6); He saves from sin all who come to Him through Jesus Christ; He adopts as His own all those who come to Him; and He becomes, upon adoption, Father to His own (John 1:12; Romans 8:15; Galatians 4:5; Hebrews 12:5–9).

God the Son

We teach that Jesus Christ, the second Person of the Trinity, possesses all the divine excellencies, and in these He is coequal, consubstantial, and coeternal with the Father (John 10:30; 14:9).

We teach that God the Father created according to His own will, through His Son, Jesus Christ, by whom all things continue in existence and in operation (John 1:3; Colossians 1:15–17; Hebrews 1:2).

We teach that in the incarnation (God becoming man) Christ surrendered only the prerogatives of deity but nothing of the divine essence, either in degree or kind. In His incarnation, the eternally existing second Person of the Trinity accepted all the essential characteristics of humanity and so became the God-man (Philippians 2:5–8; Colossians 2:9).

We teach that Jesus Christ represents humanity and deity in indivisible oneness (Micah 5:2; John 5:23; 14:9–10; Colossians 2:9).

We teach that our Lord Jesus Christ was virgin born (Isaiah 7:14; Matthew 1:23, 25; Luke 1:26–35); that He was God incarnate (John 1:1, 14); and that the purpose of the incarnation was to reveal God, redeem men, and rule over God's kingdom (Psalm 2:7–9; Isaiah 9:6; John 1:29; Philippians 2:9–11; Hebrews 7:25–26; 1 Peter 1:18–19).

We teach that, in the incarnation, the second Person of the Trinity laid aside His right to the full prerogatives of coexistence with God and took on an existence appropriate to a servant while never divesting Himself of His divine attributes (Philippians 2:5–8).

We teach that our Lord Jesus Christ accomplished our redemption through the shedding of His blood and sacrificial death on the cross and that His death was voluntary, vicarious, substitutionary, propitiatory, and redemptive (John 10:15; Romans 3:24–25; 5:8; 1 Peter 2:24).

We teach that on the basis of the efficacy of the death of our Lord Jesus Christ, the believing sinner is freed from the punishment, the penalty, the power, and one day the very presence of sin; and that he is declared righteous, given eternal life, and adopted into the family of God (Romans 3:25; 5:8–9; 2 Corinthians 5:14–15; 1 Peter 2:24; 3:18).

We teach that our justification is made sure by His literal, physical resurrection from the dead and that He is now ascended to the right hand of the Father, where He now mediates as our Advocate and High Priest (Matthew 28:6; Luke 24:38–39; Acts 2:30–31; Romans 4:25; 8:34; Hebrews 7:25; 9:24; 1 John 2:1).

We teach that in the resurrection of Jesus Christ from the grave, God confirmed the deity of His Son and gave proof that God has accepted the atoning work of Christ on the cross. Jesus' bodily resurrection is also the guarantee of a future resurrection life for all believers (John 5:26–29; 14:19; Romans 1:4; 4:25; 6:5–10; 1 Corinthians 15:20, 23).

We teach that Jesus Christ will return to receive the church, which is His Body, unto Himself at the rapture, and returning with His church in glory, will establish His millennial kingdom on earth (Acts 1:9–11; 1 Thessalonians 4:13–18; Revelation 20).

We teach that the Lord Jesus Christ is the one through whom God will judge all mankind (John 5:22–23):

- Believers (1 Corinthians 3:10–15; 2 Corinthians 5:10)
- Living inhabitants of the earth at His glorious return (Matthew 25:31–46)
- Unbelieving dead at the Great White Throne (Revelation 20:11–15)

As the Mediator between God and man (1 Timothy 2:5), the Head of His Body the church (Ephesians 1:22; 5:23; Colossians 1:18), and the coming universal King, who will reign on the throne of David (Isaiah 9:6; Luke 1:31–33), He is the final judge of all who fail to place their trust in Him as Lord and Savior (Matthew 25:14–46; Acts 17:30–31).

God the Holy Spirit

We teach that the Holy Spirit is a divine person, eternal, underived, possessing all the attributes of personality and deity, including intellect (1 Corinthians 2:10–13), emotions (Ephesians 4:30), will (1 Corinthians 12:11), eternality (Hebrews 9:14), omnipresence (Psalm 139:7–10), omniscience (Isaiah 40:13–14), omnipotence (Romans 15:13), and truthfulness (John 16:13). In all the divine attributes He is coequal and consubstantial with the Father and the Son (Matthew 28:19; Acts 5:3–4; 28:25–26; 1 Corinthians 12:4–6; 2 Corinthians 13:14; Jeremiah 31:31–34 with Hebrews 10:15–17).

We teach that it is the work of the Holy Spirit to execute the divine will with relation to all mankind. We recognize His sovereign activity in creation (Genesis 1:2), the incarnation (Matthew 1:18) the written revelation (2 Peter 1:20–21), and the work of salvation (John 3:5–7).

We teach that the work of the Holy Spirit in this age began at Pentecost, when He came from the Father as promised by Christ (John 14:16–17; 15:26) to initiate and complete the building of the Body of Christ, which is His church (1 Corinthians 12:13). The broad scope of His divine activity includes convicting the world of sin, of righteousness and of judgment; glorifying the Lord Jesus Christ and transforming believers into the image of Christ (John 16:7–9; Acts 1:5; 2:4; Romans 8:29; 2 Corinthians 3:18; Ephesians 2:22).

We teach that the Holy Spirit is the supernatural and sovereign Agent in regeneration, baptizing all believers into the Body of Christ (1 Corinthians 12:13). The Holy Spirit also indwells, sanctifies, instructs, empowers them for service, and seals them unto the day of redemption (Romans 8:9; 2 Corinthians 3:6; Ephesians 1:13).

We teach that the Holy Spirit is the divine Teacher, who guided the apostles and prophets into all truth as they committed to writing God's revelation, the Bible. Every believer possesses the indwelling presence of the Holy Spirit from the moment of salvation, and it is the duty of all those born of the Spirit to be filled with (controlled by) the Spirit (John 16:13; Romans 8:9; Ephesians 5:18; 1 John 2:20, 27).

We teach that the Holy Spirit administers spiritual gifts to the church. The Holy Spirit glorifies neither Himself nor His gifts by ostentatious displays, but He does glorify Christ by implementing His work of redeeming the lost and building up believers in the most holy faith (John 16:13–14; Acts 1:8; 1 Corinthians 12:4–11; 2 Corinthians 3:18).

We teach, in this respect, that God the Holy Spirit is sovereign in the bestowing of all His gifts for the perfecting of the saints today, and that speaking in tongues and the working of sign miracles in the beginning days of the church were for the purpose of pointing to and authenticating the apostles as revealers of divine truth, and were never intended to be characteristic of the lives of believers (1 Corinthians 12:4–11; 13:8–10; 2 Corinthians 12:12; Ephesians 4:7–12; Hebrews 2:1–4).

MAN

We teach that man was directly and immediately created by God in His image and likeness. Man was created free of sin with a rational nature, intelligence, volition, self-determination, and moral responsibility to God (Genesis 2:7, 15–25; James 3:9).

We teach that God's intention in the creation of man was that man should glorify God, enjoy God's fellowship, live his life in the will of God, and by this accomplish God's purpose for man in the world (Isaiah 43:7; Colossians 1:16; Revelation 4:11).

We teach that in Adam's sin of disobedience to the revealed will and Word of God, man lost his innocence, incurred the penalty of spiritual and physical death, became subject to the wrath of God, and became inherently corrupt and utterly incapable of choosing or doing that which is acceptable to God apart from divine grace. With no recuperative powers to enable him to recover himself, man is hopelessly lost. Man's salvation is thereby wholly of God's grace through the redemptive work of our Lord Jesus Christ (Genesis 2:16–17; 3:1–19; John 3:36; Romans 3:23; 6:23; 1 Corinthians 2:14; Ephesians 2:1–3; 1 Timothy 2:13–14; 1 John 1:8).

We teach that, because all men were in Adam, a nature corrupted by Adam's sin has been transmitted to all men of all ages, Jesus Christ being the only exception. All men are thus sinners by nature, by choice, and by divine declaration (Psalm 14:1–3; Jeremiah 17:9; Romans 3:9–18, 23; 5:10–12).

SALVATION

We teach that salvation is wholly of God by grace on the basis of the redemption of Jesus Christ, the merit of His shed blood, and not on the basis of human merit or works (John 1:12; Ephesians 1:7; 2:8–10; 1 Peter 1:18–19).

Regeneration

We teach that regeneration is a supernatural work of the Holy Spirit by which the divine nature and divine life are given (John 3:3–7; Titus 3:5). It is instantaneous and is accomplished solely by the power of the Holy Spirit through the instrumentality of the Word of God (John 5:24) when the repentant sinner, as enabled by the Holy Spirit, responds in faith to the divine provision of salvation. Genuine regeneration is manifested by fruits worthy of repentance as demonstrated in righteous attitudes and conduct.

Good works are the proper evidence and fruit of regeneration (1 Corinthians 6:19–20; Ephesians 2:10), and will be experienced to the extent that the believer submits to the control of the Holy Spirit in his life through faithful obedience to the Word of God (Ephesians 5:17–21; Philippians 2:12b; Colossians 3:16; 2 Peter 1:4–10). This obedience causes the believer to be increasingly conformed to the image of our Lord Jesus Christ (2 Corinthians 3:18).

Such a conformity is climaxed in the believer's glorification at Christ's coming (Romans 8:17; 2 Peter 1:4; 1 John 3:2–3).

Election

We teach that election is the act of God by which, before the foundation of the world, He chose in Christ those whom He graciously regenerates, saves, and sanctifies (Romans 8:28–30; Ephesians 1:4–11; 2 Thessalonians 2:13; 2 Timothy 2:10; 1 Peter 1:1–2).

We teach that sovereign election does not contradict or negate the responsibility of man to repent and trust Christ as Savior and Lord (Ezekiel 18:23, 32; 33:11; John 3:18–19, 36; 5:40; Romans 9:22–23; 2 Thessalonians 2:10–12; Revelation 22:17). Nevertheless, since sovereign grace includes the means of receiving the gift of salvation as well as the gift itself, sovereign election will result in what God determines. All whom the Father calls to Himself will come in faith, and all who come in faith the Father will receive (John 6:37–40, 44; Acts 13:48; James 4:8).

We teach that the unmerited favor that God grants to totally depraved sinners is not related to any initiative of their own part or to God's anticipation of what they might do by their own will, but is solely of His sovereign grace and mercy (Ephesians 1:4–7; Titus 3:4–7; 1 Peter 1:2).

We teach that election should not be looked upon as based merely on abstract sovereignty. God is truly sovereign, but He exercises this sovereignty in harmony with His other attributes, especially His omniscience, justice, holiness, wisdom, grace, and love (Romans 9:11–16). This sovereignty will always exalt the will of God in a manner totally consistent with His character as revealed in the life of our Lord Jesus Christ (Matthew 11:25–28; 2 Timothy 1:9).

Justification

We teach that justification before God is an act of God (Romans 8:33) by which He declares righteous those who, through faith in Christ, repent of their sins (Luke 13:3; Acts 2:38; 3:19; 11:18; Romans 2:4; 2 Corinthians 7:10; Isaiah 55:6–7) and confess Him as sovereign Lord (Romans 10:9–10; 1 Corinthians 12:3; 2 Corinthians 4:5; Philippians 2:11). This righteousness is apart from any virtue or work of man (Romans 3:20; 4:6) and involves the imputation of our sins to Christ (Colossians 2:14; 1 Peter 2:24) and the imputation of Christ's righteousness to us (1 Corinthians 1:30; 2 Corinthians 5:21). By this means, God is enabled to "be just and the justifier of the one who has faith in Jesus" (Romans 3:26).

Sanctification

We teach that every believer is sanctified (set apart) unto God by justification and is therefore declared to be holy and is therefore identified as a saint. This sanctification is positional and instantaneous and should not be confused with progressive sanctification. This sanctification has to do with the believer's standing, not his present walk or condition (Acts 20:32; 1 Corinthians 1:2, 30; 6:11; 2 Thessalonians 2:13; Hebrews 2:11; 3:1; 10:10, 14; 13:12; 1 Peter 1:2).

We teach that there is also, by the work of the Holy Spirit, a progressive sanctification by which the state of the believer is brought closer to the standing the believer positionally enjoys through justification. Through obedience to the Word of God and the empowering of the Holy Spirit, the believer is able to live a life of increasing holiness in conformity to the will of God, becoming more and more like our Lord Jesus Christ (John 17:17, 19; Romans 6:1–22; 2 Corinthians 3:18; 1 Thessalonians 4:3–4; 5:23).

In this respect, we teach that every saved person is involved in daily conflict—the new creation in Christ doing battle against the flesh—but adequate provision is made for victory through the power of the indwelling Holy Spirit. The struggle nevertheless stays with the believer all through this earthly life and is never completely ended. All claims to the eradication of sin in this life are unscriptural. Eradication of sin is not possible, but the Holy Spirit does provide for victory over sin (Galatians 5:16–25; Ephesians

4:22–24; Philippians 3:12; Colossians 3:9–10; 1 Peter 1:14–16; 1 John 3:5–9).

Security

We teach that all the redeemed, once saved, are kept by God's power and are thus secure in Christ forever (John 5:24; 6:37–40; 10:27–30; Romans 5:9–10; 8:1, 31–39; 1 Corinthians 1:4–8; Ephesians 4:30; Hebrews 7:25; 13:5; 1 Peter 1:5; Jude 24).

We teach that it is the privilege of believers to rejoice in the assurance of their salvation through the testimony of God's Word, which, however, clearly forbids the use of Christian liberty as an occasion for sinful living and carnality (Romans 6:15–22; 13:13–14; Galatians 5:13, 25–26; Titus 2:11–14).

Separation

We teach that separation from sin is clearly called for throughout the Old and New Testaments, and that the Scriptures clearly indicate that in the last days apostasy and worldliness shall increase (2 Corinthians 6:14–7:1; 2 Timothy 3:1–5).

We teach that, out of deep gratitude for the undeserved grace of God granted to us, and because our glorious God is so worthy of our total consecration, all the saved should live in such a manner as to demonstrate our adoring love to God and so as not to bring reproach upon our Lord and Savior. We also teach that separation from all religious apostasy and worldly and sinful practices is commanded of us by God (Romans 12:1–2; 1 Corinthians 5:9–13; 2 Corinthians 6:14–7:1; 1 John 2:15–17; 2 John 9–11).

We teach that believers should be separated unto our Lord Jesus Christ (2 Thessalonians 1:11–12; Hebrews 12:1–2) and affirm that the Christian life is a life of obedient righteousness that reflects the teaching of the Beatitudes (Matthew 5:2–12) and a continual pursuit of holiness (Romans 12:1–2; 2 Corinthians 7:1; Hebrews 12:14; Titus 2:11–14; 1 John 3:1–10).

THE CHURCH

We teach that all who place their faith in Jesus Christ are immediately placed by the Holy Spirit into one united spiritual Body, the church (1 Corinthians 12:12–13), the bride of Christ (2 Corinthians 11:2; Ephesians 5:23–32; Revelation 19:7–8), of which Christ is the Head (Ephesians 1:22; 4:15; Colossians 1:18).

We teach that the formation of the church, the Body of Christ, began on the Day of Pentecost (Acts 2:1–21, 38–47) and will be completed at the coming of Christ for His own at the rapture (1 Corinthians 15:51–52; 1 Thessalonians 4:13–18).

We teach that the church is thus a unique spiritual organism designed by Christ, made up of all born-again believers in this present age (Ephesians 2:11–3:6). The church is distinct from Israel (1 Corinthians 10:32), a mystery not revealed until this age (Ephesians 3:1–6; 5:32).

We teach that the establishment and continuity of local churches is clearly taught and defined in the New Testament Scriptures (Acts 14:23, 27; 20:17, 28; Galatians 1:2; Philippians 1:1; 1 Thessalonians 1:1; 2 Thessalonians 1:1) and that the members of the one spiritual Body are directed to associate themselves together in local assemblies (1 Corinthians 11:18–20; Hebrews 10:25).

We teach that the one supreme authority for the church is Christ (1 Corinthians 11:3; Ephesians 1:22; Colossians 1:18) and that church leadership, gifts, order, discipline, and worship are all appointed through His sovereignty as found in the Scriptures. The biblically designated officers serving under Christ and over the assembly are elders (also called bishops, pastors, and pastor-teachers; Acts 20:28; Ephesians 4:11) and deacons, both of whom must meet biblical qualifications (1 Timothy 3:1–13; Titus 1:5–9; 1 Peter 5:1–5).

We teach that these leaders lead or rule as servants of Christ (1 Timothy 5:17–22) and have His authority in directing the church. The congregation is to submit to their leadership (Hebrews 13:7, 17).

We teach the importance of discipleship (Matthew 28:19–20; 2 Timothy 2:2), mutual accountability of all believers to each other (Matthew 18:5–14), as well as the need for discipline of sinning members of the congregation in accord with the standards of Scripture (Matthew 18:15–22; Acts 5:1–11; 1 Corinthians 5:1–13; 2 Thessalonians 3:6–15; 1 Timothy 1:19–20; Titus 1:10–16).

We teach the autonomy of the local church, free from any external authority or control, with the right of self-government and freedom from the interference of any hierarchy of individuals or organizations (Titus 1:5). We teach that it is scriptural for true churches to cooperate with each other for the presentation and propagation of the faith. Each local church, however, through its elders and their interpretation and application of Scripture, should be the sole judge of the measure and method of its cooperation. The elders should determine all other matter of membership, policy, discipline, benevolence, and government as well (Acts 15:19–31; 20:28; 1 Corinthians 5:4–7, 13; 1 Peter 5:1–4).

We teach that the purpose of the church is to glorify God (Ephesians 3:21) by building itself up in the faith (Ephesians 4:13–16), by instruction of the Word (2 Timothy 2:2, 15; 3:16–17), by fellowship (Acts 2:47; 1 John 1:3), by keeping the ordinances (Luke 22:19; Acts 2:38–42) and by advancing and communicating the gospel to the entire world (Matthew 28:19; Acts 1:8; 2:42).

We teach the calling of all saints to the work of the service (1 Corinthians 15:58; Ephesians 4:12; Revelation 22:12).

We teach the need of the church to cooperate with God as He accomplishes His purpose in the world. To that end, He gives the church spiritual gifts. He gives men chosen for the purpose of equipping the saints for the work of the ministry (Ephesians 4:7–12), and He also gives unique and special spiritual abilities to each member of the Body of Christ (Romans 12:5–8; 1 Corinthians 12:4–31; 1 Peter 4:10–11).

We teach that there were two kinds of gifts given the early church: miraculous gifts of divine revelation and healing, given temporarily in the apostolic era for the purpose of confirming the authenticity of the apostles' message (Hebrews 2:3–4; 2 Corinthians 12:12); and ministering gifts, given to equip believers for edifying one another. With the New Testament revelation now complete, Scripture becomes the sole test of the authenticity of a man's message, and confirming gifts of a miraculous nature are no longer necessary to validate a man or his message (1 Corinthians 13:8–12). Miraculous gifts can even be counterfeited by Satan so as to deceive even believers (1 Corinthians 13:13–14:2; Revelation

13:13–14). The only gifts in operation today are those nonrevelatory equipping gifts given for edification (Romans 12:6–8).

We teach that no one possesses the gift of healing today, but that God does hear and answer the prayer of faith and will answer in accordance with His own perfect will for the sick, suffering, and afflicted (Luke 18:1–6; John 5:7–9; 2 Corinthians 12:6–10; James 5:13–16; 1 John 5:14–15).

We teach that two ordinances have been committed to the local church: baptism and the Lord's Supper (Acts 2:38–42). Christian baptism by immersion (Acts 8:36–39) is the solemn and beautiful testimony of a believer showing forth his faith in the crucified, buried, and risen Savior, and his union with Him in death to sin and resurrection to a new life (Romans 6:1–11). It is also a sign of fellowship and identification with the visible body of Christ (Acts 2:41–42).

We teach that the Lord's Supper is the commemoration and proclamation of His death until He comes, and should be always preceded by solemn self-examination (1 Corinthians 11:28–32). We also teach that, whereas the elements of Communion are only representative of the flesh and blood of Christ, participation in the Lord's Supper is nevertheless an actual communion with the risen Christ, who indwells every believer, and so is present, fellowshipping with His people (1 Corinthians 10:16).

ANGELS

Holy Angels

We teach that angels are created beings and are therefore not to be worshiped. Although they are a higher order of creation than man, they are created to serve God and to worship Him (Luke 2:9–14; Hebrews 1:6–7, 14; 2:6–7; Revelation 5:11–14; 19:10; 22:9).

Fallen Angels

We teach that Satan is a created angel and the author of sin. He incurred the judgment of God by rebelling against his Creator (Isaiah 14:12–17; Ezekiel 28:11–19), by taking numerous angels with him in his fall (Matthew 25:41; Revelation 12:1–14), and by introducing sin into the human race by his temptation of Eve (Genesis 3:1–15).

We teach that Satan is the open and declared enemy of God and man (Isaiah 14:13–14; Matthew 4:1–11; Revelation 12:9–10); that he is the prince of this world, who has been defeated through the death and resurrection of Jesus Christ (Romans 16:20); and that he shall be eternally punished in the lake of fire (Isaiah 14:12–17; Ezekiel 28:11–19; Matthew 25:41; Revelation 20:10).

LAST THINGS

Death

We teach that physical death involves no loss of our immaterial consciousness (Revelation 6:9–11), that the soul of the redeemed passes immediately into the presence of Christ (Luke 23:43; Philippians 1:23; 2 Corinthians 5:8), that there is a separation of soul and body (Philippians 1:12–24), and that, for the redeemed, such separation will continue until the rapture (1 Thessalonians 4:13–17), which initiates the first resurrection (Revelation 20:4–6), when our soul and body will be reunited to be glorified forever with our Lord (Philippians 3:21; 1 Corinthians 15:35–44, 50–54). Until that time, the souls of the redeemed in Christ remain in joyful fellowship with our Lord Jesus Christ (2 Corinthians 5:8).

We teach the bodily resurrection of all men, the saved to eternal life (John 6:39; Romans 8:10–11, 19–23; 2 Corinthians 4:14), and the unsaved to judgment and everlasting punishment (Daniel 12:2; John 5:29; Revelation 20:13–15).

We teach that the souls of the unsaved at death are kept under punishment until the second resurrection (Luke 16:19–26; Revelation 20:13–15), when the soul and the resurrection body will be united (John 5:28–29). They shall then appear at the Great White Throne judgment (Revelation 20:11–15) and shall be cast into hell, the lake of fire (Matthew 25:41–46), cut off from the life of God forever (Daniel 12:2; Matthew 25:41–46; 2 Thessalonians 1:7–9).

The Rapture of the Church

We teach the personal, bodily return of our Lord Jesus Christ before the seven-year tribulation (1 Thessalonians 4:16; Titus 2:13) to translate His church from this earth (John 14:1–3; 1 Corinthians 15:51–53; 1 Thessalonians 4:15–5:11) and, between this event and His glorious return with His saints, to reward believers according to their works (1 Corinthians 3:11–15; 2 Corinthians 5:10).

The Tribulation Period

We teach that immediately following the removal of the church from the earth (John 14:1–3; 1 Thessalonians 4:13–18) the righteous judgments of God will be poured out upon an unbelieving world (Jeremiah 30:7; Daniel 9:27; 12:1; 2 Thessalonians 2:7–12; Revelation 16), and that these judgments will be climaxed by the return of Christ in glory to the earth (Matthew 24:27–31; 25:31–46; 2 Thessalonians 2:7–12). At that time the Old Testament and tribulation saints will be raised and the living will be judged (Daniel 12:2–3; Revelation 20:4–6). This period includes the seventh week of Daniel's prophecy (Daniel 9:24–27; Matthew 24:15–31; 25:31–46).

The Second Coming and the Millennial Reign

We teach that, after the tribulation period, Christ will come to earth to occupy the throne of David (Matthew 25:31; Luke 1:31–33; Acts 1:10–11; 2:29–30) and establish His messianic kingdom for 1,000 years on the earth (Revelation 20:1–7). During this time the resurrected saints will reign with Him over Israel and all the nations of the earth (Ezekiel 37:21–28; Daniel 7:17–22; Revelation 19:11–16). This reign will be preceded by the overthrow of the Antichrist and the False Prophet, and by the removal of Satan from the world (Daniel 7:17–27; Revelation 20:1–7).

We teach that the kingdom itself will be the fulfillment of God's promise to Israel (Isaiah 65:17–25; Ezekiel 37:21–28; Zechariah 8:1–17) to restore them to the land that they forfeited through their disobedience (Deuteronomy 28:15–68). The result of their disobedience was that Israel was temporarily set aside (Matthew 21:43; Romans 11:1–26), but will again be awakened through repentance to enter into the land of blessing (Jeremiah 31:31–34; Ezekiel 36:22–32; Romans 11:25–29).

We teach that this time of our Lord's reign will be characterized by harmony, justice, peace, righteousness, and long life (Isaiah 11; 65:17–25;

Ezekiel 36:33–38), and will be brought to an end with the release of Satan (Revelation 20:7).

The Judgment of the Lost

We teach that following the release of Satan after the 1,000-year reign of Christ (Revelation 20:7), Satan will deceive the nations of the earth and gather them to battle against the saints and the beloved city, at which time Satan and his army will be devoured by fire from heaven (Revelation 20:9). Following this, Satan will be thrown into the lake of fire and brimstone (Matthew 25:41; Revelation 20:10), whereupon Christ, who is the Judge of all men (John 5:22), will resurrect and judge the great and the small at the Great White Throne Judgment.

We teach that this resurrection of the unsaved dead to judgment will be a physical resurrection, whereupon receiving their judgment (John 5:28–29), they will be committed to an eternal conscious punishment in the lake of fire (Matthew 25:41; Revelation 20:11–15).

Eternity

We teach that after the closing of the millennium, the temporary release of Satan, and the judgment of unbelievers (2 Thessalonians 1:9; Revelation 20:7–15), the saved will enter the eternal state of glory with God, after which the elements of this earth are to be dissolved (2 Peter 3:10) and replaced with a new earth, wherein only righteousness dwells (Ephesians 5:5; Revelation 20:15; 21:1–27; 22:1–22). Following this, the heavenly city will come down out of heaven (Revelation 21:2) and will be the dwelling place of the saints, where they will enjoy forever fellowship with God and one another (John 17:3; Revelation 21–22). Our Lord Jesus Christ, having fulfilled His redemptive mission, will then deliver up the kingdom to God the Father (1 Corinthians 15:24–28), that in all spheres the triune God may reign forever and ever (1 Corinthians 15:28).

WHAT IT MEANS TO BE A CHRISTIAN

Being a Christian is more than identifying yourself with a particular religion or affirming a certain value system. Being a Christian means you have embraced what the Bible says about God, mankind, and salvation. Consider the following truths found in Scripture.

God Is Sovereign Creator

Contemporary thinking says man is the product of evolution. But the Bible says we were created by a personal God to love, serve, and enjoy endless fellowship with Him. The New Testament reveals it was Jesus Himself who created everything (John 1:3; Colossians 1:16). Therefore, He also owns and rules everything (Psalm 103:19). That means He has authority over our lives and we owe Him absolute allegiance, obedience, and worship.

God Is Holy

God is absolutely and perfectly holy (Isaiah 6:3), therefore He cannot commit or approve of evil (James 1:13). God requires holiness of us as well. First Peter 1:16 says, "You shall be holy, for I am holy."

Mankind Is Sinful

According to Scripture, everyone is guilty of sin: "There is no man who does not sin" (1 Kings 8:46). That doesn't mean we're incapable of performing acts of human kindness. But we're utterly incapable of understanding, loving, or pleasing God on our own (Romans 3:10–12).

Sin Demands a Penalty

God's holiness and justice demand that all sin be punished by death (Ezekiel 18:4). That's why simply changing our patterns of behavior can't solve our sin problem or eliminate its consequences.

Jesus Is Lord and Savior

The New Testament reveals it was Jesus Himself who created everything (Colossians 1:16). Therefore He owns and rules everything (Psalm 103:19). That means He has authority over our lives and we owe Him absolute allegiance, obedience, and worship. Romans 10:9 says, "If you confess with your mouth Jesus as Lord, and believe in your heart that God raised Him from the dead, you shall be saved." Even though God's justice demands death for sin, His love has provided a Savior who paid the penalty and died for sinners (1 Peter 3:18). Christ's death satisfied the demands of God's justice and Christ's perfect life satisfied the demands of God's holiness (2 Corinthians 5:21), thereby enabling Him to forgive and save those who place their faith in Him (Romans 3:26).

The Character of Saving Faith

True faith is always accompanied by repentance from sin. Repentance is agreeing with God that you are sinful, confessing your sins to Him, and making a conscious choice to turn from sin (Luke 13:3, 5; 1 Thessalonians 1:9) and pursue Christ (Matthew 11:28–30; John 17:3) and obedience to Him (1 John 2:3). It isn't enough to believe certain facts about Christ. Even Satan and his demons believe in the true God (James 2:19), but they don't love and obey Him. True saving faith always responds in obedience (Ephesians 2:10).

Good Questions to Ask a Prospective Senior Pastor

These questions are to assist you in the interview with your primary candidate. They are designed to promote discussion. Please select the questions that would stimulate important discussion for your church and add other questions to go with them. These questions are a compilation of my own thought and a number of other unpublished lists I have acquired over the years from those who have taught on candidating. Contributors include Jim George, Dan Dumas, and Jack Hughes—all of whom are, or have been, associated with The Master's Seminary.

Doctrinal Questions

1. What is your position on the inerrancy of Scripture?
2. What role does repentance play in faith (define both repentance and faith)?
3. Regarding salvation, discuss the relationship between God's sovereignty and man's responsibility.
4. Is justification by faith alone?
5. How does the Roman Catholic view of justification differ from the Protestant view of justification?
6. Does the Roman Catholic gospel differ from that of the Bible?
7. Discuss some key passages that teach about the total depravity of man.
8. Discuss the relationship between positional sanctification and progressive sanctification.
9. Describe any differences you have with pre-millennial dispensationalism.
10. Please outline the end-times events that the Bible refers to.
11. Do you believe that God has a future plan for Israel? If so, what is it?
12. What kind of fellowship and/or partnership do you foresee between yourself and believers in the Charismatic movement?
13. Do you believe that tongues, prophetic revelation, and miraculous gifts have ceased?

14. What does the Bible teach about women's roles in the church?
15. How important is it to believe in a six-day creation?
16. What are the means that you intend to pursue for church growth?
17. Is it possible for Christ to be Savior of someone's life, but not Lord?
18. According to the Bible, what are biblical grounds for divorce and remarriage?
19. Does divorce necessarily disqualify a man for ministry or an elder for service?
20. Should "altar calls" be practiced in the church?
21. What is the earliest age appropriate for baptism and communion?
22. Describe the mode and method of baptism you prefer and explain why.
23. What does the Bible teach about tithing, and how should that apply to our church?
24. According to the Bible, who will experience the wrath of God for all eternity?

Practical Ministry Questions
1. Are the Scriptures sufficient to handle any spiritual or emotional issue?
2. How would you use the Scriptures in your counseling ministry?
3. What other essential resources (if any) would you rely upon for counseling people with particular problems?
4. Do you believe it is possible to integrate secular psychology with Christianity?
5. Are you equipped to counsel any spiritual or emotional problem?
6. Can you walk us through a typical counseling session between you and a couple in the church having marriage problems—how you would start, what passages you would take them to, what kind of homework you would assign them, how often you would plan to meet with them, etc.
7. Describe your understanding of how the church should practice church discipline (according to Matthew 18).
8. Please give an example of an issue in which you would not pursue church discipline.
9. What is an issue in which you would pursue church discipline?
10. What kind of music do you prefer in church worship?
11. Describe your philosophy of music in corporate worship.

12. What kind of balance between hymns, choruses, and other worship music would you like to see in this church?

13. Describe any concerns you would have with church music ministry.

14. List some unbiblical practices of worship that are common today.

15. Describe how you typically address the issue of sin while preaching.

16. How would you respond to an eight-year-old boy who wants to be baptized?

17. What qualifies someone to baptize another believer?

18. What ordinances, if any, should the church practice besides baptism and communion?

19. Who should administer the Lord's Supper?

20. Can you give some examples of Christian liberty?

21. Please define legalism and give some examples of it.

22. Describe the kinds of activities that our children and youth ministries should be involved with.

23. Are you satisfied with our current Sunday-school curriculum?

24. Are you aware of the missionaries we are currently supporting?

25. What area of foreign missions should a church focus on (church planting, church strengthening, mercy ministries, supporting organizations, etc.)?

26. Please describe an ideal men's, women's, and adult church ministry.

27. Name and discuss some current Christian books that concern you.

28. Would you be willing to marry two unbelievers who called our church for a wedding?

29. What should be the process to become a member of a church?

30. What doctrinal differences should prevent someone from becoming a member of this church?

31. Is baptism a prerequisite for membership? If so, which modes are acceptable?

Philosophy of Ministry Questions

1. What is your philosophy of ministry?

2. What is the purpose of the weekly gathering of the church?

3. Do you believe that the Bible expects a plurality of leaders in a local church?

4. What is the role of a senior pastor?

5. What means do you intend to use to equip people to do the work of ministry (Eph. 4:11–16)?

6. What is the role of the staff? Explain your philosophy in working with a staff.

7. Have you managed a staff before? If so, how many people did this involve?

8. What have been your major contributions to the work of the church, and what would you like to accomplish in the future?

9. What is the purpose and nature of evangelism?

10. What should be our church's involvement with short-term missions?

11. Define success and discuss how it may or may not relate to pastoral ministry.

12. What are the marks of spiritual growth in a congregation?

13. Define discipleship and explain how it should be implemented in the local church.

14. If you become our pastor, how many years do you think it will take you to be effective in ministry?

15. Who would you prefer to lead the worship services?

16. Define expository preaching.

17. Do you typically preach consecutively through a book of the Bible, verse by verse?

18. How often do you preach topical messages?

19. Describe how your topical message might differ from an expositional message.

Personal Questions

1. Are you aware of anything in your life that would disqualify you for ministry according to the standards laid out in 1 Timothy 3 and Titus 1?

2. What do you feel are your strengths and weaknesses?

3. What are your chief interests and recreational activities?

4. What should and shouldn't a church expect from a pastor's wife?

5. What does your wife see as her role in supporting you in your ministry?

6. Who are your favorite authors and why?

7. Please list three books (besides the Bible) that have impacted your life in a profound way and explain why.

8. What books have you recently read?

9. Have you ever been asked to leave a church or ministry position? If so, please explain the circumstances and give us names of those we might want to contact.

10. Are there any questions about yourself that you are hoping we won't ask, or that you think we should ask?

11. What books of the Bible have you preached through?

12. Do you have recordings of all your sermons? If so, could we select five passages that you have preached on in the past and listen to those recordings?

Financial Questions

1. Through what kinds of expenditures would it be appropriate for a church to enter into debt (salaries, property, building renovations, etc.)?

2. What advice would you give a church that wanted to get out of debt?

3. Do you think it is wise for a church to be externally audited?

4. What percentage of a church budget should go toward missions?

Staffing Questions

1. What should be the roles of elders and deacons in the church?

2. Are you aware of our current paid staff and their positions?

3. Discuss the importance of a staff that is united in its philosophy of ministry.

4. In your estimation, who should the staff report to?

5. What do you think our process should be for adding staff?

6. What are your secretarial needs and desires?

Pastoral Duties

1. In order of priority, please list what you would see as your duties and responsibilities if you were the pastor of this church.

2. Please walk us through what an average working week would look like for you as the pastor of our church (nights away from family, days off, office hours, etc.).

3. What annual conferences do you, or would you like to, attend?
4. How many Sunday services per year do you think you would be out of the pulpit in a typical year (vacations, guest speakers, conferences, sick leave, etc.)?
5. How long should a sermon be?
6. Describe how you intend to be involved in evangelism at our church.

Appendix C

Checklist for Clarity in a Call

I first received a version of this list in 1999 from The Master's Seminary Admissions office. There was no bibliographic information and I do not know who first drafted these questions. I have made some changes and I encourage each committee to adjust them as necessary. These are difficult questions for a candidate to raise after he is called. Sometimes, churches also neglect to inform their new pastors of the details that this appendix confirms. It will be beneficial for both parties to have a signed copy of these details to help clarify questions down the road. Some pastors may not want these financial issues to influence their decision-making process. If the new pastor does not want to deal with these questions early on (which may be right), it may be helpful for him to ask an elder from his home church to come and discuss these issues on his behalf. When the time is right, he can confirm or ask questions about these issues.

1. Will the church provide moving expenses? If yes, how much?_____
2. Does the church provide housing for the pastor and his family? If yes, in which form?
   Parsonage _____
   Allowance _____
   If allowance, how much?_____
3. Does the church provide utilities or allowance? If allowance, how much?
   Electricity _____
   Phone _____
   Water _____
   Other _____
4. Will the church assist the pastor in purchasing a home? If yes, complete the following: The church provides downpayment as a gift/loan in the amount of _____ at an interest rate of _____ to be repaid at _____ monthly intervals. Amount to be paid in full within _____ days of termination as pastor.
5. Monthly salary to begin: _____ with a review for increase at the end of _____.

How often will reviews be considered thereafter?_____

6. Who makes recommendations for salary increases? _____

7. Is a monthly car allowance provided? If yes, state the amount
  per month _____ and
  per mile _____ for distant travel on church business.

8. Does the church provide insurance coverage? If yes, how much for
  health _____
  life _____ and
  retirement _____ ?

9. Does the church provide an annual book allowance? If yes, state annual amount: _____

10. How many weekly days off does the church provide? _____

11. Does the church provide annual paid vacation? If yes, state number of weeks
  1st year _____
  2nd year _____
  thereafter _____

12. Is pulpit supply paid by the church for vacation absences? Yes/No

13. List the number of weekdays off and Sundays away that the pastor is given each year for
  conferences:
  _____ (weekdays)
  _____ (Sundays)
  other preaching invitations:
  _____ (weekdays)
  _____ (Sundays)
  other _____:
  _____ (weekdays)
  _____ (Sundays)

14. Is pulpit supply paid by the church for those absences? Yes/No

15. Are conference fees and travel expenses paid for both the pastor and his wife when he attends conferences? Yes/No

16. Does the church provide time off for bereavement? If yes, state how much _____

17. Is the pastor eligible for a sabbatical at the end of each seven-year term? Yes/No

18. Is the church willing to pay for the pastor's further education expenses (Th.M., D.Min., or other)? Yes/No

19. Does the church provide time off for illness? If yes, state how much time annually _____

20. Are salary benefits paid during times of illness? If so, for how long? _____

21. Is a supply minister paid by the church in case of an illness? If so, for how long? _____

22. Does the church provide an annual physical examination for the pastor? Yes/No

23. Is the pastor designated as the supervisor of all other staff? If not, who is designated, and for which staff? _____

Achtemeier, Elizabeth, *So You're Looking for a New Preacher: A Guide for Pulpit Nominating Committees* (Grand Rapids, MI: Eerdmans, 1991)

Adams, Jay E., *Marriage, Divorce, and Remarriage in the Bible: A Fresh Look at What Scripture Teaches* (Grand Rapids, MI: P&R, 1986)

Balswick, Judith K., and **Balswick, Jack O.,** *Authentic Human Sexuality: An Integrated Christian Approach* (Downers Grove, IL: InterVarsity Press, 1999)

Beale, David O., *In Pursuit of Purity: American Fundamentalism since 1850* (Greenville, SC: Unusual Publications, 1986)

Belz, Joel, "Farewell to Anger," in *World Magazine*, 14/38 (Oct. 2, 1999)

——"Relativism at Fuller," in *World Magazine*, 21/25 (July 1, 2006)

Borthwick, Paul, *How to Choose a Youth Pastor* (Nashville: Thomas Nelson, 1993)

Calvin, John, *Commentary on the Book of the Prophet Isaiah*, vol. 8, *Calvin's Commentaries*, trans. by William Pringle (Grand Rapids, MI: Baker, 2005)

——*Commentaries on the Epistles to Timothy, Titus, and Philemon*, vol. 21 (Grand Rapids, MI: Baker, 2005)

Carter, Tom, *Spurgeon At His Best* (Grand Rapids, MI: Baker, 1988)

Catherwood, Christopher, *Five Evangelical Leaders* (Fearn: Christian Focus, 1994)

Chapell, Bryan, *Christ-Centered Preaching: Redeeming the Expository Sermon* (Grand Rapids, MI: Baker, 1994)

Dallas Seminary Placement Office, *The Search: Helpful Hints for a Successful Pastoral Search Process* (Dallas: Dallas Theological Seminary, 2006)

Dart, John, "U.S. Funds Evangelical–Muslim Project," in *Christian Century*, 120/26 (Dec. 27, 2003)

Dean, Jamie, "Classroom Christianity," in *World Magazine*, 22/4 (Jan. 27, 2007)

Dever, Mark, *Nine Marks of a Healthy Church* (Wheaton, IL: Crossway, 2004)

Dingman, Robert W., *In Search of a Leader: The Complete Search Committee Guidebook* (Ventura, CA: Regal Books, 1989)

Dollar, George W., *A History of Fundamentalism in America* (Greenville, SC: Bob Jones University Press, 1973)

Edwards, Brian, *Shall We Dance? Dance and Drama in Worship* (Welwyn: Evangelical Press, 1984)

Edwards, Jonathan, *The Works of Jonathan Edwards*, vol. 1 (Carlisle, PA: Banner of Truth, 1990)

Erickson, Millard J., *The Evangelical Left: Encountering Postconservative Evangelical Theology* (Grand Rapids, MI: Baker, 1997)

Bibliography

Eveson, Philip H., *Travel with Martyn Lloyd-Jones: In the Footsteps of the Distinguished Welsh Evangelist, Pastor and Theologian* (Leominster: Day One, 2004)

Gilchrist, Jack, *The Vacant Pulpit* (Valley Forge, PA: The Judson Press, 1969)

Grudem, Wayne, (ed.), *Biblical Foundations for Manhood and Womanhood* (Wheaton, IL: Crossway, 2002)

——*Systematic Theology* (Grand Rapids, MI: Zondervan, 1994)

Harrison, Paul V., "Pastoral Turnover and the Call to Preach," in *Journal of the Evangelical Theological Society,* 44/1 (March 2001)

Hendricksen, William, and **Kistemaker, Simon J.,** *Exposition of Thessalonians, the Pastorals, and Hebrews* (New Testament Commentary; Grand Rapids, MI: Baker, 1995)

Hoehner, Harold W., *Ephesians: An Exegetical Commentary* (Grand Rapids, MI: Baker Academic, 2002)

Hughes, Jack, *Expository Preaching with Word Pictures* (Fearn: Mentor, 2001)

Jefferson, Charles Edward, *The Minister as Shepherd* (Fincastle, VA: Scripture Truth, 1989/ Fort Washington, PA: CLC Publications, 2006)

Johnson, Wesley E., *The Right Pastor: Seeking God's Man for Your Church* (Schaumburg, IL: Regular Baptist Press, 2001)

Kent, Homer, Jr., *Ephesians: The Glory of the Church* (Chicago: Moody, 1971)

Kistemaker, Simon J., *Exposition of the First Epistle to the Corinthians* (New Testament Commentary; Grand Rapids, MI: Baker, 1993)

Kreider, Glenn R., "Sinners in the Hands of a Gracious God," Jan. 1, 2004, at www.bible.org

Lawson, Steven J., *Famine in the Land: A Passionate Call for Expository Preaching* (Chicago: Moody, 2003)

Lischer, Richard, "The Promise of Renewal," in **Lischer, Richard,** (ed.), *The Company of Preachers: Wisdom on Preaching, Augustine to the Present* (Grand Rapids, MI: Eerdmans, 2002)

Lloyd-Jones, D. Martyn, *Preaching and Preachers* (Grand Rapids, MI: Zondervan, 1972)

——*Studies in the Sermon on the Mount,* 2 vols. (Grand Rapids, MI: Eerdmans, 1960)

Lummis, Adair T., "What Do Lay People Want in Pastors?" in *Pulpit & Pew,* Winter 2003

Lutzer, Erwin W., *Pastor to Pastor: Tackling the Problems of Ministry* (Chicago: Moody, 1987)

MacArthur, John F., *Acts* (MacArthur New Testament Commentary; Chicago: Moody, 1996)

——*Colossians and Philemon* (MacArthur New Testament Commentary; Chicago: Moody, 1992)

——*1 Corinthians* (MacArthur New Testament Commentary; Chicago: Moody, 1984)

——*Different By Design: Discovering God's Will for Today's Man and Woman* (Wheaton, IL: Victor Books, 1994)

——*Ephesians* (MacArthur New Testament Commentary; Chicago: Moody, 1986)

——"Frequently Asked Questions about Expository Preaching," in **MacArthur, John F., Mayhue, Richard,** and **Thomas, Robert L.,** (eds.), *Rediscovering Expository Preaching: Balancing the Science and Art of Biblical Exposition* (Dallas: Word, 1992)

——*The MacArthur Study Bible* (Nashville: Word, 1997)

——"The Mandate of Biblical Inerrancy: Expository Preaching," in **MacArthur, John F., Mayhue, Richard,** and **Thomas, Robert L.,** (eds.), *Rediscovering Expository Preaching: Balancing the Science and Art of Biblical Exposition* (Dallas: Word, 1992)

——*Titus* (MacArthur New Testament Commentary; Chicago: Moody, 1996)

——*The Vanishing Conscience* (Dallas: Word, 1994)

——(ed.), with The Master's College Faculty, *Think Biblically! Recovering a Christian Worldview* (Wheaton, IL: Crossway, 2003)

Malphurs, Aubrey, *The Dynamics of Church Leadership* (Grand Rapids, MI: Baker, 1999)

Marsden, George M., *Fundamentalism and American Culture* (New York: Oxford University Press, 1980)

——*Understanding Fundamentalism and Evangelicalism* (Grand Rapids, MI: Eerdmans, 1991)

Mayhue, Richard L., "Rediscovering Expository Preaching," in **MacArthur, John F., Mayhue, Richard,** and **Thomas, Robert L.,** (eds.), *Rediscovering Expository Preaching: Balancing the Science and Art of Biblical Exposition* (Dallas: Word, 1992)

McCune, Rolland D., "The Self-Identity of Fundamentalism," in *Detroit Baptist Seminary Journal*, vol. 1 (1996)

Morgan, Jill, *A Man of the Word: Life of G. Campbell Morgan* (London: Pickering & Inglis, 1951)

Murray, Iain H., *Evangelicalism Divided: A Record of Crucial Change in the Years 1950 to 2000* (Carlisle, PA: Banner of Truth, 2000)

O'Brien, Peter T., *Colossians and Philemon* (Word Biblical Commentary, vol. 44; Nashville: Thomas Nelson, 1982)

"Pastoral Search Survey," 1999–2003, Mainstream Oklahoma Baptists, at www.mainstreambaptists.org/mob/pastor_survey.htm; accessed Jan. 2011

Pearson, Roy, *The Preacher: His Purpose and Practice* (Philadelphia: Westminster Press, 1962)

"Pensacola Christian College Articles of Faith," at www.pcci.edu; accessed Dec. 2010

Pettegrew, Larry, "Evangelicals, Paradigms, and the Emergent Approach," in *The Master's Seminary Journal*, 17/2 (Fall 2006)

Scott, Donald M., *From Office to Profession: The Transformation of the New England Ministry, 1750–1850* (Philadelphia: University of Pennsylvania Press, 1978)

Bibliography

——Pastors and Providence: Changing Ministerial Styles in Nineteenth-Century America (Evanston, IL: Seabury-Western Theological Seminary, 1975)

Spurgeon, C. H., "God's Providence," a sermon on Ezekiel 1:15–19, in the *Metropolitan Tabernacle Pulpit*, 54/3114 (October 15, 1908; repr. Pasadena, TX: Pilgrim Publications, 1978)

Stitzinger, James F., "The History of Expository Preaching," in **MacArthur, John F., Mayhue, Richard,** and **Thomas, Robert L.,** (eds.), *Rediscovering Expository Preaching: Balancing the Science and Art of Biblical Exposition* (Dallas: Word, 1992)

Stonehouse, Ned B., *J. Gresham Machen: A Biographical Memoir* (Grand Rapids, MI: Eerdmans, 1954)

Stott, John R. W., *The Preacher's Portrait* (Grand Rapids, MI: Eerdmans, 1961)

Strauch, Alexander, *Biblical Eldership: An Urgent Call to Restore Biblical Church Leadership* (Littleton, CO: Lewis & Roth, 1995)

——*A Christian Leader's Guide to Leading with Love* (Littleton, CO: Lewis & Roth, 2006)

Swindoll, Charles R., *The Tale of the Tardy Oxcart* (Dallas: Word, 1998)

Taylor, Barbara Brown, "Preaching," in **Lischer, Richard,** (ed.), *The Company of Preachers: Wisdom on Preaching, Augustine to the Present* (Grand Rapids, MI: Eerdmans, 2002)

Temple Baptist Seminary Catalog, vol. 1 (Chattanooga, TN: Temple Baptist Seminary; 54th edn., 2006–2007); also accessed at www.tntemple.edu/seminary

Thomas, Robert L., *Evangelical Hermeneutics: The New versus the Old* (Grand Rapids, MI: Kregel, 2002)

——*Understanding Spiritual Gifts: A Verse-by-Verse Study of 1 Corinthians 12–14* (Chicago: Moody, 1978)

Tidball, Derek J., *Who Are the Evangelicals?* (London: Marshall Pickering, 1994)

Umidi, Joseph L., *Confirming the Pastoral Call: A Guide to Matching Candidates and Congregations* (Grand Rapids, MI: Kregel, 2000)

Vine, W. E., *An Expository Dictionary of New Testament Words* (Old Tappan, NJ: Fleming H. Revell, 1966)

Wallace, Daniel B., *Greek Grammar beyond the Basics* (Grand Rapids, MI: Zondervan, 1996)

Wells, David F., *No Place for Truth or Whatever Happened to Evangelical Theology?* (Grand Rapids, MI: Eerdmans 1993)

Westing, Harold J., *Church Staff Handbook: How to Build an Effective Ministry Team* (Grand Rapids, MI: Kregel, 1985)

Yaconelli, Mike, "The Church Is Dead," in *The Door*, Jan./Feb. 1992

About Day One:

Day One's threefold commitment:

- TO BE FAITHFUL TO THE BIBLE, GOD'S INERRANT, INFALLIBLE WORD;

- TO BE RELEVANT TO OUR MODERN GENERATION;

- TO BE EXCELLENT IN OUR PUBLICATION STANDARDS.

I continue to be thankful for the publications of Day One. They are biblical; they have sound theology; and they are relative to the issues at hand. The material is condensed and manageable while, at the same time, being complete—a challenging balance to find. We are happy in our ministry to make use of these excellent publications.

JOHN MACARTHUR, PASTOR-TEACHER, GRACE COMMUNITY CHURCH, CALIFORNIA

It is a great encouragement to see Day One making such excellent progress. Their publications are always biblical, accessible and attractively produced, with no compromise on quality. Long may their progress continue and increase!

JOHN BLANCHARD, AUTHOR, EVANGELIST AND APOLOGIST

Visit our website for more information and to request a free catalogue of our books.

www.dayone.co.uk
www.dayonebookstore.com

Illuminated preaching
The Holy Spirit's vital role in
unveiling His Word, the Bible

JEFFREY CROTTS

978-1-84625-166-5

All true expository preachers want to experience the illumination of the Scripture in their hearts when they study and preach. Sadly, today's preaching culture promotes an imbalance in the discussion of the Spirit's role in preaching. In this Bible-soaked study, Jeffrey Crotts defines and applies the seemingly forgotten doctrine of illumination. Preachers who long for illumination during their personal study and preaching will be enriched as they read and apply this scholarly yet pastoral work on the priceless doctrine we call illumination.

I'm thankful for Jeff Crotts' balanced and sharply focused emphasis on the Holy Spirit's illuminating ministry ... Here is a sound, biblical antidote to the shallow superficiality and silly pragmatism that have commandeered so many pulpits today.
JOHN MACARTHUR, PASTOR-TEACHER OF GRACE COMMUNITY CHURCH, SUN VALLEY, CALIFORNIA, USA

A commendable balance characterizes the author's efforts and product ... May this book rescue many contemporary preachers from theologically aberrant methods by the Spirit's illumination of God's words from his

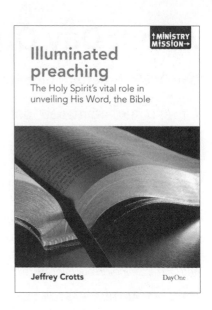

Illuminated preaching
The Holy Spirit's vital role in
unveiling His Word, the Bible

↑MINISTRY MISSION→

Jeffrey Crotts   DayOne

Word. May they come to understand where the power of true change comes from and be liberated from ultimately ineffectual tactics.
GEORGE J. ZEMEK, ACADEMIC DEAN, THE EXPOSITORS SEMINARY, USA

Jeffrey Crotts was raised in a Christian family in Virginia Beach, Virginia. At the age of 17 he became a Christian, and at 18 sensed a call to preach. He trained at Liberty University and The Master's Seminary, as well as a variety of ministry internships. In 1994 he met Judith, a Biblical Counseling and English major at The Master's College. They were married in 1997. They moved to Little Rock, Arkansas in 1998 when Jeffrey joined the pastoral staff of the Bible Church of Little Rock. He now ministers as senior pastor at Anchorage Grace Church in Alaska. They have been blessed with six children.

JERRY WRAGG

978-1-84625-200-6

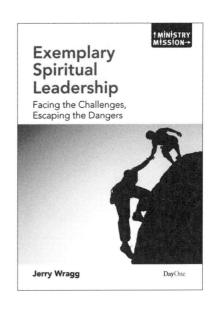

Exemplary
Spiritual
Leadership
Facing the Challenges,
Escaping the Dangers

↑MINISTRY
MISSION→

Jerry Wragg   DayOne

What is it that compels a group of people to follow the leadership and vision of one person? Why are the insights and pursuits of certain individuals more persuasive than those of others?

In this book, Jerry Wragg investigates how leadership should be characterized in the church, and how biblical leadership must differ from the kind of leadership promoted in the world. He explores the dynamics of leadership, particularly the character traits that need to be built up or eradicated in leaders, the dangers that leaders face and temptations to which they are particularly prone, and the development of future leaders: how to recognize leadership potential and encourage leadership gifts in the next generation. Throughout, Jerry Wragg writes honestly and offers pastoral encouragement and practical guidance that will help all men placed in church leadership positions.

Jerry Wragg was born and raised in California. Although exposed to Christian training through his parents' example and his own involvement in church, he didn't come to faith in Christ until after he was married and serving in the United States Air Force. After he was discharged, he graduated from The Master's Seminary with a Masters degree in Ministry and served as an associate pastor and personal assistant to Dr. John MacArthur at Grace Community Church, California. In 2001, he accepted the call to be pastor-teacher at Grace Immanuel Bible Church in Jupiter, Florida, where he is currently ministering. He has taught on church leadership, biblical counseling, theology and Bible survey courses, marriage and family, and parenting. In addition, Jerry serves as Board Chairman for The Expositors Seminary, Jupiter, Florida. He and his wife, Louise, have four adult children and are the proud grandparents of three grandsons and one granddaughter.

ERIC E. WRIGHT

384PP PAPERBACK

978–1–84625–198–6

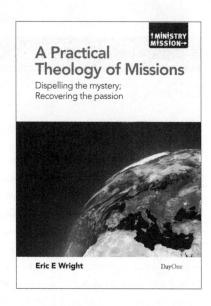

A Practical Theology of Missions
Dispelling the mystery;
Recovering the passion

Eric E Wright   DayOne

↑MINISTRY
MISSION→

What is the church's work of missions, and how should we carry it out? In this thorough study, Eric Wright roots missions solidly in the biblical text while giving modern, real-life examples of how missionary principles can be applied practically. He covers subjects such as missions and God's kingdom, the validity of mission boards, the role of providence, the necessary spiritual gifts, the multi-ethnic nature of ideal churches, how to avoid dependency, the priority of church planting versus humanitarian ministries, and short-term versus life-long missionary commitment.

A good understanding of biblical theology provides the basis for effective cross-cultural missionary work in *A Practical Theology of Missions* ... I highly recommend his effort.
RUDOLPH H. WIEBE, LECTURER AT THE TORONTO BAPTIST SEMINARY FOR TWENTY-NINE YEARS AND A PRINCIPAL LECTURER AT THE FEDERAL COLLEGE OF EDUCATION, PANKSHIN, NIGERIA, WEST AFRICA SINCE 2004.

This book is the climax of Eric Wright's full life as missionary, pastor and author ... It
distils decades of missionary experience and research, reflection and devotion. The book is thorough and balanced, and yet it is an inspiring book to read.
REVD GEOFF THOMAS, PASTOR SINCE 1965 OF ALFRED PLACE BAPTIST CHURCH, ABERYSTWYTH, WALES, UK

Eric E. Wright grew up in Toronto, Canada. He and his wife, Mary Helen, were called to missionary service in the Muslim world, ministering in Pakistan for sixteen years. There Eric became co-founder of the Open Theological Seminary. After returning to Canada, Eric pastored Long Branch Baptist Church, Toronto, served as interim pastor in six other churches, and taught both the history and theology of missions at Toronto Baptist Seminary. Eric and Mary Helen have three married children and nine grandchildren. They live in Salem, Ontario.

Biblical shepherding of God's sheep
The use and abuse of authority
by church officers

STEVEN MARTIN, (ED.)

978–1–84625–195–5

"Tend my sheep" is the awesome task given to those who have been called and equipped by the Holy Spirit to be overseers of the church of God. Leadership in the local assembly must be biblical and balanced if the church is to properly discharge its commission from the Lord Jesus Christ.

Recent trends in leadership methods have made it more necessary than ever that Christ's shepherds "be on guard for yourselves and for all the flock." The application of biblical church authority is one of the crucial issues facing Christians today.

This work deals forthrightly with the hard questions about leading God's people on the local-church level. Representing the mature thought of men who have spent many years guiding Christians, *Biblical Shepherding of God's Sheep* is an anthology of essays dealing with various aspects of the issue of church authority. The true nature of an "ideal" church, the proper way of reformation, the danger of the abuse of church discipline and the relationship of authority to individual freedom are some of the topics handled here.

Leaders reproduce themselves and put their stamp indelibly upon a congregation. This influence can in turn make or break a church's influence in the world. These essays provide the tools needed for the self-examination, correction and growth of all those concerned to see Christ's style of shepherding safeguarded among his flock.

Contains contributions from:

Leon Blosser

Walter Chantry

Paul Clarke

Erroll Hulse

Donald R. Lindblad

Steven L. Martin

Thomas Nettles

Henry Rast

Ernest Reisinger

James Renihan

John Thornbury

Biblical
Shepherding of
God's Sheep

The use and abuse of authority
by church officers

↑MINISTRY
MISSION→

Steven Martin, Editor   DayOne

MIKE ABENDROTH

176PP PAPERBACK

978-1-84625-108-5

Since preaching is God's ordained means of disseminating truth, it is vital that Bible teachers preach well and congregations listen well. This study of Jesus Christ's preaching will assist both the preacher and the congregation in their quests to honor the Lord with their respective responsibilities in worship.

While there are many definitions and descriptions of preaching today, preaching like Jesus must be the unchanging standard for all who dare teach the Bible. Preaching fads come and go, yet the manner and method of the Lord's preaching is always relevant, right, and worthy to be emulated.

What you win them with is what you win them to. Preaching is God's way of proclaiming the foolishness of the gospel to the weak and despised, all to His own glory. The world will always despise preaching, but when the church likewise questions God's wisdom and starts using alternatives, a major problem exists. Abendroth calls his readers back to the pre-eminence of preaching through the example of the Lord Himself. Encouraging and challenging.

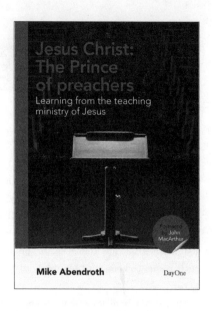

JAMES WHITE, AUTHOR OF SCRIPTURE ALONE, PULPIT CRIMES, THE GOD WHO JUSTIFIES, *AND* THE KING JAMES ONLY CONTROVERSY.

Mike Abendroth was born in Omaha, Nebraska. He was saved by God's intervening grace in 1989. After his father died, he bought a study Bible and began reading it beginning with Genesis. He graduated from The Master's Seminary (M. Div., 1996) and became the pastor of Bethlehem Bible Church, West Boylston, Massachusetts (1997). Mike has been married to Kimberly for 18 years and has three daughters and one son. He has been preaching expository sermons on a weekly basis for 15 years. One of Mike's passions is teaching men to teach the Bible expositionally. He is an Adjunct Professor of Theology at the Southern Baptist Theological Seminary, where he teaches homiletics.

Counsel one another
A Theology of Personal Discipleship

PAUL TAUTGES

192PP PAPERBACK

978–1–84625–142–9

Today, churches are increasingly placing their confidence in Christian psychology as the answer to their need for the ministry of counseling. But counseling is not primarily the work of the professional: it is a crucial way for believers in Christ to demonstrate biblical love toward one another within a gospel-centered, truth-driven, and grace-dispensing church environment. That is the main point of this book.

Solidly rooted in the belief that the Scriptures are sufficient for every soul-related struggle in life, and totally committed to the truth that the Holy Spirit is competent to accomplish the work of sanctification, this paradigm-shifting book will challenge every believer.

In his companion work, *Counsel Your Flock*, Paul concentrated on the role that teaching shepherds have in leading God's people to spiritual maturity by faithfully equipping them for effective ministry. Here he biblically presents, and thoroughly defends, every believer's responsibility to work toward God's goal to conform us to the image of His Son—a goal that will not be reached apart from a targeted form of discipleship, most often referred to as "counseling."

This book gets it right! Comprehensive and convincing, *Counsel One Another* shows how true biblical counseling and preaching fit hand-in-glove. Those who preach, teach, or counsel regularly are sure to benefit greatly from this helpful resource.
JOHN MACARTHUR, PASTOR-TEACHER, GRACE COMMUNITY CHURCH, SUN VALLEY, CALIFORNIA

Dr. Paul Tautges has served Immanuel Bible Church in Sheboygan, Wisconsin as pastor-teacher since 1992. He is also the author of *Delight in the WORD: Biblical Counsel for Everyday Issues* and is a biblical counselor certified with the National Association of Nouthetic Counselors (NANC) and the International Association of Biblical Counselors (IABC). Paul and his wife Karen have nine children.